SING TO THE LORD A NEW SONG

THE HISTORICAL SERIES OF THE REFORMED CHURCH IN AMERICA
NO. 74

SING TO THE LORD A NEW SONG

Choirs in the Worship and Culture of
the Dutch Reformed Church in America,
1785–1860

David M. Tripold

WILLIAM B. EERDMANS PUBLISHING COMPANY
Grand Rapids, Michigan / Cambridge, UK

Wm. B. Eerdmans Publishing Co.
2140 Oak Industrial Drive SE, Grand Rapids, Michigan 49503
PO Box 163, Cambridge CB3 9PU UK
www.eerdmans.com

Printed in the United States of America

Library of Congress Cataloging-in-Publication Data

Tripold, David M.
 Sing to the Lord a new song : choirs in the worship and culture of
the Dutch Reformed Church in America, 1785-1860 / David M.
Tripold.
     p. cm. -- (The historical series of the Reformed Church in
America ; no. 74)
 Includes bibliographical references (p.   ) and index.
 ISBN 978-0-8028-6874-9 (pbk. : alk. paper)
 1. Choirs (Music)--History. 2. Church music--Reformed Church in
America--History. 3. Reformed Church in America--Liturgy--History.
4.
 Reformed Church in America--History. I. Title.
 BX9525.M87T75 2012
 264'.0573202--dc23
                                  2012006894

To my wife, Maggie

The Historical Series of the Reformed Church in America

The series was inaugurated in 1968 by the General Synod of the Reformed Church in America acting through the Commission on History to communicate the church's heritage and collective memory and to reflect on our identity and mission, encouraging historical scholarship which informs both church and academy.

www.rca.org/series

Contents

Illustrations

Tables

Acknowledgments

Though this study has taken just under two years, it is the result of a lifelong journey for which I have accrued more debts than I can enumerate. The effort was inspired by the great music teachers, choral directors, choir members, colleagues, and friends in music and liturgical studies with whom I have studied or whom I have known since the time I joined a church choir as a teenager. Moreover, it evolved from the even earlier and steadfast support and encouragements of my parents, Edward and Lois Tripold; my sister, Dr. Diane Haviland; and my brother, Edward Tripold.

Many people have provided tangible help in locating and interpreting materials. I especially thank Russell Gasero, archivist for the Reformed Church in America; Marsha Blake, librarian of the Gardner A. Sage Library of the New Brunswick Theological Seminary; Dr. James D. Folts, historian for the First Church, Albany, New York; Laura Lee Linder, historian for the First Reformed Church, Schenectady, New York; Dr. Gregg Mast, president of New Brunswick Theological Seminary; Dr. Daniel J. Meeter, pastor of the Old First Reformed Church in Brooklyn, New York; Mary Brotherton, historian for the Old

Brick Reformed Church, Marlboro, New Jersey; the Reverend James Hart Brumm, pastor and teacher at Blooming Grove Reformed Church, Rensselaer, New York; the late Karen Schakel, administrator for the Van Raalte Institute at the Theil Research Center at Hope College, Holland, Michigan; Dr. Elton Bruins, scholar at the Theil Research Center, for his gracious assistance in locating many items; Stephen L. Pinel, archivist of the Organ Historical Society at Westminster Choir College of Rider University, for his expert help in finding relevant material; and Dr. Robin Leaver, whose vast knowledge of liturgical studies and music makes even brief conversations deeply informative occasions.

I am grateful to the faculty of Drew University and especially the late Dr. James White, whose wide-ranging knowledge of liturgical studies and extraordinary kindness helped me advance through the Ph. D. coursework; Dr. Neil Alexander, who taught me the mechanics of scholarship; my dissertation committee: Dr. John Witvliet, for his encouragement and insightful questions and comments produced from expertise in both music and liturgy; Dr. Kenneth Rowe, whose prescient observations and advice in so many facets of this study challenged me to ask new questions at every turn; and especially to Dr. Anne Yardley, who suggested this project and whose constant invaluable guidance has allowed it to grow beyond what I ever could have achieved independently.

The help and encouragement of colleagues, friends, and family have also made this work possible. I am grateful to my colleague and friend Dr. John J. Burke, former Music and Theatre Arts Department chair at Monmouth University, for making my path smooth and to my adored music and theater colleagues Sheri Anderson, Fred Del Guercio, Laura Dubois, Ron Frangipane, Michael Gillette, Christie Reder, Nicole Ricciardi, Dr. Gloria Rotella, and George Wurzbach. I am also grateful and blessed to be a member and the organist/choir director of the Colts Neck Reformed Church, where members have asked me regularly how my work was going. I am especially thankful for our senior pastor and my dear friend, the Reverend Scott Brown, who has offered much valuable advice and insight and has endured my constant updates on this project. My wonderful children, Amy and Greg, have generously tolerated my absenteeism while researching and writing, and my loving wife, Maggie, has given me unending support and carried many of my other loads along the way. None of this would have taken root nor been nurtured to fruition had she not decided to take this journey too.

Introduction

In the sixteenth century a fierce struggle for religious freedom gave rise to John Calvin's (1509-64) reformed theology in the Netherlands, which displaced Catholicism and other Protestant trends and ultimately gained preeminence in all seventeen provinces as a national faith. According to James White, Calvin's theology "tended to be the most cerebral and didactic in its moral earnestness,"[1] a pattern reproduced in the worship and culture of followers who today, in several denominational groups, call themselves "Reformed."

> Whatever did not positively contribute to the congregational celebration of the Word and Sacrament as commanded by Scripture was discarded. Elaborate vestments and ceremonies, chanting and singing by choirs, and all things that primarily satisfied the aesthetic senses of the worshipper were abandoned.[2]

Calvin's congregations sang versifications of the psalms and a few other scriptural texts contained in the *Genevan Psalter*. The tunes were sung

---

[1] James H. White, *A Brief History of Christian Worship* (Nashville: Abingdon, 1993), 107.
[2] Howard G. Hageman, *Lily among the Thorns* (New York: Half Moon Press, 1953), 148.

unaccompanied, in unison, and led by a children's choir or an individual who "lined out" each phrase. When the Dutch colonized North America (the first church established in 1628), this worship tradition was transplanted to the New World, where it remained entrenched for 150 years.[3]

But a radical change had unfolded in Dutch Reformed worship and music culture in America by the late eighteenth century, when the "regular" singing movement brought about the widespread institution of singing schools in towns and churches. The movement had gained access to the Dutch Reformed Church during the course of the First Great Awakening through the introduction of English hymnody, especially the hymnody of Isaac Watts (1674-1748). Furthermore, in the early nineteenth century a church music reform movement in the Northeast disseminated a more "scientific" method of music pedagogy, along with a vast repertoire of "cultured" European music and the indigenous compositions of a few zealous American composer/ educators. Many Dutch Reformed churches adopted this movement's mission and repertoire. Although the emergent taste for "cultured" music contradicted the very precepts of the Reformed tradition, choirs began to appear in Dutch Reformed worship in America by the late eighteenth century.[4] By the mid-nineteenth century a majority of Dutch Reformed Church congregations were using choirs and organs in worship on a regular basis. The use of hymnody alongside psalmody, the incorporation of choirs and their Anglo-American repertoire, and the playing of organs in the church constituted an "Americanization" of the musical culture of the Dutch Reformed Church.[5]

While it seems unusual for such a longstanding worship tradition to give way to a new and radically different one, it is only fair to say that

[3]   While the relationship between Calvinism and the Dutch Reformed Church is complex, matters of music until the nineteenth century were essentially clear-cut: one authorized book with one preferred manner of musical performance.

[4]   The Netherlands state church endured a cultural upheaval when, along with other "liberal" measures, the national administration directed the use of a new hymnal in the early nineteenth century. Although the mother church remained a mirror to the Reformed Church in America even after America's independence, as a rule, church choirs did not proliferate there as they did in the United States.

[5]   In *The Americanization of the Dutch Church* (Ph.D. diss., Univ. of Oklahoma, 1969), John Pershing Luidens concluded that the Americanization of the Dutch Reformed Church "was the result of a novel environment and of cultural interaction; it began slowly during the brief tenure of the Dutch, was vastly forwarded under the British, and achieved its final form in the early years of the American republic," 392. He stated further, "The entering wedge was language, and it was Dutch which gave way during the work-day week. As the English population increased, their tongue became the medium of business, administration and the courts," 394.

the other "mainline" Protestant traditions in nascent America adopted the same musical paradigm, including the doctrinally equivalent Presbyterian Church. Conformity was requisite to survival, its pressures exerted in all avenues of life, economic, political, and cultural. What is truly remarkable is the degree to which choirs and organs influenced this changing religious culture.

By assembling a picture of choral activity in American Dutch Reformed churches from the late eighteenth century until 1860, one can argue that the development of choirs played a distinctive role in altering a longstanding Dutch Reformed pattern of worship. Furthermore, by incorporating an Anglo-American choir repertoire as a substitute for Dutch psalmody and by embracing the social structures of American choirs, these nascent Dutch Reformed choirs made an important contribution toward their churches' assimilation into American culture. It is notable that choirs, organs, and the music they provided played an extremely significant role in establishing and maintaining the uniquely American culture of the Dutch Reformed Church. As a result, choirs and their leaders had an enormous impact on changing patterns of Dutch Reformed worship, ecclesiastical culture, social values and moral practices, and even the finances of individual churches.

Contents Summary

Chapter 1 traces the events leading to the formation of Calvin's church in the Netherlands, along with an overview of Dutch Reformed worship and music. The chapter posits that a spirit of tolerance and ecumenism held by the Dutch, including Calvin's own latitude in worship music, led to the eventual admission of hymns and organs in worship. These values were transmitted to the New World, where connections can be made among hymn singing, organs, and the "New Way" of singing that led to the formation of choirs.

The pathway of Americanization for the Dutch and its bearing on worship, music, and ecclesiastical culture is traced in chapter 2, highlighting the impact of the Great Awakening and the settling of a bifurcation in the Dutch Reformed Church in favor of an independent American classis. As the Dutch in America adopted English language and customs, they also adopted English language worship and hymnody as part of their remaking into an American denomination. Singing schools, instituted as a means to improve congregational singing, changed the church's ecclesiastical culture and worship radically. As a result, choirs were formed from singing school graduates to extend the learning to the congregation and to lead the singing in weekly public worship.

Chapter 3 surveys the types of forerunner and ancillary choir and musical innovations that led to or strengthened the organization of institutional church choirs.[6] Evidence of singing schools, Sabbath school choirs, choral societies, and sacred music conventions and concerts in Dutch Reformed churches, along with an appendix of concert programs, provides a categorical summary of the wide-ranging choral activities and types of repertoire employed. This chapter documents the use of musical instruments, including the organ, with tables of evidence collected from specific churches.

The statistical makeup of the institutional church choir, its leaders, and a timeline of musical innovations in individual churches form chapter 4. The impact of the choir on Dutch Reformed worship and ecclesiastical culture is discussed, along with information on choir location, performance opportunities, choir behavior, and choral sound. Attention is paid to the role of Thomas Hastings and other church music reformers in influencing choir agendas and to the changing role of women in the Dutch Reformed Church as a result of instituting choirs.

Chapter 5 examines tunebook use in the Dutch Reformed Church as a means to understand the choral repertoire used and the manner in which it was performed in worship. A valuable discovery, a tunebook used at the First Church, Albany, in the 1820s containing hand-written notations about modes of performance, aids this discussion.

Chapter 6 includes a case study of First Church Albany, summary statements, further thoughts, and five appendixes.

This book provides historical context by integrating the areas of world history, American history, church history, liturgical history, architecture, and music history. Through these lenses, I have sought to identify the causes of church choir development in the American Dutch Reformed Church and to assess the impacts of choirs on its ecclesiastical culture.

A newly recorded audio CD accompanies this book, offering readers an opportunity to hear examples of the institutional church choir repertoire herein described. Pieces recorded on the CD that are discussed in chapter 5 are flagged in the text. I was assisted in making

---

[6]   I use the term, *institutional choir*, throughout this book to distinguish professionally led church choirs that participated in the full realm of ecclesiastical activity, including weekly worship, weddings, funerals, installation services, anniversary exercises, and other church occasions, from a former group of church choirs that were composed of singing school graduates who banded together to teach and aid congregational singing.

this recording by an eleven-voice choir drawn from the Colts Neck Reformed Church Senior Choir and the Chamber Choir of Monmouth University. Gleanings obtained from articles and sacred music concert reviews found in the *Christian Intelligencer* and period music journals, instructions for singing found in tunebooks, Thomas Hasting's *Dissertation on Musical Taste* (unfurling a musical aesthetic philosophy he had acquired at the dawn of his mission to reform church music), and Nathaniel Gould's 1853 state-of-the art book, *Church Music in America*, guided our endeavor to replicate period institutional church choir musical performance. To the best of our ability, we have avoided a bias for present-day vocal arrangement, choral sound, and other trademarks of contemporary musical interpretation and performance practice.

PART I

From Tolerance to Ecumenism:
How the Reformed Church in America
Came to Allow Choirs

CHAPTER 1

Foundations of Tolerance and Ecumenism in the Reformed Church in the Netherlands

Under the *laissez-faire* rule of Holy Roman Emperor and King of Spain Charles V (1500-1558), the Dutch enjoyed a prosperous, open, and largely self-governing society that embraced the Renaissance, participated in the Reformation, and experimented with new social and political ideas.[1]

The Dutch mercantile empire was the envy of Europe, their inheritance customs rejected the primogeniture of England and elsewhere in favor of a system that apportioned a man's estate first to his widow and then more or less equally among his children. Dutch and Flemish artists of this era are still counted among the masters of all time. The Dutch configuration of church and state,

[1] In 1549 Charles united the seventeen provinces of the Netherlands, separating them from the empire and from France. According to church historian Howard G. Hageman in *Lily among the Thorns: History, Faith and Worship of the Reformed Church in America*, "In the early days of the Reformation, Charles, who had come to the imperial throne, was enormously popular in the Netherlands. In both appointments and privileges, he tended to favor the land of his birth. Nowhere in all his wide European domain was he more popular than in the Low Countries and, as he himself confessed, there was no place in Europe that he liked better," 31.

forged in the bitter struggle between the Netherlands States-General and Spain, in many ways anticipated the formulation of the United States.[2]

A vast network of worldwide trade routes exposed the Dutch to people of all races, religions, and cultures abroad and at home, equipping them with an uncommon bearing of tolerance and openness. They offered safe haven to some of the most radical thinkers of the time but often chose the *via media* between rivaling factions to maintain internal solidarity. This ethos played a role in their adopting the ecumenical creeds, confessions, and liturgies of the Reformed faith, and even in introducing organs and hymns into their worship.

Seeds of Humanism and Reform

Presaging the Reformation, the humanistic and pietistic teaching of Gerhard de Groote (1340-1384) inspired a religious community called the Brethren of Common Life, or *Devotio Moderna*. The Common Life schools implemented significant and popular reforms in Dutch Roman Catholicism and social life including reading the Bible, preaching and praying in the vernacular, and ministry and education for common people.[3] The Brotherhood produced the theologian Thomas à Kempis (1380-1471), whose pattern of pietism was captured in the book *The Imitation of Christ*,[4] and Desiderius Erasmus (1466-1536), the founder of biblical criticism and utmost figure in prefiguring the Reformation in the Netherlands.[5]

A man of exceeding charm, wit, urbanity, he was distinguished most of all by his prodigious erudition, which he directed to one purpose—the revival of Christianity by means of a humanistic program, at once intellectual and ethical. A true man of the Renaissance, he believed that the way to correct the immediate past was to return to the remote past, to the world of the classics,

[2]   Randall Balmer, "The Historiological Neglect of Religion in the Middle Colonies," in *Pulpit, Table, and Song: Essays in Celebration of Howard Hageman*, ed. Heather Murray Elkins and Edward C. Zaragoza, Drew Studies in Liturgy, no. 1 (Lanham: Scarecrow Press, 1996), 104.

[3]   Albert Hyma, *The Christian Renaissance: A History of the 'Devotio Moderna,'* 2nd ed. (Hamden: 1965).

[4]   Thomas à Kempis or one of his followers authored *The Imitation of Christ*.

[5]   At the Common Life school in Deventer, Erasmus studied with the Greek and Latin scholar Rudolf Agricola (1444-1486), whose New Testament translations made an important contributed to the vernacular reading and biblical scholarship movement.

the Bible, and the early church fathers. Using those classical and Christian sources, the scholar, working in tandem with the schools and the printing press, could set off a revolution; the scholar could actually generate enough intellectual and ethical force to purge Western Catholic society of its disorders. For Erasmus, therefore, the worst of all stumbling blocks were, first, *obscurantism*, the failure of intellectualism, and second, *pusillanimity*, any faintheartedness in ethical determination.[6]

Erasmus's books, *Enchiridion* and the lighthearted *In Praise of Folly*,[7] placed him at the forefront of liberal Catholic reform. The consummate humanist, his political commentary, *The Complaint of Peace*, written in the Netherlands in 1517, condemned the brutality and futility of war. However, war was to be another agent of reform in the Netherlands. Charles V's persecutions of Lutherans and Anabaptists in the northern provinces had been severe but irregular, but with failing health and the pressures of his administration he abdicated to his son Phillip II (1527-1598) in 1566.[8] Phillip subsequently installed Ferdinand of Toledo (1508-1583), the Duke of Alva, as the Netherlands regent. What followed was one of the bloodiest and most protracted battles for political and religious freedom in European history.[9]

The Birth of the Reformed Church in the Netherlands

By the mid-sixteenth century, John Calvin's success in Geneva had ignited a well-organized Reformed movement that spread into the French-speaking southern Netherlands provinces.[10] In 1563 an initiative to promote unity and mutual support among congregations

---

[6]   Bard Thompson, *Humanists and Reformers: A History of the Renaissance and Reformation* (Grand Rapids: Eerdmans, 1996), 333-34.

[7]   Johan Huizinga, *Erasmus and the Age of Reformation* (Princeton: Princeton Univ. Press, 1984). *In Praise of Folly's* gentle lampoons of both the clergy and institution of Roman Catholicism were especially effective in drawing public attention to the need for church reform.

[8]   John T. McNeil: *The History and Character of Calvinism* (London, Oxford and New York, 1954).

[9]   The "Blood Council" executed eighteen thousand people in six years. When the Spanish *Alcabala* was imposed, a 10 percent tax on all goods sold, William the Silent's (1533-1584) resistance movement forced Alba's retreat in 1573. An "Eighty Years War" ensued, with the Netherlands gaining full independence at the Treaty of Westphalia in 1648.

[10] The French-speaking Netherlanders from the southern provinces were known as Walloons, the same group that formed the majority of first settlers in New Netherland and who founded the first Reformed Church in North America.

resulted in calling the first annual synod meeting in Antwerp.[11] In 1566, the synod adopted Guido de Bres's confession of faith, known as the Belgic Confession.[12] Another synod in the German City of Wezel in 1568 embraced the standard of the Heidelberg Catechism. Supplying insights from all Protestant branches, this completely biblical and most ecumenical confession of the Reformation found a middle ground between the increasingly inflexible Lutheran and Calvinist doctrines. Through its three-part division of guilt, grace, and gratitude, the pastoral catechism offers a practical and experiential approach to daily Christian life in a warm, personal, and comforting tone.[13] At the synod in Emden in 1571 Calvin's Presbyterian mode of church government was adopted. It set forth procedures for calling a minister and made provision for forming classes and individual church consistories. The pattern of government remains essentially the same in the Reformed family of churches today.[14]

[11]   Even before the arrival of the Duke of Alva, Spanish officials had intensified their persecution of heretics in the Netherlands. Reformed congregations concealed their religious identities by adopting organizational pseudonyms, such as the "Society of the Vineyard" for the congregation in Antwerp and the "Society of the Lily" for the church in Oudenaarde.

[12]   The thirty-seven articles of the Belgic Confession are reprinted and described in *Ecumenical Creeds & Reformed Confessions* (Grand Rapids: Board of Publications of the Christian Reformed Church, 1979). To convince Phillip II to tolerate Reformed Protestantism in the Netherlands, De Bres's confession articulated a Reformed doctrine that showed continuity with ancient Christian creeds while distancing Reformed beliefs from Anabaptist teachings.

[13]   Elector Frederick III (1515-1576) commissioned Zacharius Ursinus (1534-1583), a professor of theology at Heidelberg University and former student of Zurich theologian Peter Martyr (1557-1526), and court preacher Caspar Olevianus (1536-1587) to prepare the Heidelberg Catechism to promote the cause of Calvinism and to quiet the controversies between Lutheran and Reformed factions in the region. The 129 questions of the catechism that are the basis for Reformed religious instruction of youth and for guiding pastors and teachers were adopted by the synod in Heidelberg and first published with a preface by the Christian prince in 1563. In 1566 Peter Datheen (1531-1588), the pastor of the exiled Dutch congregation at Frankenthaal, translated the catechism and appended it to the Dutch form of the *Genevan Psalter*. In the Netherlands and later in America, pastors were obliged to cover the points of doctrine of the entire catechism in the course of a year, for which the questions and answers were divided into fifty-two "Lord's Days" installments. In 1833 the *Constitution of the Reformed Protestant Dutch Church in America* was amended to allow for the entire catechism to be covered once in four years.

[14]   See Richard R. De Ridder, with Peter H. Jonker and Leonard Verduin, *The Church Orders of the Sixteenth Century Reformed Churches of the Netherlands Together with their Social, Political, and Ecclesiastical Context* (Grand Rapids: Calvin Theological Seminary, 1987) for rich documentation and a fascinating study of the differing regional views of church polity, struggles between civil and ecclesiastical authorities for control,

The horrific persecutions that followed did not deter the Reformed church's advance into the northern provinces, where John Calvin's theology displaced Catholicism and other Protestant trends and became entrenched as a national faith linked with the cause of political freedom. From its inception, the witness of the Dutch Reformed Church has been both evangelical and ecumenical, a unique pairing among early Protestant claimants who sought not only to oppose Roman Catholicism but also to champion a particular theological stance against other Protestant communions. But divisions between Protestants often led to tragedy and suffering, a consequence that the Dutch could not abide.[15] With the doctrinal standards and the modes of church governance in place, what remained to be added was an official liturgy.[16]

Liturgy and Music in the Reformed Church

The eclectic roots of the Reformed Church extended beyond its confessions, creeds, and adopted forms of church government to its Palatinate liturgy.[17] Completed in 1563, the liturgy was translated by Peter Datheen in 1566, approved by the Synod of Wezel in 1568, ratified

---

and the growing consensus among the churches shortly after the Netherlands' release from Spanish control.

[15] Russell Shorto, *The Island at the Center of the World* (New York: Vintage Books, 2004) and "All Political Ideas are Local" *New York Times* (Oct. 8, 2005), where he posited that Dutch tolerance was the unique sociological ground upon which the Island of Manhattan was settled. "Dutch Protestants, however, had experienced horrific violence at the hands of the Spanish Inquisition, and many had had enough of religious absolutism. Tolerance became codified into Dutch law, and Dutch cities, which had high concentrations of minorities, flourished."

[16] Daniel J. Meeter, *Meeting Each Other in Doctrine, Liturgy, and Government*, Historical Series of the Reformed Church in America, no. 24 (Grand Rapids: Eerdmans, 1993). The doctrinal standards consist of three confessions: the Belgic Confession, the Heidelberg Catechism, and the Canons of Dort (added after the Synod of Dordrecht in 1618-19) and three ecumenical creeds: the Apostles Creed, which is contained in the Heidelberg Catechism, and the Nicene and Athanasian creeds, which were added during the drafting of the Constitution of the Reformed Dutch Church in the United States of America in 1793. The constitution presents the rules of church government in four chapters: offices; ecclesiastical assemblies; doctrine, sacraments, and usages; and Christian discipline.

[17] The handiwork of Ursinus and Olevianus draws from Marten Micron's (1523-1559) summary in *de Christelycke Ordinancien* (1554) and Johannes à Lasco's (1499-1560) *Forma ac Ratio* (1555), prepared for the London refugees and greatly influenced by Zwingli; the *Liturgia Sacra* (1551) of Valerand Pullain (1515-c. 1560), for the French refugees in London; a translation of Calvin's *La Forme de Prieres* (1545), which was originally based on Martin Bucer's (1491-1551) *Grund und Ursach* (1524); and the Lutheran preaching service of the *Kirchenordnung* of Wurttemberg (1561).

in the Dutch city of Dordrecht (Dort) in 1574, and, with revisions, canonized at Dort in 1619.[18] Adherence to the liturgy was mandated by the constitution. However, since the liturgy does not constitute a complete order of worship but a collection of formularies and prayers, pastors were free to add elements, as Hageman observed:

> So far as the requirements are concerned, a Sunday morning service could have consisted of nothing but the opening prayer, the sermon, the closing prayer with the Lord's Prayer, and the Benediction, with a psalm or two sung at appropriate intervals. I have no doubt that many services had no more content than that; a visit to the Zwinglian parts of Reformed Switzerland today would reveal scores of Sunday services built according to precisely this plan. On the other hand, by leaving the question of additions to this skeletal form completely open, a congregation could construct an order of service remarkably like that of Calvin at Strassburg or Pullain's *Litugia Sacra*. I have tried to show from various synodical actions and the words of at least one commentator that many of them did, fleshing out Dathenus' rather meager provision with votum, law, absolution, etc.[19]

Not only did the forms and prayers of the liturgy diverge radically from the obscurant mysteries and congregational passivity of the Roman Mass, they were distinguishable from other Protestant communions because of a pervasive pedagogical tone:

> The liturgical forms we inherited from the Synod of Dort were often criticized for being too didactic, but the Netherlands Liturgy was designed specifically to be strong in teaching. It tended to focus on the evangelical promises more than the doxological mysteries. It tended to go deep rather than lofty, aiming for the "comfort" of the soul rather than the inspiration of the spirit. Its

[18] Bard Thomson: "The Palatinate Liturgy, Heidelberg, 1563," [trans. with notes by Bard Thompson] in *Theology and Life* 6/1 (Spring 1963), 49-67. See also James Hastings Nichols, *Corporate Worship in the Reformed Tradition* (Philadelphia: Westminster, 1968) and Bertus Polman, *Church Music and Liturgy in the Christian Reformed Church of North America* for a complete listing of the liturgy sources and commentary; and Kenneth E. Rowe, "The Palatinate Liturgy and the Pennsylvania Germans" in Elkins and Zaragoza, *Pulpit, Table, and Song*, 53-76, for a historical summary and a colonial American perspective on the liturgy.

[19] Howard G. Hageman. "The Liturgical Origins of the Reformed Churches," in John H. Bratt, ed., *The Heritage of John Calvin*, Heritage Hall Lectures, 1960-1970 (Grand Rapids: Eerdmans, 1973), 125.

whole purpose was to teach the people how to live in comfort and die in peace. It was a catechetical liturgy.[20]

Two Sunday services were stipulated—a morning preaching service, then an afternoon pedagogically based service.[21] A scripture reading preceded the morning service. The *voorzanger* then led the congregation in singing one to several psalms. The *domine* (minister) and elders entered toward the end of the singing, at which time the minister commenced the service by saying the *Votum* (Psalm 124:8) and the *"Grace and peace be unto you..."* apostolic greeting. Then the minister read Datheen's lengthy prayer of confession, followed by a prayer of illumination, the Lord's Prayer, and a metrical version of the Decalogue sung by the congregation. The minister then read from scripture and gave an expository sermon followed by another confession, modeled on the Württemberg form, containing a scriptural promise of redemption and the double proclamation of forgiveness and judgment based on the *Forma ac Ratio*.[22] Concluding prayers from Calvin's rite, or substituted prayers for festival occasions, followed the absolution, ending with the Lord's Prayer, a sung psalm, and the Aaronic Benediction (Num. 6:24-26).

When the Lord's Supper was offered, a formulary appended the morning preaching service after the sermon and intercessions consisting of the minister reading the Words of Institution (1 Cor. 11), Calvin's "fencing of the table" directive, a prayer of approach, an epiclesis, the Lord's Prayer, and the Apostles Creed.[23] The people came forward and stood at the table to receive Communion. Though a Saturday preparation service preceded Sunday Communion, Polman points out that few actually received the elements, since the denouncement of the "fencing of the table" and the minister's interjected listing of the

---

[20] Meeter, *Meeting Each Other*, 173.

[21] The Sunday afternoon service included the Creed, the Lord's Prayer, and sermons preached on the questions of the Heidelberg Catechism arranged in a lectionary style. The musical formula was similar to the morning preaching service. There were also weekday morning and evening prayer services, of which the Wednesday and Friday prayer services included psalm singing. See Nichols, *Corporate Worship*, 78-82. I am indebted to Bertus Polman, *Church Music and Liturgy*, for the following liturgy reconstructions.

[22] Rowe, "The Palatinate Liturgy," 59. Calvin was unable to convince the Genevan magistrates to allow the pronouncement of absolution by the minister after the confession.

[23] The Synod of Dordrecht in 1574 authorized the Lord's Supper to be observed every two months. Polman suggests that in this period the sacrament may have been offered only every three months.

congregation's sins caused many to feel unworthy to participate in the Lord's Supper.[24]

By the late eighteenth century, the pattern of worship in the Netherlands had changed considerably. The most conspicuous and far-reaching challenge to the liturgy came with the introduction of free prayer, as all fixed prayers became expendable in the eyes of a growing pietistic wing.[25] This development came as a challenge because, in another paradox with the supposed distancing from Catholicism, Reformed worship relied increasingly on the preaching and prayer of the minister, offering few places for congregational participation but for the music.

As many churches still contained organs, organists were employed to play preludes and postludes. They also replaced the *voorzanger* in accompanying the psalms and played *tussenspelen* (interludes) between the lines. The preservice scripture and singing was now located within worship after the *Votum*. Additionally, the congregation sang a psalm before and after the first confession, one after the post-Communion prayer of thanksgiving, and frequently another psalm midway through the sermon. By this time many churches had also begun singing hymns.[26] While the persistence of psalm singing is traceable to an adherence to Calvin's theology of music, the accretions of organ use and hymnody are not and must be considered as probable paths to the eventual acceptance of choirs. Therefore, it is necessary to examine the implementation of hymns and organs, but first to see if Calvin may have somehow invited an opportunity for these digressions.

A Closer Look at Calvin's Prescription for Worship Music

Congregational singing was a cherished part of Reformed worship from the start. In the Palatinate, the Lutheran manner of chanting lections and the majority of German hymns were rejected in favor of Calvin's formula for psalm singing.[27]

The psalms can stimulate us to raise our hearts to God and arouse us to ardor in invoking as well as in exalting with praises

---

[24]   Polman, *Church Music and Liturgy*, 43.
[25]   The pietists were known as Labadists after the preacher Jean de Labadie (1610-1674) began his free prayer campaign. See Nichols, *Corporate Worship*, and Hageman, *Pulpit and Table*.
[26]   See John Julian, "Dutch Hymnody," *Dictionary of Hymnology*, 2 vols. (Grand Rapids: Kregel, 1985, rep. of 2nd rev. ed., 1907), 1526-30.
[27]   Rowe, "The Palatinate Liturgy," 62. The *Genevan Psalter*, although available after 1562, was not nearly as popular in the region as Ambrosius Lobwasser's (1515-1585) *Psalter des konihlichen Propheten Davids* (Leipzig, 1573).

the glory of His name. Moreover by this one will recognize of what advantage and consolation the pope and his creatures have deprived the church, for he has distorted the psalms, which should be true, spiritual songs, into a murmuring among themselves without any understanding.[28]

Calvin's theology of worship music evolved from a nearly Zwinglian skepticism in his first writings in the *Institutes of the Christian Religion* (1536) to an impassioned endorsement of music when he drafted the organizational articles for the church in Geneva in 1537 to a neo-Platonist viewpoint upon his return to Geneva in the *Epistle to the Reader* (1542-43). This evolution points to the theologian's reforming nature and his openness to the cultural and liturgical conditions that he encountered.[29]

What repertoire other than the psalms Calvin might have admitted remains speculative, for the best evidence of his theology

[28]   References to Calvin's works will be cited in this chapter using the recognized abbreviations for two edited collections, *OC* = *Ioannis Calvini Opera quae supersunt omnia*, ed. Wilhelm Baum, Edward Cunitz, and Edward Reuss, 59 vols. (Brunsvigae: A. Swetschke and Son, 1843-48) and *OS*= *Ioannis Calvini Opera Selecta*, ed. Peter Barth, Wilhelm Niesel, and Dora Scheuner, 5 vols. (Munich: C Kaiser; 1926-62). English translation sources such as John Calvin, *Institutes of the Christian Religion* [1536], trans. Ford Lewis Battles (Grand Rapids: Eerdmans, 1975); John Calvin, *Institutes of the Christian Religion* [1559], ed. John T. McNeill, trans. Ford Lewis Battles, Library of Christian Classics, vols. 20-21(Philadelphia: Westminster, 1960); and John Calvin, *Theological Treatises*, trans. J.K.S. Reid, Library of Christian Classics, Vol. 22 (Philadelphia: Westminster, 1954) are used here along with those of Charles Garside Jr., "The Origins of Calvin's Theology of Music: 1536-1543," *Transactions of the American Philosophical Society* 4 (1969). The passage cited above is from Calvin's *Articles concernant l'organisation de l'église et du culte à Geneve, proposes au conseil par les ministres*, Jan. 16, 1537, found in *OC* X1:12; *OS* 1:375, trans. Garside, 10.

[29]   Garside's article pinpointed the rapid shift in Calvin's theology of music and served to contextualize the events within Calvin's life and pastoral situation. It has set off a stream of writings that have aimed to better comprehend the prolix cultural, sociological, and spiritual circumstances under which Calvin and his congregations lived and worshiped, and that have improved our understanding of the nature and use of the *Genevan Psalter*. Some important contributions in this area have been made by Robert Homer Leslie, Jr., "Music and the Arts in Calvin's Geneva: A Study of the Relation between Calvinistic Theology and Music and the Arts, with Special Reference to the *Cent cinquante pseaumes* (1538) of Pascal de L'Estocart" (Ph.D. diss., McGill Univ., 1969); Natalie Z. Davis, "From 'Popular Religion' to Religious Cultures," in *Reformation Europe: A Guide to Research*, ed. Steven Ozment (St. Louis: Center for Reformation Research, 1982), 321-41; and John D. Witvliet, "The Spirituality of the Psalter in Calvin's Geneva," in *Worship Seeking Understanding: Windows into Christian Practice* (Grand Rapids: Baker Academic, 2003), 203-29.

of worship music is found in the *Genevan Psalter* (1562), which he supervised.[30] His subjective establishment of poles between music that is neither "light nor frivolous" as opposing music that contains "weight and majesty" leaves the door ajar for speculations about what he would have admitted to worship.[31] By acknowledging a "great difference between the music which one makes to entertain men at the table and in their houses,"[32] and music that would be suitable for worship, Calvin revealed not the recipe for a particular repertoire,[33] but an ever-pastoral concern for the edification and spiritual growth of his congregation. With this definition in mind and given Calvin's extraordinary change in attitude about music in the seven years between 1536 and 1543, one can only imagine whether Calvin might have amended his prescription for unison and unaccompanied psalm singing in worship to embrace the polyphonic settings of the *Genevan Psalter* sung by the faithful in their homes.[34] Although there is no evidence to support the contemporaneous use of polyphonic psalm settings in worship, their

[30]   Pierre Pidoux, *Le Psaltier Hugenot du XVIe Siecle*, 2 vols. (Basel: Edition Baerenreiter, 1962), and an earlier work, Orientin Douen's *Clement Marot et le Psautier Huguenot*, 2 vols. (Paris: 1878-79, rep. Nieuwkoop, 1967). In Strassburg, Calvin published the *Aulcuns Pseaumes et Cantiques mys en chant* (1539), which included nineteen psalm versifications, mostly by Clement Marot (1497-1544), and a few by his own hand, along with settings of the Ten Commandments, the Lukan Canticles, and the "Strassburg Credo." The eighteen tunes accompanying these are mostly attributable to the composers Matthias Greitter (c.1495- c.1550) and Wolfgang Dachstein (1487-1553). In 1542 Calvin returned to Geneva and enlisted the poet Theodore Beza (1519-1605) and the composer Louis Bourgeois (1510-1561) to complete the project. By 1562, the collection, hereafter referred to as the *Genevan Psalter*, comprised all 150 canonical psalms, the Ten Commandments, the Apostles Creed, the *Nunc Dimittis*, and the three Lukan Canticles. Bourgeois and a "Maitre Pierre" may have used Gregorian chant sources to craft the tunes. For a discussion of *Genevan Psalter* tune sources see Jan R. Luth, "Where do Genevan Psalms Come From," *Reformed Liturgy and Music* 5 (1993): 41-42, and Piet van Amstel, "The Roots of Genevan Psalm Tunes," *Reformed Music Magazine* 3 (1992), 54.
[31]   *Epistle to the Reader* (1542), *OC* VI: 169-70; *OS* 2:15, Garside trans., 18. Calvin credited Augustine with having made this analogy, yet it has not been determined where, if at all, this it appears in Augustine writings.
[32]   *Epistle to the Reader* (1542), *OC* VI: 169-70; *OS*2:15, Garside, trans., 19.
[33]   In "Church Music in Reformed Europe" in *Protestant Church Music: A History*, ed. Friedrich Blume et al. (New York: Norton, 1974), 507-90, Walther Blankenburg referred to Calvin's intent to develop a "sacred style," opposing Luther, who was willing to adapt secular tunes to sacred texts, 517.
[34]   Blankenburg, "Church Music in Reformed Europe"; Pierre Pidoux, "Polyphonic Settings of the Genevan Psalter: Are They Church Music?" *Cantors at the Crossroads*, ed. J. Riedel (St. Louis: Concordia, 1967), 70-71; Mildred E. Bisgrove, *Sacred Choral Music in the Calvinistic Tradition of the Protestant Reformation in Switzerland and France from 1541-1600* (Ph.D. diss., New York Univ., 1968); and Witvliet, "Spirituality of the Psalter," 203-29.

use in home and school must have been widespread,[35] as they endowed the populace with musical literacy and artistic sensibilities in spite of worship practices.[36]

Especially germane to this study was Calvin's prescription that children's voices,[37] rather than a precentor, lead the psalm singing in worship. Witvliet noted that what Calvin prescribed constitutes a choir,[38] not the *schola cantorum* of Catholicism, but a new invention, a choir to teach and lead congregational singing of the psalms. As we shall see, those wishing to admit choirs to worship in Dutch Reformed churches in the late eighteenth and early nineteenth centuries often cited Calvin's theological and practical precedent. Moreover, the argument against choirs was based on a divergence from Calvin's pattern, where choirs had ventured beyond congregational leadership by singing anthems.

Dutch Psalmody and Hymnody

While paraphrases and translations of psalms into Dutch existed from the earliest years of the Common Life brotherhood, a collection

---

[35] Calvin would have been aware of the four-part psalter settings produced by composers Louis Bourgeois in 1547 and Claude Goudimel (c. 1514-1572) in 1565. Polyphonic settings of Genevan tunes were also made by Jacob Arcadelt (c.1505-1568), Pierre Certon (c. 1510-1572), Clement Janequin (c. 1485-1558), Claude Le Jeune (c. 1528-1600), and the Netherlands composers Jacobus Clemens non Papa (c.1510-c.1555) and Jan Pieterszoon Sweelinck (1561-1621). Witvliet states, in "Spirituality of the Psalter" (222), that more than two thousand polyphonic settings of the Genevan tunes and texts were produced in the era.

[36] In his dissertation, *Church Music and Liturgy in the Christian Reformed Church of North America*, Bertus Polman cited the thesis of Arthur P. Schoep, "The Harmonic Treatment of the Dutch Psalter of the 18th and 19th Centuries" (M.M. thesis, Eastman School of Music, 1945), which explored the gradual reharmonization of psalms (many of which were formerly modal) into major and minor tonalities. To accommodate reharmonization, the tunes had to be modified and the rhythmic language subdued to an *isorhythmic* pattern, that is, with notes of largely the same value. Nicholas Temperley's "Old Way of Singing," 511-44, pointed out that the "New Way" of singing psalms was far slower and lacked the rhythmic vitality and melodic interest of the "Old Way," leading to a gradual disdain for singing psalms. Another issue that blurred the line between Calvin's idea of a sacred repertoire and "the music which one makes to entertain men at the table and in their houses" was the increased practice of "contrafacta," the coupling of Genevan tunes with secular texts or, vice versa, the coupling of psalm texts with secular tunes. For a discussion of this practice see Witvliet, "Spirituality of the Psalter," 225-26.

[37] "The manner of proceeding seemed especially good to us, that children, who beforehand have practiced some modest church song, sing in a loud distinct voice, the people listening with all attention and following heartily what is sung with the mouth, till all become accustomed to sing communally." *OS*, 1:375; *OC* X1:12, *Treatises* 54 as cited in Witvliet, "Spirituality of the Psalter," 211.

[38] Ibid.

titled *Souterliedekens* was the first designed for Protestant use.[39] Jan Utenhove's (c.1520-1566) *De Psalmen Davidis* (1566), prepared for the refugee congregation at the Austin Friars monastery in London, included some of his versified songs for the Ten Commandments; the songs of Mary, Simeon, and Zachary; the Lord's Prayer; Apostle's Creed; and Luther's *Glaubenslied* (Song of Faith).[40] However, Peter Datheen's *CL Psalmen Davids* (1566) gained preeminence and remained exclusively used until the last quarter of the eighteenth century, even when challenged by Philips van Marnix van Sint Aldegonde's (1540-1598) more eloquent *Het Boeck der Psalmen Davids* in 1580.[41]

Indeed, Datheen had done little but adapt and translate the *Genevan Psalter*, including its tunes, to remain in sync with the French church. It contained versifications for the 150 psalms and settings for the Ten Commandments, the Lord's Prayer, the Lukan Canticles, two settings of the Apostles Creed, and five prayer hymns, although the prayer hymns were excised at the Synod of Dort in 1619.[42] Heeding long-standing complaints about its amateurishly written verse and numerous mismatches between textual and music accents, Datheen's psalter was finally replaced in 1773 by a composite psalter with theologically trendy

[39] Samuel J. Lenselink, *De Nederlandse Psalmberijmingen van De Souterliedekens tot Datheen*, Doc. diss. (Assen, 1959) and Henry Bruisma: *The Souterliedekens and Its Relation to Psalmody in the Netherlands*, Ph. D. diss. (Ann Arbor: Univ. of Mich., 1949). See also Blankenburg, "Church Music in Reformed Europe," 566-67. The ingenious use of popular song in *Souterliedekens* collection concealed its Protestant purpose and protected users from the authorities. Although at times repressed by Spanish authorities, the *Souterliedekens* popularity made thirty-three editions possible by 1613, including a three-part arrangement by Clemens non Papa in 1556-57.

[40] In *Gooslty Psalmes & Spirituall Songes' English & Dutch Metrical Psalms from Coverdale to Utenhove 1535-1566*, Robin A. Leaver explored the "common origins and parallel development" of English and Dutch metrical psalmody, providing evidence of a much more united Protestant movement, along with its implications for sacred music, than previously thought.

[41] In *Church Music and Liturgy in the Christian Reformed Church of North America*, Polman described how the popularity of Datheen's psalter, compounded by the lobbying efforts of its printers, consistently trumped attempts to replace it with Marnix's psalter during the series of general synods that led up to the Great Synod of Dort in 1619. By the time of the Great Synod, the "Datheen Psalter had prevailed by common consent!" 22.

[42] See Meeter, *Meeting Each Other*, for a translation and commentary on the Articles of Dort. Section III, "Of Doctrines, Sacraments and Usages," Art. LXIX states, "The 150 Psalms of David; the ten commandments; the Lord's Prayer; the 12 articles of the Christian faith; the songs of Mary, Zachariah, and Simeon versified, only, shall be sung in public worship. The churches are at liberty to adopt, or omit that entitled, "O thou, who art our Father God!" All others are prohibited, and where any have been already introduced, they shall be discontinued as soon as possible" 87.

deistic overtones.[43] Although containing the traditional appendages of the Decalogue, two settings of the creed, the canticles, and morning and evening hymns, there were evidently not enough hymns to appease a growing pietistic faction.[44]

A tension over the use of hymns existed from the earliest days of the Reformation in Holland. One of the first attempts to incorporate hymns into worship was instigated by the Calvinist, antipredestination sect called the *Remonstrants*, who published a collection of eighty-five hymns in 1615 titled *Hymnische Lofzangen*.[45] John Julian reported that hymns were sung at festivals and that the synods of Drenthe and Friesland around 1638 had recommended their use. Willem Sluiter (1627-1673) published *Psalmen, Gezangen, en Geestelijke Leidereen* (1659) and ten books of *Gezangen* in 1661. "His books spread rapidly, and soon formed together with the Bible and psalm-book the whole religious library of the country people."[46] Julian also suggested that the improved poetry of the psalter might have further instigated a desire for hymnody among the educated and clerical classes.[47] In 1805 the national church presented a 192-hymn collection, titled *Evangelische Gezangen*. In 1816 church officials decreed that one hymn, at least, was to be sung at each worship service.

The Organ in Dutch Reformed Worship

In his thought-provoking article, "The Organ Controversy in the Netherlands Reformation to 1640," Henry A. Bruinsma traced the gradual acceptance of the organ into Dutch Reformed worship by the mid-sixteenth century.[48] He noted that where the iconoclastic followers of Calvin in France, Geneva, and in the southern provinces of the Netherlands dismantled or destroyed organs along with altars, stained glass windows, and the statuary of Catholicism, the magistrates of northern province towns preserved church organs for use in regularly

---

[43] The English-speaking Reformed congregation in Amsterdam adopted the Tate and Brady Psalter in 1772.

[44] Julian, "Dutch Hymnody," 1527. The evening hymn was a setting of *Christe, Qui lux es et dies*.

[45] Blankenburg, "Church Music in Reformed Europe," 566. The Synod of Dort rejected the collection in 1618.

[46] Julian, "Dutch Hymnody," 1528.

[47] Ibid.

[48] *Journal of the American Musicological Society* 7 (Fall, 1954), 205-12. For a recent examination of the organ controversy, see Randall Dean Engle, *A Devil's Siren or an Angel's Throat? The Organ Controversy in the Netherlands from Calvin to Huygens* (Ph.D. diss., Univ. of Wales, 2006).

scheduled concerts taking place before and after worship services.[49] The 1574 Synod of Dorderchт's edict, "Concerning the playing of the organ in the church, we hold that it must be entirely abolished,"[50] did not hold, as municipalities cherished their valuable and attractive instruments and had long been accustomed to organ recitals and the use of the organ in earlier Roman Catholic worship.[51]

The debates shifted from whether or not to use organs to what organists should be playing. Still, it was not until the influential book of Constantijn Huygens, *Gebruyck of Ongebruyck van 't Orgel inde Kercken der Vereenighde Nederlanden* (Leiden, 1640),[52] that the organ entered the mainstream of Dutch Reformed worship. Huygens's ingenious argument hinged on the improvement of congregational singing, which he said, "sounds to us more like howling and screaming rather than like human singing."[53] His guidelines for organ use became the standard for the way psalms and hymns are introduced and for the playing of preludes, postludes, and other soloed organ music.[54]

Nicholas Temperley recognized that Reformed music split into "two streams": those which held on to the "Old Way," that is, a static metrical psalm repertoire sung unison, unaccompanied, and led by a song leader; and the "New Way," which "integrated the new congregational song into the art-music tradition; the use of organs, choirs, music books, and the leadership of professional musicians automatically 'regulated' the hymnody or psalmody and kept it in touch with developments in art music."[55]

---

[49] For instance, Bruinsma recounts that the city of "Delft, in 1612, required evening recitals in the winter once on Monday, Wednesday, Friday and Saturday, from 5-6 p.m., after the afternoon church services, plus a performance before every daily church service," 209.

[50] N.C. Kist, "Het Kerkelijke Orgel-Gebruik bijzonder in Nederland," *Archief voor Kerkelijke Geschiedenis inzonderheid van Nederland* X (1840), 246.

[51] The most important organist/composer of the period was Jan Pieterszoon Sweelinck (1561-1621), organist of the Amsterdam Oude Kerk. He was a renowned teacher of organ. His students Jacob Praetorius (c. 1530-1586), Heinrich Scheidemann (c.1595-1663), Samuel Scheidt (1587-1654), Gottfried Scheidt (1593-1661), and Paul Siefert (1586-1666) gave rise to the so-called north German Baroque organ school.

[52] Trans. Erica Smit-Van Rotte as *Use and Non-Use of the Organ in the Churches of the United Netherlands* (New York, 1964).

[53] Bruinsma, "The Organ Controversy," 211.

[54] Bruinsma pointed out that in some of the rural areas of the Netherlands the organ was not introduced until the nineteenth century and that "a few schismatic groups in the Netherlands have resisted the introduction of organs until the present day" (212).

[55] Temperley, "Old Way of Singing," 514.

It is, indeed, the presence or absence of organs that demarcates the two practices. Organs were banned completely in Scotland and among dissenting groups in England until the nineteenth century. They were almost unknown in parish churches in England between 1570 and 1660, and still lacking in most country churches (because they could not afford them) until the nineteenth century, though present in cathedrals and the larger town churches.[56]

Accepting Temperley's "two steams" thesis, we might conclude that the Reformed Church in the Netherlands for some time straddled the two practices, using organs but holding to a fixed repertoire of psalms. The church ventured even closer to the "New Way" by replacing the *Genevan Psalter* in the late eighteenth century by a book that, in design and in performance practice, more closely aligned with the art music of the day, and by adding hymns to the official church repertoire in the early nineteenth century. Nevertheless, the "New Way" ingredients did not precipitate the forming of many church choirs in the Netherlands as it had in other European Protestant traditions.[57] For the Dutch Reformed Church, that innovation would arrive on American soil.

---

[56] Ibid., 515.
[57] In "Church Music in Reformed Europe," Walter Blackenburg notes that in the present-day Netherlands, choirs in the conservative *Gereformeerde Kerk* are unheard of, while the more liberal *Hervormde Kerk* does admit choirs, 586. However, community and professional choirs have flourished in the Netherlands since the early nineteenth century, often performing treasured classics of sacred music to eager audiences.

CHAPTER 2

The Americanization of the Dutch Reformed Church as a Catalyst for Innovations in Worship and Music

For forty years the Dutch Reformed Church was the official church in New Netherland. Its body grew modestly on American soil. Traditional disciplines and forms of worship were maintained in spite of occasional disputes between Dutch West India Company officials and local ecclesiastical authorities, as well as protracted and frustrating dealings with the distant Classis of Amsterdam, especially in supplying ministers. After the conquest of New Netherland in 1664, British governors attempted to supplant the Dutch Reformed Church with the Church of England and convert the language and customs of the Dutch to their own. Nevertheless, the Dutch church survived and continued to expand in colonial America, securing the only British royal charter for a non-Anglican church in 1696.[1]

---

[1]   David D. Demarest, *History and Characteristics of the Reformed Protestant Dutch Church*, 2nd ed. (New York: Board of Publication of the Reformed Protestant Dutch Church, 1856); Luidens, *Americanization*; Arie R. Brouwer, *Reformed Church Roots: Thirty-Five Formative Events* (New York: Reformed Church Press, 1977); Gerald F. De Jong, *The Dutch Reformed Church in the American Colonies*, Historical Series of the Reformed Church in America, no. 5 (Grand Rapids: Eerdmans, 1978); Randall H. Balmer, *A*

19

At this time, immigration from the Netherlands nearly ceased. Within two generations, the majority of church members had been American born, although ministers still needed to be procured through the Classis of Amsterdam. Time and environment gradually Americanized a growing and diverse population and produced a distinctive, but bifurcated, Dutch Reformed Church with conservative and pietistic wings. The conservative wing retained theologically orthodox views of faith, worship, and church governance and tended to be loyal to the British crown. The pietistic wing consisted of younger, American-born members who had taken part in America's Great Awakening. They shunned Reformed orthodoxy, adopted unique forms of worship, and sought both independence from England and from the Classis of Amsterdam.

The Reverend John Henry Livingston's (1746-1825) plan of union succeeded in reuniting the church in 1772. After independence was won from Great Britain, he emerged the leader of a new American denomination. By the turn of the nineteenth century he had drafted an English-language constitution, translated the liturgy, directed the publication of a psalter/hymnal, and laid the groundwork for an American seminary. Livingston succeeded in steering a central course through the conservative and pietistic parties. However, his preface to the liturgy invited a radical digression from the received liturgical forms, and his foresight to add 135 hymns to a new English psalter placed the Reformed Dutch Church squarely within the mainstream of American Protestantism.

The acceptance of church choirs into Dutch Reformed worship in America is attributable to the gradual Americanization of the church and its need to survive in a democratic church environment. This chapter will look at the first Dutch Reformed worship traditions in America, the tensions and subterfuges caused by British control, and the aspects of Americanization that ultimately made way for church choirs.

Transplanted Worship Traditions in New Netherland

The first worship services in the colony were probably held in private homes or outdoors. Then a mill loft was renovated to

---

Perfect Babel of Confusion: Dutch Religion and English Culture in the Middle Colonies (New York: Oxford Univ. Press, 1989); Donald J. Bruggink and Kim N. Baker, *By Grace Alone: Stories of the Reformed Church in America*, Historical Series of the Reformed Church in America, no. 44 (Grand Rapids: Eerdmans, 2004).

accommodate the growing congregation. A *krankenbezoeker* (comforter of the sick), Bastien Jansen Krol (b. 1595), probably officiated with Jan Huygens, a *ziekentrooster* (finder of the sick) who arrived in 1626.[2] In 1628 Jonas Michaelius (1577-c.1640) was sent to New Netherland by the Dutch West India Company to be the congregation's first ordained minister.[3] Michaelius recounted the first worship service in a 1628 letter to the Reverend Adrianus Smotius, minister in Amsterdam:

> At the first administration of the Lords Supper which was observed, not without great joy and comfort to many, we had fully fifty communicants, Walloons and Dutch, a number whom made their first confession of faith before us, and exhibited their church certificates. Others had forgotten to bring their certificates with them, not thinking that a church would be formed and established here; and some who brought them, had lost them unfortunately in a general conflagration, but they were admitted upon satisfactory testimony of others to whom this was known, and also upon their daily good deportment, since one cannot observe strictly all the usual formalities in making a beginning under such circumstances.[4]

The passage above confirms Howard Hageman's assertion that from its onset in colonial America "the life of the Reformed Church was liturgical."[5] The liturgy brought over by Michaelius, which had been approved at the Synod of Dort in 1618, consisted of three items: two

---

[2]   The office of comforter could be expanded to permit the holder to read scripture, prayers, and sermons; provide catechetical instruction; do missionary work; but not administer Holy Communion. Shortly after arriving at Fort Orange, Krol returned to the Netherlands to request a minister be sent to New Netherland. The company deemed the settlement too small to warrant the services of a minister and returned Krol to the colony in 1626 with permission to baptize and marry until such time as a minister could be sent.

[3]   Peter Minuit and Jan Huygens were elected elders. Bastien Krol was elected deacon.

[4]   De Jong, *The Dutch Reformed Church in the American Colonies*, 18, previously cited in A. Eekhof, *Jonas Michaeleus: Founder of the Church in New Netherland* (Leyden: Sijthoff, 1926), 130.

[5]   Howard Hageman, *Pulpit and Table: Some Chapters in the History of Worship in the Reformed Churches* (Richmond: John Knox, 1962), 39-40, where he noted that the liturgy was used for Sunday worship and weekday instruction. Based on a report from the Rev. Henry Selyns (1636-1701), pastor of the New York congregation (1682-1701), to the Amsterdam Classis in 1698, it was customary for the reception of catechumens to take place on Easter Monday, Ascension Day, and Pentecost Monday, confirming that church year festivals were being observed in North American Dutch Reformed churches.

prayers—one before and one after the sermon—and a benediction.[6] Unaccompanied psalm singing, lined out in the manner described in the first chapter, was the only authorized music. On Manhattan Island a plain wooden church building was erected in 1633. It was replaced in 1642 by a stone church built within Fort Amsterdam and named after Holland's patron, St. Nicholas.

The Entanglements of Church and State

From the time of Michaelius's arrival, the Classis of Amsterdam had supervised ecclesiastical affairs in New Netherland. Yet the remote authority was often circumvented by the pecuniary interests of West Indies Company agents and, later, challenged by the colonial clergy under its auspices.

> Not only was the company directly responsible for the support and maintenance of the religious life in New Netherland, but indirectly its decision affecting land tenure, trading regulations, wages and salaries, and extent of colonization were of vital importance to the Church.[7]

The entanglements of church and state in the Netherlands sparked tensions in colonial New York.[8] The Michaelius letter to

---

[6]   The fixed *votum*, approved at the Synod of 1574, probably began each service (although perhaps because it was universally practiced, it is missing from many printed liturgies and seldom referred to in contemporary worship accounts). To appease the Mennonite faction, the prayer of confession and the absolution were excised at the Synod of Dort (1618-19). Bound with Datheen's psalter was an order for the Lord's Supper and Baptism, the Heidelberg Catechism, and the Belgic Confession.

[7]   Luidens, *Americanization*, 24.

[8]   Ibid., 5. "As Europeans, the first settlers brought with them religious assumptions commonly shared by the people of the colonizing era. They accepted the principle of religious uniformity within a state, with disabilities for competing religions. All were accustomed to a close relationship between Church and State that cast them in mutually supporting roles. Furthermore, the transplanted churches were regarded merely as extension of a Mother Church." See also Balmer, *A Perfect Babel*, 7. The state-enforced persecution of the Arminian party leaders after the Synod of Dort was a digression from the religious tolerance embraced by the Dutch in the Netherlands. The Calvinist (Gomarist) majority felt endangered by the Arminians' attempt to integrate radically differing theological views into the established church. On the other hand, had the Arminians wished to form an independent religious communion in Holland, the matter would have been easily dispatched. So recent were these events when the New Netherland colony was planted that already strong sentiments for a clear division between church and state would have been understandably magnified by the utopianism inherently felt by New World settlers.

Adrianus Smotius stressed that "political and ecclesiastical persons can greatly assist each other, nevertheless the matters and offices belonging together must not be mixed but kept separate, in order to prevent all confusion and disorder."[9] To the chagrin of the Amsterdam Classis and colonial clergy, the company directors-general often granted religious tolerance throughout the New Netherland period.[10] In 1640 the company relinquished its commercial monopoly and modified its land and governing policies, thereby "attracting a more aggressive type of settler."[11]

When Peter Stuyvesant replaced William Kieft as director-general, he was zealous to restore Dutch Reformed religious order.[12] But in 1650 the West India Company advocated lighter restrictions on religious freedom to further encourage non-Reformed Hollanders to settle in New Netherland. The Amsterdam Classis exerted pressure on the company to pass a resolution in 1654 not to permit Lutheran pastors in New Amsterdam, nor to allow any other form of public worship other than the "true Reformed." But the restrictions were short-lived with the impending takeover of New Netherland.[13]

Tallying and Transition

At the time of the British invasion in 1664 there were thirteen Dutch Reformed congregations in the province of New Netherland: four in the Hudson Valley, five on Long Island, two in New Jersey,

---

[9]   Hugh Hastings, *Ecclesiastical Records of the State of New York*, 7 vols. (Albany: James B. Lyon, 1901-1916), I, 55.
[10] Known for his ignominious Native American war campaign, William Kieft (1597-1647), director-general from 1638-1647, had given religious freedom to English settlers adhering to Presbyterian doctrines. This permitted the refugee church in Europe to continue in America, where German and French Reformed adherents with their varying religious customs and liturgies joined the Dutch Reformed constituency. Quakers, Mennonites, Jews, Lutherans, and Roman Catholics (although few at this time) settled in the region too, but were not permitted to build houses of worship during the New Netherland period.
[11] See Luidens, *Americanization*, 28.
[12] Ibid., 34, and www.collegiatechurch.org/history.html, 3-4. Stuyvesant, director-general from 1647-64, forbade drinking in taverns during church services and directed saloons to close at nine p.m. Dancing, playing games, pleasure rides, and even children playing or shouting in the streets on the Sabbath was forbidden. In 1648 he insisted that there be morning and afternoon preaching, which all were required to attend. In 1657 Stuvesant prohibited labor on the Sabbath and, in 1664, required schoolmasters to catechize their children every Wednesday in the presence of elders and ministers of the church.
[13] Company officials frequently reproached Stuyvesant for his religious intolerance and blocked his many attempts at instituting a theocracy in New Netherland.

one on Staten Island, and one in Delaware. In the four decades of Dutch control a total of fifteen Dutch Reformed ministers had been dispatched; eleven were present at the British invasion, but only six were active.[14]

Article eight of the surrender agreement permitted the Dutch to "enjoy the liberty of their consciences in Divine Worship and church discipline."[15] Richard Nicholls (1624-72), the conquering fleet captain who became New York's first governor, spoke fluent Dutch and maintained tolerant views toward the Dutch church. During his four-year administration (1664-68), he may have enabled a false sense of security that British control of the colonies would not precipitate much change. But soon after Nicholls's tenure, British officials began an orchestrated attack on the prevailing Dutch culture that gradually replaced Dutch law, language, customs, and patterns of faith with English equivalents in the American colonies.

The Ploy to Anglicize

Emigration from the Netherlands all but ceased after the surrender of New Netherland to the British.[16] The authority of the National States General, exercised through the political control and economic support of the Dutch West Indies Company, was summarily cut off. The Classis of Amsterdam continued to supervise the Reformed Church but was without legal authority in British territory. With the

---

[14]   Ibid., 50. The *post-acta* (after Dort) articles of the constitution required a formally educated, parochially installed clergyman and schoolmaster for each congregation. The first Dutch university was founded in Leiden in 1575, in part to provide churchmen for the Reformed conversions in the northern provinces and for the rapidly expanding Dutch empire abroad. The universities of Groningen and Utrecht were established in 1614 and 1636, respectively, to meet the same need. Based on the church's constitution, Article XXVII of the West India Company patroonship charter required proprietors to "endeavor to find ways and means whereby they may support a minister and schoolmaster." Adam Roelantsen, founder of the Collegiate School in 1638, still in existence today, was the first schoolmaster sent to New Netherland. Frequently, the schoolmaster performed the role of *voorlezer* and *voorzanger*, described in the previous chapter. By 1664 there were nine common schools in the eleven chartered towns of New Netherland, and one Latin school in New Amsterdam.

[15]   Hastings, *Ecclesiastical Records of the State of New York*, I, 557-58.

[16]   Only about half of the roughly eight thousand people who emigrated from the Netherlands to colonize New Netherland were Dutch. In 1644 Governor Kieft reported that eighteen languages were spoken in the vicinity of the fort. At the time of the British conquest there were about 235,000 English-speaking people in all of New Netherland. However, Manhattan did remain predominantly Dutch for many years.

appointment of Governor Edmund Andros (1637-1714), England heightened its Anglicizing tactics with covert and open assaults on the Dutch church and culture.[17]

Dealing a strong blow to the Dutch church, the Ministry Act of 1691-93 made the Anglican Church in Manhattan and in the outlying areas of Westchester, Queens, and Richmond the established church in the region. While other communions could exist under British control, the measure required all religious groups to contribute to the sustenance of the Anglican Church. The Consistory of New York obtained a victory when it was granted a royal charter in 1696, the only charter granted in colonial America to a church other than Anglican.[18] However, the protection of the charter did nothing to mitigate the most serious threat to the Dutch church in the colonies—its dire shortage of ministers. The slow-moving Dutch Reformed polity that supplied ministers to its colonial churches had resulted in numerous pulpit vacancies, whereby only sporadic visits to congregations from overextended Dutch clergy could be expected.[19] Adding to the woes of the Dutch church, the Society for the Propagation of the Gospel sent sixty missionaries to the New York colony from 1702-76.[20] The losses to the Dutch church were severe as many individuals, and even whole congregations, yielded to the Anglican Church.

---

[17]   In 1675 Andros (governor from 1674-81) authorized full communion between the Anglican and Dutch churches, permitting Anglican clergy to celebrate the sacrament in Dutch churches. Frequent attempts by governors were made to install Anglican pastors in Dutch churches. Andros even coerced Dutch clergy to examine and ordain Dutch clerical candidate Peter Tesschenmaker (d. 1690) in 1679. By this action, Tesschenmaker became the first Dutch Reformed minister to be ordained by an American ecclesiastical body. He was first installed in New Castle, Delaware.

[18]   The charter authorized the New York Consistory to own and manage properties and to conduct church affairs, including calling a minister. British governors, such as Edward Hyde, a.k.a., Lord Cornbury (1661-1732), governor from 1701-08, still meddled in Dutch church affairs, especially in the churches outside the reach of the New York collegiate charter.

[19]   After New Netherland was ceded to the British, the financial burden of calling and supporting Dutch ministers fell upon each congregation. (The disenfranchised West India Company had previously assumed most of these costs.) Initially, to placate the majority Dutch population, British officials taxed the colonies to support Dutch churches. But the effort was, at best, halfhearted and soon ceased altogether. According to Bruggink and Baker, in *By Grace Alone* (38), there were 9 ministers for 23 churches in 1696, 13 ministers for 40 churches in 1721, and 41 ministers for 100 churches by 1772.

[20]   In 1710, society missionary Thomas Barclay reported to London that in Schenectady, New York, about a hundred Dutch families were his constant hearers. There had been no Dutch pastor there for five years. The pulpit in nearby Albany was also vacant at the time.

The most pervasive Anglicizing influences, however, were not the calculated assaults on the church but the effects of time passing in the environment of colonial America under British rule. Daily life and business came to be conducted predominantly in English.[21] Adopted English customs and intermarriage gradually eroded the Dutch language and ways in America. By the mid-eighteenth century, Dutch parochial schools had nearly vanished and were replaced by English schools. By the mid-eighteenth century even domestic and church architecture had adopted English forms.[22]

The Dutch Church in America Receives the Great Awakening

Some of the Dutch resisted the forces of Anglicization. The same group held Dutch clergy in contempt for aligning with the social stratum of the wealthy merchant class. Breeching the silent rift between Dutch social classes, the Leisler Controversy[23] produced violent confrontations between factions and instigated dispersions of large numbers of working class "Leislerians" from Manhattan to Long Island, up the Hudson River, or into New Jersey. Here they awaited a new light.

The sectarian impulse in religion rises out of some experience of social dislocation, in this case the political ferment of the post-Leisler years which resulted eventually in the exclusion of

---

[21]   Balmer, *A Perfect Babel.* By the late seventeenth century, the outlook of the Dutch on church and state separation had changed, as ties to Dutch law and modes of government vanished. Dutch men were deserting the church to take advantage of English law, which allowed them to prepare separate wills from their wives. John P. Luidens makes this observation in *Americanization*, "With the settlement of America, the patterns of thought and habits of conduct resulting from these assumptions eroded with each generation; under the influence of novel time-space and environmental factors, a new set of American assumptions was fashioned, infusing both thought and action. In common with other religious bodies, the Dutch Reformed Church experienced these changes, so that by the middle of the eighteenth century a majority of the clergy and members had accepted the new outlook," 5.

[22]   Appendix 5.

[23]   The overthrow of Roman Catholic James II in 1688 and the accession of William III and Mary II in England portended fear in the colonies of a Jacobite uprising and a possible Catholic French invasion. The vehemently Protestant champion of the lower classes, Jacob Leisler (1640-1691), led an insurrection in 1689, took control of the fort on Manhattan, and established a provisional government. But opposition to Leisler by the colonial upper classes, enjoined by a British retaking force, led to the fort's surrender in 1691. The leader's subsequent execution conferred on him a hero's status among lower classes and crystallized their enmity for the aristocracy.

Leislerians from political and ecclesiastical office in New York. When conditions of social change render a particular group marginal to the broader society, that group reaches for a new interpretation of its social experience and turns very often to articulate charismatic leaders who themselves are alienated in one form or another from the dominant social group.[24]

Whereas contemporary Henry Selyns represented the institutional clergy, those holding orthodox views and using prescribed liturgical forms, Guiliam Bertholf (1656-1726) in the Raritan Valley of New Jersey and Bernardus Freeman (1660-1743) in Long Island were among the first pietist leaders of the newly bifurcated Dutch church.[25] The interposing revival movement gained considerable momentum after Theodorus Jacobus Frelinghuysen (1691-c.1747) was called to itinerate in several villages in the Raritan Valley in 1720. This climate of revivalism sowed the seeds of the First Great Awakening (1726-1755).[26]

Frelinghuysen emerged as the apologist for those alienated from the Dutch reestablishment, as religious ecstasy and spiritual piety were aligned with political displacement, economic discontent, and ecclesiastical dissent.[27]

Controversies raged between Frelinghuysen and the orthodox wing of the church throughout the era.[28] In 1735, after fifteen years of

---

[24] Balmer, *A Perfect Babel*, 103.
[25] By the end of the seventeenth century, pietism in the Netherlands had become widespread under leaders like William Ames (1576-1633), Gyspertus Voetius (1589-1676), Jacobus Van Lodensteyn (1620-77), and Jacobus Koelman (1632-95). As a youth in Sluis, Zeeland, Guiliam Bertholf was influenced by the pietistic preaching of Koelman, who, desiring to "purify" the Dutch Reformed Church, eschewed all ceremonialism and formalism as the false trappings of Roman Catholicism.
[26] George Whitefield (1714-70) and Jonathan Edwards (1703-58) were the movement's most notable leaders. A thorough treatment of the Great Awakening can be found in Martin Ellsworth Lodge, *The Great Awakening in the Middle Colonies* (Ph.D. diss., University of California, Berkeley, 1964), where he examines the many precursors to and path of the Great Awakening through the role and response of each religious group in the region.
[27] Balmer, *A Perfect Babel*, 108. See also Joel R. Beeke, ed., *Forerunner of the Great Awakening: Sermons by Theodorus Jacobus Frelinghuysen*, Historical Series of the Reformed Church in America, no. 36 (Grand Rapids: Eerdmans, 2000).
[28] Aside from his disavowal of church order and prescribed liturgical forms, Frelinghuysen incensed the orthodoxy by associating with Presbyterian pietist Gilbert Tennent (1703-64), holding a regenerative view of the sacrament of Communion (subjective means of grace), and by ordaining his student, John Henry Goetschius (1717-74).

arbitrating discord, the wearied Classis of Amsterdam finally assented to the constant pleas of colonial clergy for an American ecclesiastical body, but it denied the confederation the power to examine and ordain its ministers.[29] The matter was rejoined in 1747, whereby a *coetus* was formed, but only to settle internal disputes. In 1753 the group reorganized into a classis.

Those in favor of the *coetus* were often the younger, American-born and educated ministers who were theologically fashioned by the Great Awakening. They lay within the pietistic wing of the church that Frelinghuysen chartered. Their mission was to expand the church through the pathways of renewal and evangelism. Therefore, training and ordaining their own ministers was a practical means to the end they sought. Brouwer summarized the long-term impact of the pietistic wing on the church:

> The pietism which Frelinghuysen typified has been a continuing, although largely informal, theme in our denominational life. Our educational institutions, mission organizations, and church societies for women, youth and men, as well as a great many voluntary organizations outside the church, owe their existence to the influence of pietism. [30]

In 1754 the Consistory of New York suddenly withdrew its support for the *coetus*. A small group of ministers led by Johannes Ritzema (1707-94) formed an opposing union called the *conferentie*.[31] Aside from the issue of ordination, the *coetus* desired an academy to train ministers in the colonies. The *conferentie* instead pursued a Dutch divinity chair at the newly founded Kings College (Columbia University). The chasm between the two parties widened into a tragic schism lasting seventeen years. The *conferentie* supporters accused those aligning with the *coetus* of heresy. The *coetus* supporters accused the *conferentie* ministers of lacking regeneration and falling from their faith. Congregations were

---

[29] Gerardus Haeghort's (c.1705- c.1776) failure to convince the Amsterdam Classis in the 1730s to permit the formation of an American federation to examine and ordain ministers locally removed the primary motivation for the group's continuance. The survival of the Dutch Reformed tradition in the colonies was inextricably linked to the number of ministers competing in a democratic church environment. The protracted time that it took to obtain ministers from the Netherlands or to send candidates to the Netherlands for examination and ordination consigned the church to a constant and severe shortage of ministers.

[30] Brouwer, *Reformed Church Roots*, 51.

[31] The *conferentie* comprised older, European-educated clergy who held orthodox views and adhered to traditional church polity.

torn apart as individuals lined up on both sides.[32] The losses to the church were significant, prompting clerical candidate John Livingston to attempt to settle the dispute and reunite the church.

In 1768, while preparing for the ministry in Utrecht, Livingston drafted his first plan of union. However, it failed to gain support from either party. In 1771 he composed a new plan of union containing thirty-nine articles, which was favorably received. The plan put forth an organization of general and regional bodies, established a theological professorship, and recognized the authority of the "General Body" to examine and ordain ministers. Ratified by the Classis of Amsterdam in 1772, the Plan of Union was the manifesto of a wholly independent American church.[33]

The American Revolution erupted just as the church had made its internal peace.[34] As a rule, the Dutch clergy and members who sided with the patriot cause had also embraced the pietistic doctrine of the Great Awakening and strongly favored an American independent classis. When the war ended, it became apparent that it had been predominantly the pietist group who had salvaged the Dutch church in America, established it as an American denomination, framed its constitution, underwrote its first seminary, and guided it further into the American mainstream. The effects of American pietism challenged the Dutch Reformed doctrine of worship as a received discipline, as can be seen in this passage from the preface to *The Constitution of the Reformed Dutch Church in the United States* (1793):

> Her mode of Worship is expressed in the Liturgy, where forms of several prayers are given, without any idea, however, of restraining her members to any particular terms of fixed standards for prayer. Firmly believing, that the gifts of the Holy Spirit for the edification

---

[32] Brouwer, *Reformed Church Roots*, 62-63. Some divided congregations met in the same church but on alternate Sundays. In the 1760s an ordination at the church in Poughkeepsie was held outdoors because members of the *conferentie* had preemptively seized the church building.

[33] The first charter for Queens College (Rutgers) was obtained from George III in 1766. A second charter in 1770 provided that a member of the Reformed Protestant Dutch Church was to serve as the college president and as a professor of divinity. The New Brunswick, New Jersey, location was chosen because of its position between New York and the German Reformed churches in Pennsylvania, from which students could be obtained. Livingston was appointed the institution's first professor of divinity in 1784.

[34] John W. Beardslee, III, "The Reformed Church and the American Revolution," in James W. Van Hoeven, ed., *Piety and Patriotism*, Historical Series of the Reformed Church in America, no. 4 (Grand Rapids: Eerdmans, 1976), 17-33.

of Zion in every age, are promised and bestowed, the reformed
Dutch Church judges it sufficient to shew in a few specimens the
general tenor and manner in which public worship is performed,
and leaves it to the piety and gifts of her ministers to conduct
the ordinary solemnities of the Sanctuary, in a manner they judge
most acceptable to God, and most edifying to his people.[35]

The preface affirmed using adapted and free prayer in public worship,
one of the defining traits of the pietistic party's evangelical worship
style. As a Netherlands-trained clergyman, Livingston well knew that his
recommendation had violated the precept of a constitutional church
liturgy set 150 years earlier at the Synod of Dort. The implications of
this were nothing short of revolutionary, for the liturgy could only be
changed through an amendment to the constitution. Furthermore,
pastors were, and are still, periodically required to pledge allegiance
to the church constitution. Thus, Livingston's preface authorized
pastors to break with constitutional law by not using the prescribed
forms of prayer. The orthodox wing might have mounted an attack on
Livingston if their numbers and influence had not been so diminished
since America's independence. But the fact remained that Livingston's
vision was for a uniquely American church, one that did survive in a
democratic church environment, and one that witnessed significant
changes in its worship.

The Impacts of the English-Language Change and the Great Awakening on Dutch Reformed Worship and Music

In 1764, Archibald Laidlie (1727-79) was called by the Consistory
of New York to preach in English to a growing number of individuals
who no longer understood Dutch. The appointment produced a
schismatic reaction in the church that continued even after the General
Synod officially designated English as the language of worship in 1816.
Regional classes or, sometimes, individual churches were left to decide
if or how to implement the language change. Some churches found
compromise to be the best solution. They held parts of the service
in English but preached in Dutch, or alternated Dutch and English
services.

The Old Brick Reformed Church in Marlboro, New Jersey, a
village church sixty miles from New York City, introduced English-

---

[35] *The Constitution of the Reformed Church in the United States of America* (New York: William Durell, 1793), v-vi..

language services "on a limited basis" in 1765.[36] In 1785 its consistory ordered that the percent of English services be in proportion to the Dutch and English subscriptions for "Sallery."[37] As a result, by 1789, only three services a year were held in the Dutch language. At the Niskayuna Reformed Church near Schenectady, New York, a vote to make English the language of worship was taken in 1816. By a vote of ninety-six to six the language change passed. Shortly thereafter, the six who had voted against the resolution recast their votes to make the measure unanimous.[38]

The churches that introduced English to the spoken parts of worship also needed to address congregational singing. However, the solution to singing in English was more complicated than simply locating an English translation of the Old Testament psalms. English singing challenged the longstanding pattern of faith that Datheen had instituted in his translation of the *Genevan Psalter* by raising the question of whether or not just the Old Testament psalms would be sung or if English hymns would be permitted in worship. By this time, many congregations had discovered the Christian interpretations of the psalms and other hymnody of Isaac Watts (1674-1748).[39] From the perspective of Christian doctrine and experience, Watts packaged lyrics in a tantalizingly subjective and emotional language. With the tide of the Great Awakening, Watts's hymnody traveled promiscuously

[36] Joseph W. Hammond, *Sing to The Lord! A History of Music at the Old Brick Reformed Church in Marlboro, New Jersey*, unpub. paper (Freehold, NJ, 1994), 5. See also Mary Brotherton, ed., *The History of the Old Brick Reformed Church: In Celebration of the Three Hundredth Anniversary 1699-1999* (Marlboro, NJ: Old Brick Reformed Church, 1999), 203.

[37] In most churches of the era, the receipts from pew rentals (a fee assessed annually to occupy a particular seat in the sanctuary) and privately pledged funds underwrote the minister's salary and the other church operating expenses.

[38] Scott Haefner, et al., *A Serving People: A History of the Niskayuna Reformed Church 1750-2000* (Niskayuna, NY: The Consistory, 2000), 29.

[39] In 1706 and 1707, respectively, Isaac Watts published *Horae Lyricae: Poems Chiefly of the Lyrical Kind* and *Hymns and Spiritual Songs in Three Books*. In 1719 he released *The Psalms of David Imitated in the Language of the New Testament and Applied to the Christian State of Worship*. See Stephen A. Marini, *Sacred Song in America: Religion, Music, and Public Culture* (Urbana: Univ. of Illinois Press, 2003), who says, "The crucial moment in the emergence of the new poetics of worship was the system of praise proposed and carried out by Isaac Watts," 75. By 1800 forty-seven editions of *Hymns and Spiritual Songs* and ninety-nine of the *Psalms of David* were published in America (76), and the flood gates had opened for a league of new hymn writers like Charles Wesley (1707-88), Augustus Toplady (1740-88), Reginald Heber (1783-1826), and Americans Samuel Davies (1723-61), Timothy Dwight (1752-1817), and Peter Cartwright (1785-1872).

across denominational lines.[40] The English singing solution depended on each church's relative allegiance to the texts, meters, and tunes of Dutch psalmody.

An early attempt at compromise between Dutch Reformed and American traditions occurred after the Collegiate Church of New York adopted English as the language of worship in 1767. The New York Consistory could have selected the 1757 Dutch translation of the Tate and Brady psalter, a worthy psalm translation with English tunes that had been well received in the English-speaking Reformed Church in Amsterdam. But, while the consistory was willing to break with the Dutch language, it was not yet willing to abandon a cherished repertoire of Genevan tunes. Therefore, a middling solution was implemented to prepare a book with Genevan tunes and English texts, packaged in the archaic Dutch musical type.[41] The initiative was predisposed to failure when the committee consigned the work to Francis Hopkinson (1737-91), lawyer, musician, and signer of the Declaration of Independence, since it appears that he spoke little or no Dutch and resorted to adapting the English texts of the Tate and Brady psalter to the Genevan meters. Adding to its literary woes, the beleaguered *Psalms of David...For Use of the Reformed Protestant Dutch Church of the City of New York* (1767) sold only about half of the two thousand books printed.[42]

---

[40]   Henry Wansey attended an afternoon service at the North Dutch Reformed Church June 1, 1794, and heard Watts's hymns and metrical psalms. See Henry Wansey, *Journal of an Excursion to the United States of America in the Summer of 1794*, published as D.J. Jeremy, ed., *Henry Wansey and his American Journal* (Philadelphia: American Philosophical Society, 1970), 84, and cited in John Ogasapian, *Music of the Colonial and Revolutionary Era* (Westport: Greenwood, 2004), 153.

[41]   See Daniel J. Meeter, *The 'North American Liturgy': A Critical Edition of the Reformed Dutch Church in North America, 1793* (Ph.D. diss., Drew Univ., 1989) for a detailed account of these early psalter/hymnals. See also James L. H. Brumm, *Singing the Lord's Song: A History of the English Language Hymnals of the Reformed Church in America* (New Brunswick: Historical Society of the Reformed Church in America, 1990) for a historical survey of all the denomination's hymnals, and James H. Brumm, ed. *Liturgy Among the Thorns: Essays on Worship in the Reformed Church in America*, Historical Series of the Reformed Church in America, no. 57 (Grand Rapids: Eerdmans, 2007), chap. 4.

[42]   A nearly concurrent effort with the Hopkinson psalter was titled *A collection of the psalm and hymn-tunes, used by the Protestant Reformed Dutch Church of the City of New York, agreeable to that Psalm book, published in English, In four parts, viz, tenor, bass, treble and cantor* (1774). Published by Hodge and Shober, editor and circulation unknown, the collection reveals a second break with Calvin's worship doctrine by venturing away from unison singing, offering harmonizations to a presumed musically literate audience. See Carleton Sprague Smith, "The 1774 Psalm Book of the Reformed Protestant Church in New York City," *Musical Quarterly*, vol. 34, no 1. (Jan 1948), 84-96, and Allen Perdue Britton, Irving Lowens, completed by Richard Crawford, *American Sacred Music Imprints, 1698-1810: A Bibliography* (Worchester, MA: American Antiquarian Society, 1990), 474-75 (No. 397).

The language change created a stir regarding music at the aforementioned Old Brick Reformed Church. In 1785 the consistory voted to permit the gallery to be used free of charge,[43] but indicated that subscribers and singers have preferential seating, for "carrying on the different parts of the music."[44] The records indicate that a choir of younger members of the congregation had been formed to lead the singing of apparently *harmonized* versions of English psalms and hymns. A contentious period arose between conservative and liberal sides. It was settled in favor of the younger faction in February 1787 by a consistory resolution, arranged in a biblically exegetical query and answer format.[45] The introduction of harmonized psalms and hymns

[43] Responding to the evangelical edict of the Great Awakening, many churches at this time began suspending pew rentals in galleries as an inducement to indigents, slaves, and Native Americans.

[44] Hammond, *Sing to The Lord!*, 6. See also Theodore W. Wells, *Brick Church Memorial, 1699-1877* (Freehold: James S. Yard, 1877), 43.

[45] Ibid., 7-9, (obtained from the *Consistory Minute Book, 1709-1826*, entry dated April, 26, 1789). Query three asked, "What tunes are to be sung?" It was answered, "Resolved unanimously, that we find no particular mode or tune limited, or pointed out in God's word. Query four asked, "May then every one sing what Psalm or tune he please? It was answered, "Resolved, that every one has a right to Sing what Psalm tune he please, by himself; but when he sings in Consort, he ought so to sing that the voice harmonises with those with whom he sings, which we support by the exhortation of the Apostle in 2 Cor 14: 40, let all things be done decently and in order. Query five asked, "Is it sutable for a Christian to sing a cheerful tune?" It was answered, "Resolved unanimously, that it is sutable for a Christian on a cheerful occasion to sing a cheerful tune, which we support by the exhortation of the Pst in the 33 Psalm v 1, Rejoice in the Lord o ye Righteous; for Praise is comely for the upright. And it is sutable on mournfull occasions to sing in a mournfull tone of the voice. So David sung in the 55th Psalm v 1, Ye mourn in complaint and make a noise. Hence it is that musitioners have formed music on two keys, the one is called the sharp Key, sutable to be used on cheerful occasions; the other is called the flat key, and sutable to be used on mournfull occasions." The final query nine asked, "What is then the resolve of the Consistory with respect to the Improvement & practice of musick in the unighted Congregations of their care and charge?" It was answered, "Resolved that the consistory, not wishing to Lord over God's Heritage, will not with stern command say to our congregations, you shall or you shall not improve nor Practice in any collection of Psalm tunes whatever, we leave the Christian where God hath left him, to the liberty of his own conscience to sing in private what Psalm tune or tunes he please, and when he sings in consort, we recommend him to sing with order and decency, as the Apostle would have all things should be done, and we would further recommend that under present circumstances such tunes be sung as have been most usually practised heretofore in our congregations, or such plain and easy tunes as the congregation can most easily join with, giving opportunity to sing on new improvements, for the encouragement of improving in the comely, the sweet, and delightfull art of musick, wishing that our harts and voices may hereafter, with the Saints and Angels above in more melodious strains, where is fullness of joy and pleasure evermore. Finally, Resolved, that the Resolves of this session be publickly read in our united congregations of Freehold and Middletown. Concluded with prayer, Benj: Dubois, Moderator."

at Old Brick also ushered in its first choir, an often-replicated pattern in eighteenth-century America through the impetus of the "regular" singing movement.[46]

The language change instigated a different musical innovation at the Church on the Ponds in Pompton Lakes, New Jersey. Although Benjamin Romeyn had occupied the post of chorister and reader since 1787, when occasional services in English were added around 1800, because Romeyn "did not understand the music of English hymns," John C. Stagg was appointed to lead the hymn singing in English.[47] Both remained in office until Dutch services were eliminated in 1824, prompting Romeyn's resignation. A similar situation erupted in West Hempstead, New York, when English singing was introduced in 1804 and the consistory debated whether the tunes should be sung in *unison or in three-part harmony*, an indication that a choir had probably been formed.[48] In contrast, at the Old North Reformed Church in Dumont, New Jersey, a stronghold of Dutch conservatism just across the Hudson River from New York City, Dutch psalms were still sung until 1833.[49] Moreover, in Dutch Reformed settlements in the Midwest, Dutch language worship persisted into the twentieth century.[50]

Considering this diverse worship landscape, Livingston's need to mollify and unite opposing factions while molding a unique American denomination can be appreciated. His committee produced an English psalter fashioned from a handful of those in use. Of 150 psalms, the texts by Watts comprised 51 percent, those of Tate and Brady 26 percent, and 14 percent came from the twenty-year-old Collegiate Psalter.[51] Livingston was careful to append the Heidelberg Catechism, the confession of faith, and the liturgy to *The Psalms and Hymns of the Reformed Protestant Dutch Church in North America* (1789) to

---

[46]   The "regular" singing controversy will be discussed in the next chapter.

[47]   H. G. McNomee, *The Church of the Ponds: A History with Reminiscences 1710-1935. In Commemoration of the 225th Anniversary, November 10th to December 1st 1935* (Pompton Lakes, NJ: The Bulletin, 1935), 24.

[48]   Joseph H. Whitehead, et al., eds., *1800-1900 A History of the Classis of Paramus in the Reformed Church in America: Containing the Proceedings of the Centennial Meeting of the Classis, the Historical Discourse, and the Addresses, Statistical History and the Histories of the Individual Churches* (New York: Board of Publication, R.C.A., 1902), 316.

[49]   *1724-1975. The Story of the Old North Reformed Church, Dumont, NJ* (Dumont: The Consistory, 1976), 20.

[50]   Some Reformed Church in America (RCA) congregations in the Midwest continued to sing psalms in Dutch until the last quarter of the nineteenth century. See Polman, *Church Music and Liturgy*, 60. The Christian Reformed Church, which separated from the RCA in 1857, adopted its first English psalter in 1914.

[51]   Brumm, *Singing the Lord's Song*, 19; Brumm, *Liturgy*.

remain consistent with Dutch psalters. But, as James Brumm noted, "the genius of John Henry Livingston" was his arranging the first fifty-two hymns in the order of the Heidelberg Catechism questions and to include twenty Communion hymns, since it had been the pattern of Dutch Reformed worship to sing psalms at the time of receiving the sacrament.[52]

Psalm and hymn tunes were omitted from the first several editions of the psalter/hymnal until the publishing of *The Book of Praise* (1866). During this period of tuneless psalter/hymnals, Dutch Reformed churches, along with most Protestant denominations, found it necessary to obtain one or more separate music collections, or tunebooks, to coincide with the texts of their psalter/hymnals.[53] Church officials attempted to stem the tide of unauthorized hymnals and tunebooks by periodic expansions of the psalter/hymnal.[54] In a desperate, but surely vain, attempt to hold back the use of unauthorized collections, concurrent with the announcement of a sizable revision to the psalter/hymnal in 1831, the General Synod issued a strongly worded prohibition published in the *Christian Intelligencer*.[55] By the time *The Book of Praise* was released, hymns had replaced metrical psalms in the official church repertoire and the majority of Dutch Reformed congregations had replaced the services of a *voorzanger* with those of a chorister or organist.

---

[52] Ibid.

[53] A discussion of the role of tunebooks in Dutch Reformed worship will be taken up in chapter 5.

[54] The *Psalms and Hymns of the Reformed Protestant Dutch Church in North America* (New York: Board of Publication of the Reformed Protestant Dutch Church in North America, 1789), ed. John Livingston, included 135 hymns. By mid-century the hymn total had reached 797 with the reissuance of *Psalms and Hymns* (New York: Board of Publication of the Reformed Protestant Dutch Church in North America, 1848). The number surely inflated after the General Synod in 1846 reported that six hymnals from other denominations were currently in use by Dutch Reformed churches in the United States.

[55] Vol. 2, no. 13 WN 65 (Oct. 29, 1831). "It has become fashionable of late to introduce private and unauthorized selections into the weekly lectures, and particular meetings for worship and prayer, with the design of creating greater interest and giving more powerful excitement to passions. We say nothing at present against the injury produced by exalting particular ordinances proposed by expediency over the stated and ordinary divine institutions, but we would direct the attention of the churches, to the mischief that may finally result from the indiscriminate use of unauthorized version of the psalms, and unauthorized collections of sacred songs.... It will be well for the different classes to call the attention of their congregations, to the introduction and use of these hymns, and to discountenance the use of any other, than those duly authorized." See appendix 2 for the full text of the General Synod motion.

The Dutch Reformed Church Recast as an American Church

Recognizing that the Dutch in America had maintained their ethnic identity and culture through the doctrines and traditions of their faith, Firth Haring Fabend's book, *Zion on the Hudson: Dutch New York and New Jersey in the Age of Revivals*, explored the tensions between maintaining that identity and forging a new one through exposure to and participation in nineteenth-century American evangelicalism.

> But there is another way to see this journey. How ethnic peoples in our present multicultural society behave in the religious arena suggests that they use their churches creatively to ease their entrance into and advance their progress in their new surroundings. The theory that ethnic groups and the national churches and religious associated with them might be functionally future oriented, not anachronistically backward looking, as was once thought, can be applied to the Dutch experience in the seventeenth and eighteenth centuries. When that experience is viewed in this light, it permits the Reformed Dutch church and its adherents in nineteenth-century multicultural New York and New Jersey to be seen not primarily as defenders of Old World doctrines, standards, and traditions, as they usually have been. Rather, by regarding the church as a crucible, instead of as a fortress, forces in the denomination can be identified that worked within the crucible to produce structural and even doctrinal changes in the church, so that it might serve its needs and purposes in an American context.[56]

Fabend concluded that each newly adopted American pattern reconfigured Dutch worship and culture, whereby the former identity eroded in time and was supplanted by a mainstream American point of view. The Second Great Awakening (c.1790s-c.1840), unlike the (Calvinist) Great Awakening that had preceded it, was orchestrated by those of the Arminian persuasion who carried the message of the gospel to the American frontier through circuit ministries and revivals. However, revivals and circuit ministries were not the way of the Dutch Reformed. While obtaining a healthy increase in congregations between 1800 and 1860, mostly in the Northeast and in the Midwest,[57]

---

[56]   Firth Haring Fabend, *Zion on the Hudson: Dutch New York and New Jersey in the Age of Revivals* (New Brunswick: Rutgers Univ. Press, 2000), 3-4.

[57]   Polman, *Church Music and Liturgy*. The *Reveille* or "Great Awakening" in the Netherlands, unlike the Second Great Awakening in America, was a call to return

the denomination was eclipsed by the number of churches added by Methodists and Baptists.[58]

What did become part of the fabric of the Dutch church in America as a result of the Second Great Awakening were congregational Sunday schools, a practical substitute for the nearly defunct Dutch parochial schools.[59] Also prayer meetings for adult members were added, featuring a wider range of hymnody than was normally permitted in Sunday worship.[60] Another development of the Second Great Awakening was the advent of missionary, publication, and education societies in which the Dutch Reformed participated and sometimes led.[61] These ecumenical leagues evinced a new generic form of American Protestantism and enabled a plethora of interchurch associations.

to the creeds and polity of the Reformed Church's Calvinistic roots. Spread by the working class, the movement opposed the 1816 national *Reformeerde Kerk's* liberal reorganization, causing some of the members of the conservative wing, the *Afscheiding*, later called the *Gereformeerde Kerk*, to secede in 1834. Beginning around 1840, some of the members of this group immigrated to Michigan and Iowa, where they joined the Protestant Dutch Reformed Church in America. In 1857 several congregations seceded from the denomination, citing theological differences, to form the Christian Reformed Church. The *Reformeerde Kerk* and the *Gereformeerde Kerk* wings still exist in present-day Netherlands, each having influenced the thought and action of Dutch Reformed people in America.

58   Bruggink and Baker, *By Grace Alone*, 82-84. There were 139 Dutch Reformed churches in America in 1800. By 1830 the number had grown to 194. Between the years 1850 and 1860 the largest growth spurt added another 150 churches. See also Roger Finke and Roger Stark, *The Churching of America 1776-1790: Winners and Losers in Our Religious Economy* (New Brunswick: Rutgers Univ. Press, 1992) for a thorough discussion of the topic and comparative numbers in other denominations.

59   Sarah Van Doren organized the denomination's first Sunday school at the First Church in New Brunswick, New Jersey, in 1799.

60   A concern for the quality of hymnals and tunebooks used in prayer meetings and other social gatherings precipitated the publishing of John Knox, et al., *Sabbath-School and Social Hymns of the Reformed Protestant Dutch Church in the United States of America* (New York: Board of Managers of the General Synod Sabbath School Union, 1843) and later the *Fulton Street Hymn Book* (New York: Board of Publication of the Reformed Protestant Dutch Church in North America, 1862).

61   In 1796 Reformed, Presbyterian, and Baptist churches in New York City organized the New York Mission Society. In 1810 The American Board of Commissioners for Foreign Missions was established including Congregational, Presbyterian, Dutch, and German Reformed churches. In 1816 the American Bible Society was organized, the American Colonization Society (not a proud thing), and the United Foreign Missionary Society for work among American Indian tribes by Presbyterian, Dutch, and German Reformed churches. The American Sunday School Union was established in 1824, and in 1825 the American Tract Society was formed. In 1826 the American Temperance Society and the American Home Missionary Society were formed. The denomination also organized mission societies of its own, such as the Missionary Society of the Reformed Dutch Church in 1822, the Sabbath School Union in 1828, and the Organization of Board of Domestic Missions in 1832.

Randall Balmer noted that nineteenth-century historians, keeping with the "histories are written by victors" maxim, wrote from the perspective that the church had triumphed as an American institution.[62] As a measure of the Dutch Reformed Church's advancement in American society it adopted English as its worship language; it maintained a constitutional liturgy, but allowed pastors to exercise discretion in using it; it authorized hymn singing; and it permitted church choirs to form. Then, on equal footing with a host of rising denominations, the Dutch Reformed Church was forced to compete against those whose evangelical methods deprived it of members and threatened its survival as a communion in the United States.[63]

[62]   Balmer, *A Perfect Babel*, ix; Demarest, *History and Characteristics*; Edward Tanjore Corwin, *Manuel of the Reformed Protestant Dutch Church* (New York: Board of Publication, Reformed Church in America, 1859); Corwin, *Manuel of the Reformed Church in America*, 2nd, 3rd, 4th, and 5th eds. (New York: Board of Publication, Reformed Church in America, 1869, 1879, 1902, 1922); *Centennial Discourses: A Series of Sermons Delivered in the Year 1876*, 2nd ed., (New York: Board of Publication of the Reformed Church in America); and Edward Tanjore Corwin, *History of the Reformed Church, Dutch* (New York: Christian Literature Co., 1895).

[63]   In 1867 the General Synod officially removed the word "Dutch" from the church name. The new name became the Reformed Church in America.

PART II

Choir Development and Repertoire in the Dutch Reformed Church

CHAPTER 3

The Role of Singing Schools, Sabbath School Choirs, Choral Societies, Sacred Music Concerts, Instruments, and Organ in the Development of the Dutch Reformed Institutional Church Choir

In the first quarter of the nineteenth century, the majority of Dutch Reformed churches in America had adopted or was considering using English as the language of worship. John Livingston's translation of the liturgy and the English psalter/hymnal had made the transition inevitable.[1] However, the pervasiveness of the evangelical movement caused many clergy to digress from the constitutional liturgy, and there were rumblings that even more hymns were needed, as many churches were supplementing the official psalter/hymnal with hymnals from other denominations.[2] Thus, beyond the language change, the Dutch Reformed Church gradually was relinquishing some of its traditional forms of worship for forms common to mainstream American Protestantism.

---

[1] Brumm, *Singing the Lord's Song*, 1-71. The psalter/hymnal was revised and enlarged in 1813. In the revision, texts by Watts accounted for 78 percent of the psalms. The Genevan canticle settings were removed and 173 hymns were added. Brumm, *Liturgy*.

[2] I found period Methodist and Baptist hymnals with church members' names written in the inside covers in the archives of the Old Brick Reformed Church in Marlboro, New Jersey.

An especially diverse picture formed regarding music. To improve congregational singing many Dutch Reformed churches instituted resident singing schools and Sabbath school choirs. Some churches enlisted musical instruments to accompany congregational singing until they could afford an organ. The increased music literacy fueled an interest in choral societies and the sacred music concerts the societies sponsored, bringing a new repertoire and new techniques into vogue. In the early nineteenth century, the trend was enhanced by a northeastern church music reform movement that attracted many followers through the allure of cultured music and the promise of increased musical accomplishment through professional music leadership. Indeed, while many churches had singing schools and Sabbath school choirs, hosted choral societies and sacred music concerts, and employed instruments or organ, other churches did only some or none of these things. This chapter will examine the evidence of these musical innovations as a catalyst, aid, or mere backdrop to the development of institutional choirs in Dutch Reformed churches.

Singing Schools

As previously discussed, Nicholas Temperley posited that the bifurcation in seventeenth-century European Reformed music delineated by the terms "Old Way" and "New Way" of singing was attributable to the "New Way" use and the "Old Way" nonuse of organ.[3] The "New Way" had a latter day appearance in the American colonies prior to widespread organ-building activity,[4] as it was swept in by the tide of the First Great Awakening and the popularity of Americanized versions of Isaac Watts's hymnody[5] through the medium of singing

---

[3]   Temperley, "Old Way of Singing," 514-15.

[4]   For a thorough treatment of American organ building, see Orpha Osche, *The History of the Organ in the United States* (Bloomington: Indiana Univ. Press, 1975). See also John Ogasapian, *Music of the Colonial and Revolutionary Era* (Westport, CT: Greenwood, 2004), and *Organ Building in New York City, 1700-1900* (Braintree, MA: Organ Literature Foundation, 1977).

[5]   See Rochelle A. Stackhouse, *Language of the Psalms in Worship: American Revisions of Watts' Psalter* (Lanham, MD: Scarecrow, 1997). See also Esther Rothenbusch Crookshank, "'We're Marching to Zion': Isaac Watts in Early America," in Richard J. Mouw and Mark A. Noll, *Wonderful Words of Life: Hymns in American Protestant History and Theology* (Grand Rapids: Eerdmans, 2004), 17-41. Stackhouse quotes Louis F. Benson in *The English Hymn: Its Development and Use in Worship* (Richmond: John Knox, 1915), who said long ago that "the movement to improve singing was inevitably a movement toward the use of Watts and other hymns,"192-93 (ff. 26), and summarizes, "In one sense then, the shift to Watts' Christianized psalms and hymns meant a move to notated music and choral polyphony, and to a select group

schools.[6] Championed by a group of New England clergymen near Boston, the "regular" singing movement eschewed the prevailing slow and free manner of psalm singing and linked musical literacy and good choral technique to spiritual renewal.[7]

The last chapter identified two Dutch Reformed choirs that formed when English hymns were admitted to public worship. While it is not known if singing schools had been organized in those two churches, one may presume, because part-singing was mentioned, that the choir members read music. In effect, these choirs acted in the same manner as singing school graduates, who tried to convert their churches to "regular" singing by sitting together to lead the congregational singing. The irony of the singing schools lay in that the original

---

that could and sometimes did eventually dominate worship as had the precentor it replaced," 27.

[6]   Stephen A. Marini, *Sacred Song in America: Religion, Music and Public Culture*, and "Rehearsal of Revival: Sacred Singing and the Great Awakening in America," in *Sacred Sound: Music in Religious Thought and Practice*, ed. Joyce Irwin (Chico, CA: Scholars Press, 1983), 84-86, where he argued that the regular singing movement was a rehearsal for the Second Great Awakening, mirroring America's shift from Calvinism to Evangelicalism, and that "the universality and publicity of sacred singing made it of all religious media perhaps the most sensitive to the complex changes wrought by the Great Awakening in America," 87. There are also two good brief histories in Richard Crawford, *Introduction to American Music* (New York: Norton, 2001) and Richard Crawford, "Psalmody" in *The New Grove Dictionary of American Music*, ed. H. Wiley Hitchcock and Stanley Sadie (New York: Grove's Dictionaries of Music, 1986), 635-42.

[7]   Stanley Sadie, ed., *New Grove Dictionary of Music and Musicians,* 20 vols. (London: Macmillan, 1980), "Singing-schools," by Richard Crawford and David Warren Steel, 233-34. The diary of gentleman farmer and satirist William Byrd (1674-1744) of Westover, Virginia, attested to a singing school in the area in 1710-11. Several singing schools were reported in operation along the East Coast by the 1720s, with at least one in Philadelphia by 1753 and one in New York by 1754. Singing master Thomas Symmes's (1678-1725) book, *The Reasonableness of Regular Singing* (1720), indicated that he taught singing school in the evening to young people for their recreation and to replace the tendency for singing secular songs and ballads with a repertoire of sacred music. (Indeed, we have already encountered this line of thinking in Calvin's writings). Singing-school masters were among the first indigenous American music professionals. Among the earliest practitioners were William Billings (1746-1800), Samuel Holyoke (1762-1820), Jacob Kimball (1761-1826), Daniel Read (1757-1836), Oliver Holden (1765-1844), and Andrew Law (1749-1821). The singing school movement initiated a new industry for anthologies of music headed by pedagogical instruction, known as tunebooks. The first American published collection was James Lyon's (1735-94) *Urania; or a Choice Collection of Psalm Tunes, Anthems and Hymns* (1761), which included four-part English plain tunes along with the first printed music by Americans Francis Hopkinson, William Tuckey (1708-81), and James Lyon. William Little and William Smith published the first shape-noted collection of music, titled *The Easy Instructor*, in 1801.

purpose of the school, to improve congregational psalmody, led to the organizing of choirs who developed a separate repertoire from the rest of the congregation. Richard Crawford summarized this phenomenon.

> A third effect of the singing-school was that, by teaching Americans to sing with greater attention to the niceties of voice production and choral blend, and introducing them to musical notation as well, it inspired a wish for a more elaborate kind of music making than congregational singing could provide. In this impulse lies the beginning of the New England church choir, an institution that began to take shape shortly after mid-century.[8]

The singing school movement gradually retreated from the urban Northeast and followed the route of the westward frontier during the late eighteenth and through the mid nineteenth centuries, where evangelists adapted rote-singing methods and an accessible repertoire to frontier worship.[9]

Singing Schools in the Dutch Reformed Church[10]

The earliest record located of a singing school in a Dutch Reformed Church was this February 13, 1794, consistory resolution from Schenectady, New York:

> The Consistory taking into consideration the defective condition of Dutch Psalmody in the public worship of this church, Resolved,

---

[8] Richard Crawford, "Psalmody," Part 2, The rise of choirs and elaborate Psalmody [mid-eighteenth century], *New Grove Dictionary of American Music*, 636.

[9] General American music histories having addressed this topic include Gilbert Chase, *America's Music: From the Pilgrims to the Present*, rev. 3rd ed. (Urbana: Univ. of Illinois Press, 1987); Leonard Ellinwood, *The History of American Church Music* (New York: Morehouse-Gorham, 1953); H. Wiley Hitchcock, *Music in the United States: A Historical Introduction*, 3rd ed. (Englewood Cliffs: Prentice-Hall, 1988); Irving Lowens, *Music and Musicians in Early America* (New York: Norton, 1964); and Ogasapian, *Music of the Colonial and Revolutionary Era*.

[10] The evidence of musical activity in individual singing schools was obtained primarily from individual church records, church histories or anniversary publications, and the denomination's weekly magazine, the *Christian Intelligencer*. Following the *Magazine of the Reformed Dutch Church*, published 1826-30, the *Christian Intelligencer* was published weekly in New York City from July 1830 until 1922, when it merged with the *Mission Field*. In 1935 the magazine merged with the *Leader*, a regional Reformed Church magazine published in Holland, Michigan, since 1905, to become the *Intelligencer Leader*. In 1943 the magazine became the *Church Herald* and was published monthly until September/October 2009. A number of features from the *Church Herald* continue to be published online, as well as in the *RCA Today* magazine.

that Cornelius DeGraaf, the Chorister, shall use his endeavors, in each family of this village and elsewhere, to obtain pupils for singing, on condition that each shall pay one shilling six pence a month, the Consistory, also adding thereto for each scholar for the term of six months, one shilling six pence a month; provided a certificate be shown to the Consistory signed by Mr. DeGraaf that each scholar had diligently spent his time as he ought. Also Mr. DeGraaf in singing shall try to observe the measure of half notes and soften his voice as much as possible.[11]

This resolution provides evidence of a commonly observed cause and effect scenario played out in American sacred music as congregations adopted "regular" singing methods. First, there was agreement that congregational singing was somehow "defective." Second, many people believed that implementing a singing school would correct the problem. Third, churches charged the youth of the church, under the guidance of some qualified individual, with learning the new techniques and repertoire and passing them on to the older members of the congregation by leading the singing in weekly worship. This is how choirs were formed. The resolution from Schenectady is particularly interesting and amusing in that the singing master, Mr. DeGraaf himself, needed schooling to conform to the regimen of "regular" singing. DeGraaf was probably the church *voorzanger* before becoming its chorister. If so, some of the "Old Way" techniques of leading the congregation in psalm singing, where tempo and note values were more subjective, and where the precentor needed a resounding voice, may have been hard to break. Nevertheless, the resolution provides a charming view of the early period of "regular" singing before the more "scientific" approaches to singing and training music directors were employed.

In Readington, New Jersey, a singing school was activated by 1799. The contract for singing master Edward Cocks included the signatures of the thirty members of his first class, sixteen male and fourteen female.[12] The nearly equal gender distribution at the Readington

[11]   *Two Hundredth Anniversary of the First Reformed Protestant Church of Schenectady, NY June 20th and 21st 1880* (New York: Steam Printing House, 1880), 161.
[12]   Lorena Cole Vincent, *Readington Reformed Church, Readington, New Jersey 1719-1769* (Somerset, NJ: Published by the Consistory and Somerset Press, 1969). "That the Said Edward Cocks do Teach the Common Rules of Psalmody at the Rate of fifty cents per Schollar per quarter, or thirteen Evenings & the Each Schollar do pay the Said Edward Cocks the Sum of fifty Cents at the Expiration of Said Quarter of thirteen Evenings as Witness Our hand, the Sixteenth day of January 1799," 58.

singing school indicates that the curriculum included part-singing. The virtually exclusive use of two, three, and four-part harmonizations in period tunebooks substantiates that singing in harmony was an important goal in the singing school curriculum. Furthermore, given that the students were most likely teenagers or slightly older, female singers would have been needed to support the upper parts of the specific scoring of the period repertoire.

At the First Church, Albany, twenty members of the congregation presented the following petition to the consistory September 10, 1803:

> To the Minister, Elders and Deacons of the Reformed Protestant Dutch Church in the City of Albany: The petition of the subscribers, members of the said church and others belonging to the congregation thereof, respectfully showeth that your petitioners feel a sincere desire to promote the interests of the said church by improvements in the mode of singing. That they have for some time past conceived with regret that by reason of the encouragement given by some of the other churches in this city in indigent persons who are disposed to feel such improvement, large numbers of young persons of both sexes may be drawn off to those churches under whose patronage they are instructed in psalmody without expense. That your petitioners perceive that correct singing forms a pleasing as well as useful part of a religious worship and therefore merits the encouragement of all those who feel solicitous for the honor and prosperity of the church.
>
> Under these impressions, your petitioners have been impelled to attempt to establish a free Singing School within the city and to place it under the direction of the Reverend Board, but they are apprehensive that their best exertions will be fruitless unless you will be pleased to give them liberal aid in their valuable undertaking...[13]

The consistory appointed a Committee on Sacred Music in 1813 to implement the ten-year-old petition. Solomon St. John was hired as singing master for a small stipend, and the consistory room was used for the singing school. In 1815 Reuben Ellis was engaged as singing master for $300 for nine months, and the next May the singing school was held from 6-8 p.m. on Mondays and Thursdays during the summer.[14]

---

[13]   Robert S. Alexander, *Albany's First Church: And Its Role in the Growth of the City, 1642-1942* (Albany: First Church in Albany, 1988), 247-48.

[14]   *Our Two Hundred and Fifty Years. A Historical Sketch of the First Reformed Church, Albany, N.Y.* (Published by the Officers of the Church, 1899), 30.

In 1816 to be able to offer the "chorister" a more substantial income, an invitation was extended to "every religious society of this city" to send their children to this singing school for a nominal fee.[15]

When the Fort Miller Reformed Church in upstate New York called a Native American missionary, the Reverend Joel Wood (presided 1839-45) in 1839, the consistory heard his preinstallation queries, "What can be done to increase the number and interests of the Sabbath school?" and "What can be done to put into operation a singing school of the first order?"[16] The consistory approved the idea of a singing school and in a minute taken December 13, 1844, resolved with caution, "...that Mrs. Whiting be permitted to hold a singing school. No damage must be done to the church, and all must be orderly." The consistory further resolved "that a committee of three shall be appointed to clear the church of such spectators as shall make any disturbance in the singing school, or shall injure the house."[17] The Sabbath school motion later passed, whereby the two schools periodically joined forces to produce monthly concerts benefiting foreign missions.

The Reverend David Demarest held singing school one night per week sometime during his brief pastoral tenure (1841-43) at the Flatbush Reformed Church in New York. It also appears that about the same time Mr. James Hendricks was the director of the choir and the first to accompany singing with the bass viol.[18] But by the second quarter of the nineteenth century, the individual hired to direct the singing school was most often obtained to be the church chorister or organist, too, as was the case in even rural areas such as this in Herkimer, New York:

> The matter of singing was not allowed to fall into neglect in those days, either, for in September of the same year (1835) a committee, of which Gen. Gray was chairman, was appointed by Consistory "to employ a suitable teacher for a singing school and also secure his services as chorister of the church."[19]

---

15   Alexander, *Albany's First Church*, 249.

16   Millard M. Gifford, *The Phoenix of the North: Four Ministers and Supply Pastors Who Served the Fort Miller Reformed Church, Fort Edward, NY 1817 to 1972* (New York, 1971), 30.

17   Ibid., 32.

18   P.S. Beekman, compiler, *History of the Reformed Church of Flatbush, NY 1807-1907* (Kingston, NY: R.W. Anderson, 1907), 56.

19   Henry M. Cox, *History of the Reformed Church of Herkimer, NY from the Settlement of Herkimer County in 1723* (Herkimer: L.C. Childs, 1886), 38.

Another example of the combined positions of singing schoolmaster and chorister[20] is found in this 1880s testimony of church treasurer Stephen B. Miller at the First Reformed Church in Hudson, New York. Here he recalled with vivid detail the time before the construction of the congregation's first sanctuary in 1836:

> Shortly after the first service at the Court House, a meeting was held at the residence of Misses Catherine and Caroline Morton, at which a large and efficient choir was organized and Mr. Enoch Hubbard was permanently retained to conduct it, at a salary of one hundred and fifty dollars. It contained seven pairs of sisters, all of whom were singers of more than ordinary excellence. A singing school was established, which was held weekly at private homes until the completion of a basement, at which Mr. Hubbard was obliged to teach the rudiments of sacred music.[21]

The above examples indicate that from about the turn of the nineteenth century singing schools had gradually become an accepted, even vital, part of the Dutch Reformed Church's ecclesiastical life and one measure of its progress toward Americanization. Indeed, one can glimpse the process by which objections had been overcome in this early issue of the *Christian Intelligencer*:

SINGING SCHOOLS BLEST
From the (Utica) Western Recorder

> Those through the land, who have the interests of Zion most at heart, are in general the farthest removed from musical cultivation; and the reason assigned is, that *"singing schools are always unfavorable to the progress of vital piety."* The position taken here is not true. It is only the neglect, the abuse, the mismanagement of singing schools, which leads to the lamented evil."[22]

---

[20]   When Dutch Reformed churches began to keep records in English in the late eighteenth and early nineteenth centuries, they often used the term *chorister* as a substitute for the Dutch word *voorzanger*. Initially denoting the individual who led congregational singing (with or without the aid of instrumental accompaniment), by the mid-nineteenth century, the term *chorister* came to identify the church choir director. However, the term *organist* was often employed when one individual held both positions. Twentieth-century records substitute the term *choir director* for chorister; yet, the term *organist* is still often used to indicate the combined positions.

[21]   William H. Gleason, D.D., *1836-1886, Semi-Centennial of the First Reformed Church, Hudson, NY* (Hudson: M. Parker Williams, Register and Gazette, 1886), 32-35. The choir consisted of fourteen women and thirteen men. See chapter 4 for a list of members' names.

[22]   *Christian Intelligencer* 1, no.1, WN1 (Aug. 7, 1830), 1. (WN, indicating Whole Number, gives the total number of editions to date.)

Figure 1. The Van Lente Choir, c.1860
(courtesy of Dr. Elton J. Bruins,
Third Reformed Church, Holland, MI, and the
A.C. Van Raalte Institute at Hope College, Holland, MI)

However, in mid-Atlantic Dutch Reformed churches singing schools declined after 1850 when public school music and the pedagogy of professional church choir directors outmoded the singing school shape-note teaching methods.

The story is somewhat different in midwestern Dutch churches— where choirs were not yet admitted to worship. A well-documented choir begun by Frederick J. Van Lente, the *voorzanger* of the First Reformed Church in Holland, Michigan, was formed in 1856 after he asked the consistory to have a choir assist him in leading the singing during worship.[23] Although the consistory refused his request, a choir of twelve boys and two girls commenced as a singing school and met in member's homes until it acquired its own building for rehearsals. Van Lente's choir sang at the dedicatory service of the Third Reformed Church in Holland, Michigan, paving the way for the church's own choir by the time the congregation had moved into its new building and for a host of other choral societies in the area.[24] The Van Lente choir

---

[23] Elton J. Bruins, *The Americanization of a Congregation*, Historical Series of the Reformed Church in America, no. 26 (Grand Rapids: Eerdmans, 1995), 22-23.

[24] Ibid., 199-200. The *Holland City News,* Dec. 26, 1874, stated, "We are not wanting in singing societies." Bruins noted, "Mr. C. Van Oostenbrugge conducted a choral group which met every Thursday evening in the consistory room of Third Church. There was a musical group at the college. The choir of First Reformed Church

was still active in 1936, its directorship conferred on the children and grandchildren of its founder.

Singing schools often provided entry points for many institutional church choirs in the Dutch Reformed Church by offering pedagogical venues aimed at improving congregational song. As a rule, the singing school graduates did not disperse once the mission was accomplished, leaving the newly informed congregation to its own devices. Rather, the singers remained as a choir to lead worship and to develop a unique and separate repertoire from the congregation.

Sabbath School Choirs

With the arrival of schoolmaster Adam Roelantsen in 1633, Dutch Reformed education was transplanted to the New World, and Dutch schools affiliated with individual churches were organized throughout the settlement. Generally, it was the *voorlezer* of each congregation who taught the Heidelberg Catechism to the youth and, as Robin Leaver noted, included psalm singing as an important component of Christian education.[25] Seventeenth-century church records indicate that psalms were sung at the opening and closing of school exercises. Indeed, in 1698 the *dominie* of the church in New York proudly reported to the Amsterdam classis that the youth of the congregation were not only capable of reciting the catechism from memory, but all of the metrical "psalms, hymns, and prayers in rhyme...."[26] It is clear that learning and singing the psalms was an essential part of a Dutch Reformed Christian education from its earliest days.

Sabbath schools, also called Sunday schools, began to appear in Dutch Reformed churches around the turn of the nineteenth century. Guided by the consistory, of which the church pastor is president, and regulated by the denomination's Sunday School Union, each church supplied a Reformed Christian education to children from about the age of five to early teens. The teachers of the graded system of religious education were members of the church who, unlike teachers

---

rehearsed on Monday evenings, the choir of Third on Tuesday evenings, led by C. De Jong, and the True Reformed Church (Central Avenue Christian Reformed Church) even had a choir which rehearsed on Thursday evenings."

25   Robin A. Leaver, "Dutch Secular and Religious Songs in Eighteenth-Century New York," in *Amsterdam-New York Transatlantic Relations and Urban Identities Since 1653.* ed. George Harinck and Hans Krabbendam (Amsterdam: VU Uitgeverij, 2005), 99-115.

26   Ibid., 100. See also Daniel J. Meeter *'Bless the Lord, O My Soul': The New-York Liturgy of the Dutch Reformed Church, 1767* (Lanham, MD: Scarecrow, 1998), 1-91.

in the nearly defunct system of parochial schools, were not charged to perpetuate the Dutch language and culture. In fact, the schools were an American invention of the Second Great Awakening and were yet another pathway to the denomination's Americanization.[27]

Singing played a key role in the Sabbath school discipline. It was implemented then, as it is today, to be a powerful tool for learning and experiencing faith and as essential preparation for adult active participation in weekly worship.

From the *Sunday School Magazine*:

> We have been persuaded for a long time, that this important part [singing] of the exercises of a Sunday school, is very much neglected; nor is it matter of surprise, when we consider what place it really (not nominally) holds in the services of the sanctuary. For children adopt with great precision and facility the standards of those who are older, and (of course) wiser than themselves.[28]

The Sabbath schools provided opportunities to sing a wider range of hymns and anthems than was usually found in weekly worship, because school leaders could venture beyond the strict use of the denomination's psalter/hymnal under the guise of an educational activity. Nevertheless, concerns over the types of hymns sung in Sabbath schools—and their seepage into public worship—prompted the General Synod to publish a special collection of 331 hymns and a set of doxologies with this explanatory preface:

> To the Sabbath Schools and Churches
>
> The committee charged by the General Synod with the selection and arrangement of Hymns for the use of Sabbath Schools, under the sanction of the Synod, present the following to the Churches. With the view of increasing the matter of the authorized Psalmody of the Church, the Psalms and hymns contained in the book now in use have been excluded from the present collection; and whilst the leading object is to furnish hymns in sufficient number and variety for the use of the Sabbath Schools, others are interspersed as to render the collection suitable for the lecture-room and social worship.[29]

27 Brouwer, *Reformed Church Roots*, 88-93.
28 *Christian Intelligencer* 1, no. 4, WN 4 (Aug. 28, 1830), 16.
29 *Sabbath School Hymns and Social Hymns of the Reformed Protestant Dutch Church of the United States of America*, adopted by the General Synod, June 1843 (New York: Board of Managers of the General Synod Sabbath School Union, 1843).

The hymns were arranged in topical/catechistic sections with such titles as "The Scriptures," "Being and Attributes of God," "Creation and Providence," and "Heaven and Hell." Hymn texts were also arranged in sections by occasion such as "Worship," "Prayer," "Opening and Closing School," "Anniversary Occasions," and "Monthly Concerts."[30] Naturally, many of the texts were aimed at the youth, with accessible language and Sunday school exercises in mind. However, one cannot help but notice the more colorful poetry of many hymn texts compared to those in the authorized worship hymnal, for lines such as these are common: "Shine, Lord! And my terror shall cease, The blood of atonement apply" and "Attend to my sorrows and cries—My groanings that cannot be told."

Another feature of the Sabbath schools were public musical performances given on such special occasions as an anniversary of the Sabbath school, a church program or mission activity, dedication, or picnic. This poetic account of the combined Sunday schools' anniversary exercises of the Thousand Isles (Alexandria Bay), New York, demonstrates the emotional responses these events sustained:

> The Exercises at the grove were rendered intensely interesting by the sweet vocal music of our village choir, which sounded afar off upon the clear blue deep, and hushed the gentle murmurs of the wave upon leaving....As the islanders dipped their oars in the sparkling waters of the St. Lawrence, the village choir again struck up a beautiful hymn, and having escorted them part of the way homeward, all parted with mutual good-will.[31]

The account of the twenty-seventh anniversary of the Market Street (Manhattan) Reformed Church Sunday school in October 1848 indicated that the event generated a capacity crowd of four hundred in the church.

> ...while the singing exercises by the children were truly delightful; indeed, we think we have never heard anything sung more sweetly than the requiem or dirge for a female teacher and little member of the infant class, who had died during the year. The number of hymns was unusual, and indicated that this was to be the children's jubilee; and such it was, for they all seemed to enjoy it.[32]

---

30   Monthly concerts were not musical concerts, as we might think, but prayer gatherings.
31   *Christian Intelligencer* 19, no. 2, WN 938 (July 20, 1848), 6.
32   Ibid. 19, no. 17, WN 953 (Nov. 2, 1848), 66.

The *Christian Intelligencer* reprinted the program with this introduction, "We give the hymns sung on the occasion, for the benefit of any who may be desirous of obtaining anniversary hymns." I have included it here as it appeared there.[33]

Introductory

"Crown the Saviour" Tune "Ford" from the *New York Choralist*

II.

"Joyous Praise" (written for the occasion) Tune "Baxter" from the *S.S. Lyre*

The first verse was sung as a duet by members of the Infant Class; the second as a response, the third as a duet by members of the Senior Department; the 4th and 5th as a response; the whole school repeating the 2d, 4th and 5th chorus.

1st verse

Come, bring the song of gladsome sound,
Our youthful praise to tell;
No sweeter strains on earth are found;
None Jesus loves so well.

II. Love of Jesus

(The last two verses of the above, five in all, and also the three following hymns were written by the indefatigable superintendent of the school.)

IV. Annual Offering Tune "Fairfield" *New York Choralist*

V. Not, Here, Not Here are They
On the death of Miss Catharine Lockwood, of the Senior Department, and Mary Gray, of the Infant Class.

Tune—"Boylston"

Not here, not here are they,
To join our festal throng;
Jesus has called them far away,
To wake a nobler song.

First, our dear teacher left
Her station by our side;

---

[33] In addition to listing the texts and tune names, the program provides valuable information by listing the actual tunebooks used for the event. See chapter 5 for a detailed discussion of tunebooks.

Then she, a flow'ret scarce yet blown,
Our little sister, died.

Weep not, for they have gone
To happier homes on high;
Where, with the angels round the throne,
They'll hymn His praise for aye.

Oh, hear this lesson learn,
That death is ever nigh;
Youth's but a flow'r beside the tomb,
And, like it, soon may die.

VI. Parting Prayer Tune—"Brown" from the "Psalmodist"

The musicians used at least three tunebooks for this Sunday school anniversary program. Two of the tunebooks, The *New York Choralist* (1847) and the *Psalmodist* (1844), were prepared by the Thomas Hastings (1784-1872) and William B. Bradbury (1816-68) team and published in New York. Hastings composed the tunes named "Ford" and "Fairfield," William Bradbury composed the tune "Brown," and Lowell Mason (1792-1872) composed the tune "Boylston." They are typical "common tune" Sunday school songs consisting of eight to ten measures with verses and a refrain. The melodies move in mostly stepwise or triadic motion, the rhythms are very simple, and the harmony is rudimentary (diatonic) in four parts, although it would be easy and effective to sing the melody with just one of the harmonizing parts. Often, as has occurred here, one of the participants wrote a new poetic text for the occasion. In fact, one finds these occasional texts published often in the *Christian Intelligencer* during this era.

The account of the twenty-eighth anniversary of the Market Street Sunday school also published the names of the hymns and the text to an anthem that was sung, titled "Praise the Lord." This assessment was given:

> ...it will be seen from the list of pieces sung, which we give below, that the pupils were to be the principal actors in the scene, and they acquitted themselves well. More than this, the singing in parts was thrilling, the duets very fine; and the infant class, of some ninety dear little creatures under six years of age, who could warble more sweetly? We may ask with confidence, when did our friends present hear the anthem "Praise ye the Lord" executed with a finer combination of sweetness and skill?[34]

---

[34]   *Christian Intelligencer* 20, no. 17, WN 1005 (Nov. 1, 1849), 66.

Here we learn that Sunday school choirs could be very large, that the choirs performed a variety of musical forms, and that at some point the choir members became capable of part-singing. It stands to reason then that when the choir members reached adulthood many would have wanted to exercise their ability to sing and read music in some other venue—perhaps by joining a singing society or, as had been the case with many singing school graduates, starting or participating in a church choir. It further makes sense that the choir members may have carried forward a preference for certain forms or styles of music learned in the Sabbath school. Though there was a distinction between Sunday school music and the music used in weekly public worship, the confluence of choral activities in and around ecclesiastical life and the availability of vast amounts of music began to make the lines between the two a bit murky. Darkening the waters even more, the repertoires of choral societies in time became practically interchangeable with the music one heard in public worship.

Choral Societies

A second campaign to improve congregational singing arose in New England in the late-eighteenth century out of the desire to replace the compositions of American colonial tunesmiths in singing school tunebooks with music of greater refinement.[35] In the early nineteenth century, the movement promoted a "scientific" music pedagogy and a repertoire derived from two distinctive pathways: (1) extractions or arrangements of elaborate European art music from composers like George Frederic Handel (1685-1759), Franz Joseph Haydn (1732-1809), Wolfgang Amadeus Mozart (1756-91), and Ludwig van Beethoven (1770-1827); and (2) the simple tunes and meters of the "common tunes," culled from Reformation era sources or newly composed by movement leaders like Lowell Mason and Thomas Hastings.

According to Gilbert Chase, the reform movement operated on the "assertion of the classical concept of inherent and immutable aesthetic

---

[35] Marini, *Sacred Song in America*, who offered this definition of the new style of music: "Called English country parish music, the new style provided small rural congregations with sacred compositions that were musically accomplished, yet could be performed by a limited number of singers. It was the sort of music John and Charles Wesley heard and sang growing up in their father's Anglican parish at rural Epworth in Lincolnshire. Composers for the English country parish like William Knapp (1698-1768), John Stevenson (1761-1833), William Tans'ur (1700-83), and Aaron Williams (1731-1776) wrote in three principal forms: the plain tune, the fuging tune, and the anthem," 77.

values, grafted onto the scientific rationalism of the Enlightenment,"[36] or as Richard Crawford summarizes:

> The reform of early nineteenth-century psalmody partakes of a different spirit—one centered not on praise but on edification. Rather than God, its main recipients were the people who worshipped God.[37]

Just how pervasive the view was can be seen in this portion of an address given by the Reverend George Schenck (1816-52) prior to a concert in his church, two years before hosting Hastings and Bradbury. Under the heading, "The Cultivation of Music," Schenck rehearsed this neo-Platonic/neo-Augustinian view of music:

> Surely a Power so great ought not be neglected;—a Power which can soothe the passions or rouse the energies, which can quicken and animate the sensibilities or soften and melt to devotion the heart, ought to be cherished and directed to the noble ends for which it is both adapted and designed. Like every other Power, it may produce evil, if the great and the good do not take hold and control it.[38]

This philosophy of music prompted the establishment of choral societies in cities, suburbs, and, soon after, in rural areas.[39] Contact between churches and the societies were assured, although the societies were not usually affiliated with individual churches. However, it can safely be assumed that the society's membership was comprised of individuals who were also members of church choirs, as Paul Allwardt has surmised.[40]

By the second quarter of the nineteenth century, the church music reform campaign had created a sizable music industry in concert, tunebook, and instrument sales.[41] Hastings and Mason expanded

---

[36] Chase, *America's Music*, 134.

[37] Crawford, *Introduction to American Music*, 86.

[38] *Music: An Address Delivered in the First Reformed Dutch Church of Somerville, NJ at a Concert of Music from the "Young Ladies" of the "Somerset Institute" by the Rev. George Schenck of Bedminster, NJ* (New York: John A. Gray, 1849), 11.

[39] Shortly after being established in the Northeast, the movement advanced into the Midwest by way of cities such as Pittsburgh, Cincinnati, and Chicago.

[40] "It is believed that the societies devoted to the cultivation of sacred music were composed of members of church choirs, and that the repertories of the societies and of the choirs were to a large extent identical." (Anton) Paul Allwardt, *Sacred Music in New York City: 1800-1850*, SMD diss. (Union Theological Seminary, 1950), ii.

[41] Richard Crawford, in "'Ancient Music' and the Europeanizing of American

the enterprise in the Northeast through an ambitious lecture/concert circuit. The lectures typically ended with a concert of allied church choirs displaying lessons learned to a sizable audience,[42] while exhibiters hawked their tunebooks.[43] There are several documented lecture/concerts in Dutch Reformed churches in New York City and in the outlying suburbs. I have extracted this early account of a lecture delivered by Thomas Hastings at the Middle Dutch Church in Manhattan:

> Without any previous understanding between him and the people, he soon put into practice specimens exhibiting the correctness of views, and the practicability of introducing the monitorial system of instruction onto the Psalmody of our churches.... Let a congregation have stated meetings for improvement. Let some competent person, after the manner of Mr. Hastings, take the lead, while those who are better acquainted than the rest with the rules and practice of singing, are distributed throughout the church in little groups, and let the monitorial mode of instruction be adopted and preserved in regularity.[44]

It is interesting to note that, in the prefaces of four Hastings tunebooks, I found no specific mention of a "monitorial mode of instruction." However, the tunebook's prefaces, Hastings's book *The*

Psalmody, 1800-1810," *A Celebration of American Music: Words and Music in Honor of H. Wiley Hitchcock* (Ann Arbor: Univ. of Michigan Press, 1990), showed that the movement had essentially succeeded by 1810, fully displacing the indigenous music of the Revolutionary War era.

[42] Advertisements often invited churches to bring their entire choirs, pastor, and chorister. However, sacred music lecture/concerts were open to all spectators, as hundreds swarmed events led by the iconic Thomas Hastings. While attending a *lesser* form of entertainment could lead to moral recriminations against the attendee, attending a sacred music lecture/concert would have been considered commendable. Indeed, the events provided an excellent opportunity to make acquaintances outside of one's immediate community in a society where social convention otherwise made the courting process limiting and cumbersome. I have encountered several advertisements that offered to admit ladies for a discount or free. Intentionally or not, the lecture/concert was a vehicle for breaking Puritanical codes, while the concept of audience and its purposes was becoming increasingly pluralistic.

[43] While Mason's primary mission was to improve congregational singing by promoting music literacy and performance style, Hastings focused more on training church choirs. Both viewed training church choirs as a means to improve congregational singing.

[44] *Christian Intelligencer* 1, no. 20, WN 20 (Dec. 18, 1830), 78.

History of Forty Choirs,[45] and the music composed by Hastings provided clues as to what this method probably entailed. It seemed that the "monitorial mode" of instruction included the types of vocal exercises, commonly used today by school and church choral directors, called "warm-ups."[46] The exercises aimed to improve pitch and rhythmic accuracy, choral balance, blend, tone quality, phrasing, and other musical elements. The exercises may have been extracted from Hastings's compositions, although books of vocal exercises from the time exist and were used to "monitor" a choir's progress through the mastery of specific techniques and aspects in the music. This explanation is supported by documentation obtained from a "music convention" led by Thomas Hastings (twenty-one years after the one cited above) and William B. Bradbury at the Second (Dutch) Reformed Church of Somerville, New Jersey, in 1851. The convention lasted for two days.

> The time was occupied by the Professors in exercising the class formed in sacred and secular music, and in conveying instructions concerning the proper manner of singing and teaching. The exercises closed with a *concert*, which attracted a large audience, who apparently were gratified.[47]

The sponsoring church committee, with the pastor, George Schenck, as its vice-president, adopted this auspicious set of resolutions for the church.

> *Resolved*,
> 1. That we regard music, and especially sacred music, as happily adapted to improve the character, increase the usefulness, and multiply the enjoyments of man.
> 2. That as our Creator has given us the faculty to distinguish and appreciate the powers to utter musical sounds, and has made music an indispensable part of his worship, therefore every soul is under obligation to cultivate music.
> 3. That music in our land, as in other lands, ought to be regarded as an essential part of common school education; and that we hope the time is not distant when it shall be deemed as necessary to children to read music as to read their mother tongue.

---

[45]   Thomas Hastings, *The History of Forty Choirs* (New York: Mason Brothers, 1854).
[46]   Vocal "warm-ups" are not limited to the beginning of a choir rehearsal, but may be employed at any time to obtain a particular result in the music being practiced.
[47]   *Christian Intelligencer* 22, no. 11, WN 1103 (Sept. 18, 1851), 42.

4. That the friends of religion are called upon to use greater exertions for the cultivation and improvement of sacred music in the Church.

5. That in the cultivation of sacred music, either in the school or the choir, while attention is paid to the mechanism of the art, to time, articulation, and enunciation, especial and chief attention ought to be devoted to the expression of truth and feeling, inasmuch as sacred music is only a language for the emotions of the soul.

6. That the instruction and enjoyment received at this musical convention, make us deeply sensible of the importance of this means of improvement; and we therefore most cordially recommend to the friends of sacred music in Somerset county the appointment of such a festival at least once a year.

7. That the "Psalmista," a collection of choir melodies used in this Convention, combines excellences which render it a most desirable manual for singing-schools and choirs; and the "Alpine Glee Singer," also used in Convention, is a work most acceptable to classes and the social circle.

8. That the valuable services so kindly given by Professors Thos. Hastings and Wm. B. Bradbury, place us under lasting obligations, and while endearing to memory these names, constrain us to invoke upon them the blessing of Him whom the serve, and whose worship they are doing so much to advance.

By request of the Convention:
Peter Stryker, President."[48]

The central purpose of the musical convention was to introduce particular choral techniques and repertoire to a large audience through discussion and demonstration. Today, we call these "workshops." The conventions demonstrated what was possible and by what means improvement could be attained. Present-day workshop attendees often claim to be revitalized by having acquired new skills and ideas, but, more, by spending the duration of the workshop engaged in better music-making than in their ordinary musical situations. The music convention must have been much the same in Hastings's day and, like today's workshops, included purchasable materials to guide musicians and leaders further when they returned home.[49]

[48] Ibid., 42.
[49] The *Psalmista* (1851), compiled by Thomas Hastings and William B. Bradbury, and

By the mid 1830s church choirs and choral societies had often become an integral part of ecclesiastical life, as can be seen from the following items taken from a nineteenth-century church history of the First Reformed Dutch Church in Jamaica, New York. The first notice appeared in the *Christian Intelligencer*. The items thereafter were consistory reports.

> 1836, Feb. 10—Sacred Music. The closing performances of the school of singers, taught by Mr. John Murch, of Newtown, assisted by some members of the Jamaica Sacred Music Society, took place in Rev. Dr. Schoonmaker's church, yesterday afternoon, and evinced a constant improvement going on among us in this delightful science.[50]

> 1836.—July 4th was celebrated in the church. Wessell S. Smith was the reader, and John Mills the orator. Dr. Schoonmaker made the opening prayer, and the exercises were closed by Rev. Mr. Crane, with prayer and benediction. The Choir sang the 712 and 930th hymn of the present hymnal.[51]

> Sacred Music Society. - The regular meeting, the first Tuesday evening in April, the 7th, at 7 o'clock, at the house of Rev. Dr. Schoonmaker. Per order, N.W. Conklin, Secretary. Jamaica, March 23, 1840.[52]

> 1842—The fourth of July was celebrated on temperance principles. The order of exercises was as follows:

> Introductory Music,—"Praise Ye Jehovah!"
> Prayer, by the Rev. Garret J. Garretson
> Musical prayer for our country.
> Reading Declaration of Independence by H.O., Jr.
> Hymn,—"Columbia, Tune Thy Voice!"
> Oration, by Wm. Betts, Esq.
> Closing Anthem,—"Salvation to Our God."
> Prayer and Blessing, by the Rev. James Macdonald.

the *Alpine Glee Singer* (1850), compiled by Bradbury, were typical tunebooks of the era that combined repertoire composed or collected by the compilers and a lengthy pedagogical front section.

[50] Henry Onderdonk, J., *History of the First Reformed Dutch Church of Jamaica, N.Y*, With an Appendix by Rev. WM. H. DeHart, the Pastor (Jamaica, New York: The Consistory, 1884), 96.

[51] Ibid., 96.

[52] Ibid., 96.

About 200 ladies and gentlemen sat down to a dinner in the upper room of Union Hall Academy, with naught to promote hilarity but nature's beverage—sparkling, cold water. The Rev. Schoonmaker invoked the blessing; and thanks were returned by the Rev. W. L. Johnson. The performances of the Sacred Music Society elicited the warmest approbation. The Jamaica Volunteers made an imposing military appearance, and the Flushing Band were much admired for their musical performances.[53]

The 1842 Fourth of July ceremony demonstrated the confluence of religion, patriotism, and social action that by this time had become imbedded in American life. The above program demonstrates the role of choirs in this assimilation process, as sacred music and "a musical prayer for our country" are interwoven in the same ceremony.

Sacred Music Concerts

In New York City a sacred music concert life had grown up by the 1820s. Manhattan's first sacred music societies, like the *Handelian European,* the *St. Celia Society*, and the *New York Choral Society* (org. 1824) rivaled Boston's *Handel and Haydn Society* to sponsor notable concerts and performers, such as the first performance of Handel's *Messiah* in America with Mozart's orchestrations at St. Paul's Chapel, November 18, 1831.[54]

But not everyone approved of this form of entertainment:

Sunday Concerts.—We regret to state that a concert of sacred music was given or rather sold at Niblo's Garden on the last Lord's day evening. How many and how specious are the divices (sic) of Satan. One of the daily papers says that twenty thousand persons crossed the river on the last Sabbath to Hoboken—and speaks of this as a good beginning for the season. Other thousands, no doubt, went to Long Island, made excursion on the Rail-Road, & c. &c. What will the end be of these things? We might ask; but all these things do not move us so much as these Sunday evening concerts. They tempt to ruin those classes in society of whom, we would indulge best hopes. We say tempt to ruin, because it is the tendency of these concerts that principally excites our fears. The same arguments that sustain them, will justify attendance at other scenes. The voice of Christians should be heard deprecating

---

53   Ibid., 98.
54   *Odell's Concert Notices* (New York, 1831), 595.

such abuse of holy time. If public opinion do not exert a powerful influence, and that immediately, we fear the Sabbath will be shorn, in this city—of some of its best, its sweetest hours, for doubtless there are many of the proprietors of public places of amusement waiting the result of the present experiment on Christian feelings and forbearance. We call on you, Christians, to show by language, by example, by influence on others, that the place of week day amusement is not the Temple dedicated to the Most High, that the excitement of music is not a substitute for the emotions felt in the sanctuary, that the attendance on such scenes is not an appointed means of grace.[55]

A brief interpretation of this diatribe from a Dutch Reformed perspective reveals a concern expressed about a Sunday concert, a violation of the Sabbath. On this particular Sunday, money was exchanged, travel was undertaken, and the overall pattern of a well-spent Sabbath disrupted. Seeping into the argument was the fear of outsiders, the ever-present infidel who tempts one to ruin, a concern forwarded regularly in the *Christian Intelligencer*.

Still, the article is a thinly veiled critique from the shrinking group that resisted choirs. For the impression of a mandate to improve church music had been steadily building, and Hastings had already demonstrated that properly trained choirs could effect musical improvement. Furthermore, sacred music concerts had been proliferating in the New York area for about twenty years and had attracted a wide following. The resistance group had begun to accept the inevitability of choirs but, as can be seen from the above article, attempted to push back in whatever way possible.[56]

These concerns did little to dampen the enthusiasm for concert going, however, as ample evidence exists that Dutch Reformed churches held, and we must believe that members participated in, sacred music concerts from an early date. Table 1 offers a sample of sacred music activity in Dutch Reformed churches in New York City.

Operating on the same two principles as the town music societies, to educate and to raise the standard of church music, city societies differed by attracting more accomplished performers and leaders and were often comprised of members of many church

---

[55] *Christian Intelligencer* 5, no. 46, WN 253 (June 6, 1835), 178.
[56] Chapter 4 includes the section, "Concerns over Choir Behavior," which provides evidence of commonly lodged complaints against choirs and their members.

Table 1
Early Nineteenth-Century Sacred Music Concerts
In Dutch Reformed Churches in New York City [57]

Church	Concert Date	Other Information/Source
Middle Dutch, Nassau St.	4/21/1813	F.D. Allen, in aid of the orphan asylum/ *Odell*, Vol. II, p. 410.
South Reformed, Garden St.	10/17/1816	by the American Conservatorio under Mr. Trajetta. / *New York Evening Post* (10/5/1816).
Middle Dutch, Nassau St.	4/3/1817	by F.D. Allen and J. H. Swindells / *Odell*, Vol. II, p. 487.
Murray St.	4/20/1819	Concert of sacred music at the Associated Reformed Church (Dr. Mason's)/ *Odell*, Vol. II, p. 540f.
Middle Dutch, Nassau St.	11/30/1820	For the benefit of the Men's Missionary Society/ *Odell*, Vol. II, p. 600.
Middle Dutch, Nassau St.	3/15/1821	Sage, Earle, Allen, and Morse/ *Odell*, Vol. II, p. 604.
Murray St.	4/8/1822	F.D. Allens's annual concert of Sacred music in the Reformed Church / *Odell*, Vol. III, p. 111f.
Greenwich	6/1/1826	Concert of sacred music under the direction of Mr. M. Beam./ *New York Observer* (5/28/1826).
Vandewater St.	2/17/1831	H.H. Gear, Mrs. Austin Mme. Brichta, Fehrmann, Schott/ *Odell*, Vol. III, p. 538.

[57]   These concert notices were taken from "A Chronological List of Events" in Allwardt, *Sacred Music in New York City, 1800-1850.*

Orchard St.	3/30/1831	Featuring Mr. and Mrs. Demarest/ *Odell*, Vol. III, p. 538.
Vandewater St.	5/18/1831	Mrs. Austin, Miss Pearson, Gear, Norton, Hill, Taylor, Schoot, Mrs. Singleton / *Odell*, Vol. III, p. 539.
Broome & Greene Sts.*	12/24/1836	/ *New York Evangelist* (5/7/1836).
Ninth St. (near Broadway)*	10/25/1838 and other dates	Arranged by Mr. J. R. Price/ Redway notices, announcements, etc. on music, *Commercial Advertiser, 1838*.
Northwest Dutch Reformed Church, Franklin St.	4/24/1842	/ *New York Observer* (4/24/1842).

*See appendix 3 for concert program.

choirs.[58] The societies displayed musical prowess through sacred music concerts, which contributed to blurring the lines between Protestant denominations, as well as between church music and public music performance, professionals and amateurs, and the repertoires of sacred and secular music. Still, the sacred concerts were an acceptable form of entertainment for even staunch Calvinists who had adopted the music reform agenda. As a further inducement to attend, receipts from the concerts went either to the sponsoring church fund, since concerts were held in churches before the days of concert halls, or to charities and mission activities.

The following concert notice and program is taken from the *Christian Intelligencer* as an example of the repertoire and program order of sacred music concerts in the period studied:

[58]   Some concert promotions listed the names of participating churches and towns, with one advertisement boasting that one thousand participants were expected. See appendix 3 for a collection of several sacred music concert programs.

SACRED MUSIC FESTIVAL—Christmas Eve, 24th December 1836, in the Reformed Dutch Church, corner of Broome and Greene streets, to commence at 7 and close at 9 o'clock.

Mr. C. Rogers very respectfully informs his friends and the lovers of Cathedral Music, that more than ordinary care has been taken in the selection of Anthems for this occasion, he feels great pleasure in stating that he has secured the valuable services of Mrs. Franklin and other eminent vocal performers in order to render the concert worthy of the eve of that glorious morn in which was proclaimed "Peace on earth—good will towards men."

James Nares, Mus. Dr.
Solo Anthem by Mr. Rogers
  "O come hither all ye that fear God."
Christmas Anthem
  "Comfort ye my people."   Handel
Mrs. Franklin
  "Rejoice greatly, O daughter of Zion."   Handel
Soprano Duet
  "O praise the Lord with me."
Te Deum Laudamus,   Dr. Arnold
  "We praise thee, O God."
Solo anthem by Mr. Rogers,
  "Rejoice in the Lord, O ye righteous."   Handel
Recitation and Air by Mrs. Franklin,
  "Angels ever bright and fair."   Handel
Anthem
  "O come hither and behold the works of God." Dr. Boyce

Tickets 50 cents each, may be had at the office of the Christian Intelligencer, corner of Nassau and Ann streets; M.T. L. Chester & Co. 203 Broadway, and at the door, on the evening of the performance.[59]

This program and those in appendix 3 provide evidence that the church music reformers had been successful in creating an interest in public performance of Western European sacred music. Identified as "cathedral music" in the concert notice, the program included anthems by the English composers Samuel Arnold (1740-1802), William Boyce (1711-79), and extracted material from the *Messiah* and *Israel in*

---

[59] *Christian Intelligencer* 7, no. 22, WN 334 (Dec. 24, 1836), 87.

Egypt oratorios of George Frederic Handel.[60] There is nothing about this program to indicate that it was tailored for a Dutch Reformed audience. Indeed, any Protestant church able to support the cost of the professional talents employed through ticket sales could have sponsored this concert.

Charles H. Kaufman devotes a chapter to concert life in his book, *Music in New Jersey, 1655-1860*. Particularly striking is his comparison of population growth with the increase in public concerts. He states, "During its period of greatest growth (1830-1860) concert activity far surpassed any expectations based merely upon the increase of the state's population. Between these years the number of residents in the state slightly more than doubled, but the number of concerts increased more than five-fold."[61] He provides evidence that sacred concerts far outweighed secular concerts in the early part of the century but shows that secular concerts eventually outnumbered sacred concerts as the century drew on. The data affirms that concert life was a key component in nineteenth-century musical activity, for it is safe to say that these patterns were common throughout the Northeast. Furthermore, the sheer number of concerts and great variety of offerings indicates that concert going was a highly important part of American life, which cannot be overestimated as an Americanizing agent.

Instruments and Organ

Richard Crawford noted that, by 1800, "gallery orchestras" consisting of the treble instruments flute, clarinet, and violin, with bass support from the cello or bassoon, were used to double the voice parts of American psalmody.[62] Whereas the precentor in the Dutch Reformed Church had used a tuning fork or pitch pipe to start unaccompanied

---

[60]   The use of the term *cathedral music* is a bit misleading. While the anthems by Arnold and Boyce were composed for an English Cathedral Choral Eucharist, Handel's oratorios were not intended for worship but to be performed in their entirety in a concert setting. The idea of arranging portions of oratorios into a concert format, and likewise in public worship, originated with the *Handel and Haydn Society* in Boston and will be discussed further in chapter 5.

[61]   *Music in New Jersey, 1655-1860: A Study of Musical Activity and Musicians in New Jersey from Its First Settlement to the Civil War* (Rutherford: Fairleigh Dickenson Univ. Press; London and Toronto: Associated Univ. Press, 1981), 172.

[62]   Crawford, "Psalmody," *New Grove Dictionary*, 638. Composed in "open score," that is, without a keyboard accompaniment, eighteenth-century American psalmody was intended for public worship, singing schools, and choral societies. Crawford's discussion centers on New England Congregational churches, which began to use choirs by 1760 and employed "gallery orchestras" to accompany the choirs around 1800.

psalm singing, knowing the point at which individual churches added instrumental accompaniment could help determine when new patterns of singing and repertoire may have developed. In some churches there is mention of a choir before the employment of instruments, such as at First Albany, New York (1806), and Old Brick Reformed in Marlboro, New Jersey (1785). But in the majority of Dutch Reformed churches studied, instrumental accompaniment appears to have preceded choir formation and was used to accompany congregational singing.

Table 2 includes twelve Dutch Reformed churches that introduced instrumental music to public worship in the early nineteenth century. Included are the year(s) in which the instruments were introduced, type of instruments employed, and other information, such as player names, instrument cost, and reactions to instrumental music. If known, organ acquisitions are also listed to show when instruments were replaced by

Table 2
Musical Instruments in Dutch Reformed Churches
(**Chronologically arranged by year of first instrument implementation**)

Church / Location	Year	Instruments / Organ	Other Information
Rotterdam, NY	1820s	Flute and cello.	In the 1820s Andrew Yates Putnam, flute, and Cobus Schermerhorn, cello, "A new and increasingly popular innovation"[63]
Glen, NY	c.1835	Cello, cost $18. Organ added during pastorate of Charles Jukes (1838-1844).	Mr. Van Denburgh played bass viol "upon which he played certain accompaniments to the singing that were always solemn and appropriate to the time and place." Recollections of David Van Horne D.D.[64]

---

[63] John J. Birch (stated clerk of classis), *As the Fields Ripened: Being a History of the Schenectady Classis of the Reformed Church in America* (Schenectady Classis, 1960), 83.
[64] A. H. Van Dyke, *One Hundred Fifty Years of Service for Christ and His Church, 1795-1945* (Glen, NY: Glen Reformed Church, 1945), 44.

Albany, NY (Middle)	1836	Two flutes and cello. Pipe organ added in 1839 (see table below).	Feb. 3, 1836, petition signed by 66 members of the church to add an instrumental ensemble consisting of two flutes and a cello.[65]
Warwick, NY	1837-38	Flute, violin, and cello.	c.1837 Mr. Colton led the singing with the flute. Colton left in 1838. In 1838 William Hoyt played violin. Soon cello added, played by Jeremiah Pelton.[66]
Saugerties, NY (Flatbush)	1841	Cello	Cello played by chorister James Hendricks. David Demarest held singing school 1841-43.[67]
Second New Brunswick, NJ	1844	Flute and cello. Organ added c.1861.	Calvin Case played cello in 1844. Dispensed with cello in 1847.[68]
Marlboro, NJ (Old Brick)	c.1850	Cello and violin. Melodeon added in 1853.	In 1858 the organist became a paid position at $75 per year.[69]

[65]   Alexander, *Albany's First Church*, 250.

[66]   *(The) Record of Two Centuries 1804-2004: a compilation of two books, Warwick Reformed Church* (Warwick, NY: Bicentennial History Committee, 2004) and Taber Knox, et al., *1804-1904, The Record of a Century of Church Life of the Reformed Church, Warwick, NY* (New York: Warwick Valley Dispatch, 1904), 72-73.

[67]   P.S. Beekman, compiler, *History of the Reformed Church of Flatbush, NY, 1807-1907* (Kingston, NY: R.W. Anderson, 1907), 56-57.

[68]   *(The) One-Hundredth Anniversary of the Second Reformed Church, New Brunswick, N.J., 1843-1943* (New Brunswick: Publ. by the Consistory and Thatcher-Anderson, 1943), and *Celebration on the Fiftieth Anniversary of the Founding of the Second Reformed (Dutch) Church of New Brunswick, New Jersey, 19, 20. February, 1893* (Trenton: Publ. by the Consistory and J. L. Murphy, 1893), 12.

[69]   Brotherton, *History of the Old Brick Reformed Church*, 207. See also Hammond, *Sing to the Lord!*; A.I. Martine, *Bi-Centennial Celebration 1699-1899 Reformed Church of the Navasink and its Two Branches The First Reformed Church of Freehold Now Known as the Brick Church of Marlboro, N.J. and the Reformed Church of Holmdel Formerly Known as the White Meeting House, Tuesday, October 24, 1899* (New York: P. F. Collier, 1899); and Theodore Wells, W., *Brick Church Memorial, 1699-1877, The Days of Old and their Commemoration. Wednesday, September 5, 1877* (Marlborough, NJ: Publ. by the Consistory, 1877).

Amsterdam, NY (Glenville)	c.1850	Cello.[70]	
Readington, NJ	c.1850	Cello. Melodeon purchased in 1857 for $150.[71]	
Walden, NY	c.1850	Cello.[72] Melodeon c.1859.[73]	
Red Hook, NY (St. Johns)	c.1855	Flute and cello. Organ added c. 1855.[74]	Portion of a poem by septuagenarian first organist and Sunday school teacher Anna B. Moore read at centennial in 1888. "No pealing organ then, no traceried roof to echo and reecho back the strains, But strings of viol every holy day quivered to stately moving melodies; And often times a pipe of flute joined its deep voice."[75]

[70] Birch, *As the Fields Ripened*, 46.

[71] Lorena Cole Vincent, *Readington Reformed Church, Readington, NJ 1719-1969* (Somerset, NJ: Publ. by the Consistory and Somerset Press, 1969), 70.

[72] *One Hundredth Anniversary of the First Reformed Church, Walden, New York. April 23-30th, 1939* (Publ. by the Consistory), 22.

[73] W.H.S. Demarest, *Anniversary of the First Reformed Church, Walden , N.Y., October 1st and 2nd, 1893. The Fifty-fifth of the Church, the fifth of the Existing Pastorate* (Walden: Consistory of the First Reformed Church of Walden, 1893), 21.

[74] Norman Edwin Thomas, *A History of St. John's Reformed Church Formerly The Reformed Calvinist Church of the Upper Part of Palatine in the County of Montgomery*, rev. by the Bicentennial Historical Book Committee (St. Johnsville, NY: The Consistory and the Congregation of St. John's Reformed Church, 1947; rev. ed. St. Johnsville: The Enterprise and News, 1970), 83.

[75] V. Walter Miller and John Jurkowski, *St John's Low Dutch Reformed Church, 200th Anniversary 1788-1988* (Upper Red Hook, NY: St. John's Dutch Reformed Church, 1988), 23.

Bronxville, NY	Late 1860s c. 1870	Tuning fork	Mason and Hamlin reed organ in gallery. Mr. Prescott, one of the elders, was strongly opposed to the introduction of "mechanical music" in the service, deeming it "Popery and the work of the Devil." [76]

a keyboard. See table 3 for known pipe organ installations in Dutch Reformed churches.

Organs in the Dutch Reformed Church

Until 1820 there may have been only two Dutch Reformed churches with installed organs. An interesting story pertains to the first instrument given by Governor William Burnet (1688-1729) of New York to the South Reformed Church on Garden Street in lower Manhattan in 1727.[77] Although Burnet was a member of the nearby Trinity Episcopal Church, a church that had desired an organ since 1703,[78] it appears that Mrs. Burnet, nee Anna Maria Van Horn, may have prevailed on him to give an organ to the Dutch church.[79] A two-year contract for the first organist, Hendrick Michael Kock, provides very interesting detail on how, when, and in what style the organ was to be played.[80] The contract stipulates playing on Sunday morning, Sunday afternoon, and Wednesday preaching services, but not during Communion Sundays. Furthermore, it addresses the manner of playing to introduce psalm singing, the time when a postlude is to be played, and the requirement to play in the *Zangtrant* style, the musical style played in Dutch churches.

---

[76]   Mrs. Harry Walker and LaMont A. Warner, eds., *A History of the Reformed Church of Bronxville: in Commemoration of its Centenary November 5, 1950* (Bronxville: Consistory of the Church of Bronxville, New York, 1951), 99.

[77]   Peter T. Cameron, "A History of the Organs of the Collegiate Church of New York City, 1727-1861," *Tracker* (Journal of the Organ Historical Society) 25, no. 1 (Fall 1980), 82-85.

[78]   Hugh Hastings, ed., *Ecclesiastical Records of the State of New York*, Vol. III (Albany: State of New York, 1901-16), 1520.

[79]   Charles E. Corwin, "First Organ in New York in 1727; Story of Early Days," *Diapason* 23, no.1 (Dec. 1931), 12.

[80]   Hastings, *Ecclesiastical Records*, Vol. IV, 2397-99. See appendix 3 for Hendrick Kock's contract.

The instrument vanished after the British occupied the church during the American Revolution and was not replaced until c.1824-26. Collegiate Church records indicate that the second church to install an organ was either the Middle Collegiate or the North Reformed Church in Manhattan in 1790. However, the only evidence of the instrument is the recorded date of installation and two subsequent maintenance expenditure records.[81] Below is a table of thirty-two representative organ installations in Dutch Reformed churches.

Table 3
Organ Installations in Dutch Reformed Churches
(Chronologically arranged by year of installation)

Church/ Location	Year	Builder or Type	Other Information
South Reformed, Garden Street, NYC	1727 1824/26	Unknown, English Henry Erben[82]	Given by Governor Burnet. Organ listed in Erben printed matter in 1824. Church consistory records indicate that it was completed in 1826 at a cost of $2,000. Church destroyed by fire in 1835 and rebuilt on Murray Street.[83]

---

81 Cameron, "History of the Organs," 82-83. The maintenance expenditure records suggest that John Geib (1744-1818) may have been the organ builder.
82 For the history and significance of this American organ builder, see Stephen L. Pinel, *"Henry Erben: New York Organ Builder"* de Mixtuur, tijdschrift over het orgel, no. 60/June (Nederlands: Gerarard Verloop, 1988), 434-53; Orpha Ochse, *The History of the Organ in the United States* (Bloomington: Indiana Univ. Press, 1988); and John Ogasapian, *Organ Building in New York City: 1700-1900* (Braintree: Organ Literature Foundation, 1977).
83 Cameron, "History of the Organs," 82; *Henry Erben & Co., Organ Manufactory 235, 237 & 239 East 23rd St. Between 2d and 3rd Aves., New York* (New York: George F. Nesbitt, 1874), 1; Stephen L. Pinel, Archive # 5847 (consistory records), *Organ Historical Society* (Princeton: Westminster Choir College of Rider Univ.), 1.

Middle Collegiate or North Reformed	1790	Possibly John Geib	A record of the installation date and subsequent maintenance records provide the only evidence of the instrument.[84]
Katsbaan, NY	1820	Unknown	Probably oldest surviving organ of NY origin, 13 stops, 3 manuals, and pedal.[85]
First Schenectady, NY	1826 1862	Hall and Erben Hook and Hastings	Elder Van der Volgen and his wife in 1797 laid aside 150 pounds in their estate for the purchase of an organ.[86]
Franklin St, NYC	1826	Henry Erben[87]	
Greene St, NYC	1826	Henry Erben[88]	
Broome St, NYC	1828	Henry Erben[89]	
Thirty-Fourth St, NY	1828	Unknown	August 1828, "A request was made by the Finance Committee for permission to put an organ in the gallery free of expense to the consistory;

84   Cameron, "History of the Organs," 82-83.
85   Albert F. Robinson, ed., *The Bicentennial Tracker: In Commemoration of the Bicentennial of the United States of America 1776-1976 and the Twentieth Anniversary of the Organ Historical Society, Inc. 1956-1976* (Organ Historical Society, Inc. 1976), 24-29.
86   John J. Birch, *The Pioneering Church of the Mohawk Valley* (Schenectady: Consistory of the First Reformed Church, 1955), 106.
87   *Henry Erben & Co., Organ Manufactory*, 1.
88   Ibid.
89   Ibid.

Thirty-Fourth St, NY (continued)	1828	Unknown	after a month's deliberation it was deemed inexpedient to grant it. But the next July permission was given."[90]
Christ Church, Utica, NY	1831	Unknown	"A new organ was last week put in the Reformed Dutch Church in the village, which for richness of tone exceeds any we have before heard in this part of the country," Utica Sentinel (10/4/31). 10/3/31 Consistory Minutes: "That the key to the Organ be kept by our Treasurer & that it is not to be used for practice.[91]
North Reformed, NYC	1836	Henry Erben	May have previously owned a John Geib organ.[92]
South Reformed, Murray St, NYC	1838	Henry Erben	Cost: $2,500.[93]

---

[90] *Jubilee. The Fiftieth Anniversary of the Organization of the Thirty-Fourth Street Reformed Church of New York City. December 14-21, 1873* (New York: The Consistory, 1874), 21.

[91] Pinel, Archive #2869 (consistory records), 1-2.

[92] *Henry Erben & Co., Organ Manufactory*, 1; Cameron, "History of the Organs," 84.

[93] *Henry Erben & Co., Organ Manufactory*, 1.

Hudson, NY	1838-39	Henry Erben	Cost: $1,000.[94]
Middle Dutch, Albany, NY	1839 1848	John Meads Hook and Hastings	Meads organ: Great—8' Open Diapason, 8' Stopped Diapason, 2' Fifteenth Swell—8' Clarabella, 8' Dulciana, 4' flute, poppet-valve action, apparently no pedal. Odd no 4' stop on Great. Very early use of Clarabella stop, especially with the Dulciana on Swell.[95]
New South, Washington Square, NYC	1841 1843 1850, 54	Firth and Hall (Henry Crabb) Thomas Robjohn Richard Ferris[96]	
Peekskill, NY	1839	Henry Erben[97]	
Market St, NYC	1841	Henry Erben[98]	
Henry St, NYC	1841	Henry Erben[99]	

[94]   Ibid.
[95]   Allwardt, *Sacred Music*, 74-75; William T. Van Pelt, compiler, *The Hook Opus List, 1829-1916 in Facsimile with a Compiled List of Organs 1916-1935 and Facsimiles of Promotional Publications* (Richmond: The Organ Historical Society, 1991), 1.
[96]   Pinel, Archive #4973 (concert review), 1.
[97]   *Henry Erben & Co., Organ Manufactory*, 1.
[98]   Ibid.
[99]   Ibid.

North Dutch, Albany, NY	1845	E. and G. Hook	19 ranks enlarged in 1859 with extended open diapason, trumpet ranks on great and swell, and additional pedal rank. Cost of 1845 organ: $2,250.[100]
Rhinebeck, NY	1845	Unknown	Consistory Minute (12/8/1845): "Resolved a vote of thanks be presented to the Ladies Benevolent Association for the organ which they have presented to the church."[101]
Middle Collegiate, 4th Street and Lafayette Place, NYC	1846	Hall and Labagh	"LARGE ORGAN—The first class Organ recently erected in Collegiate Dutch Reformed Church, corner of 4th Street and Lafayette Place by Hall and Labagh will be publicly exhibited this evening."[102]
Greenwich, NY	1846	Davis and Ferris[103]	

---

[100] Alexander, *Albany's First Church*, 252-55.
[101] Frank D. Blanchard, *History of the Reformed Dutch Church of Rhinebeck Flats, New York* (Albany: J.B. Lyons, 1931), 82.
[102] Pinel, Archive #5487 (*New York Daily Tribune*, April 8, 1846), 1.
[103] Ibid., Archive #3395 (consistory and financial records), 1.

Wappinger Falls, NY (New Hackensack)	1848	Unknown	Consistory Minute (9/19/1848): "Mr. Jones on behalf of the Organ Society requested permission of the Consistory to put an organ in the Church. It was unanimous resolved that leave be granted the Organ Society to put an organ in the church provided that the Congregation do not object and the Consistory incur no expense with it now or hereafter. Resolved that the consistory take the voice of the congregation when the Organ Society think proper."[104]
Jamaica, NY	1849	Aeolian Seraphine	Purchased 12/26/1849 for $300. $70 allowed for old instrument, probably owned before 1842, based on an annotation in the deacon's ledger for an instrument repair.

[104] Maria Bockee Carpenter Tower, *The Records of the Reformed Dutch Church of New Hackensack, Dutchess County, New York*, Collections of the Dutchess County Historical Society, Vol. 5 (Poughkeepsie: 1932), 228.

Jamaica, NY continued	1851-59	Henry Erben	On May 1, 1851, Henry Erben sold the church a used two-manual, 20-stop organ for $1200, allowing $350 for its melodeon in trade. The church and organ was destroyed in a fire in 1857. The organ was insured for $1,000. An English Gothic church was dedicated October 6, 1859, with a new Erben organ. [105]
Lodi, NJ	1850	Henry Erben[106]	
Jersey City, NJ	c.1851	Unknown	Fire destroyed organ in 1851. Insurance covered much of the loss. "A new organ was promptly ordered at a cost of one thousand dollars, and the energy of the people was afresh and availability taxed."[107]

---

[105] Onderdonk, *History of the First Reformed Dutch Church of Jamaica*, 102.
[106] *Henry Erben & Co., Organ Manufactory*, 1.
[107] Benjamin C. Taylor, D.D., *Annals of the Classis of Bergen, of the Reformed Dutch Church, and of the Churches Under its Care: Including the Civil History of The Ancient Township of Bergen, in New Jersey* (New York: Board of Publications of the Reformed Protestant Dutch Church, 1857), 391.

Scotia, NY	1849 1851	Melodeon Henry Erben	Consistory Minute (10/16/1849): "The clerk of Consistory was directed to serve notice on 'the individuals' who set up the organ in the church that Consistory would not be responsible either for purchasing or renting same. The reason for this decision was the 'their present financial embarrassments.'" The organ served in the first and second church buildings until 1917. Consistory Minute (4/9/1853): "The ladies' sewing group donated $200 as part payment on a new organ."[108]
First Kingston, NY	1852	Henry Erben[109]	
Piermont, NY	1852	Henry Erben[110]	

---

[108] Donald A. Keefer, Scotia Village Historian, *A History of the Reformed Church of Scotia, New York, 1818-1968* (Scotia: First Reformed Church of Scotia, 1968), 27-28.
[109] *Henry Erben & Co., Organ Manufactory*, 1.
[110] Ibid.

Yonkers, NY	1854	Unknown	Reverend Hulbert served as a supply pastor between 1842-1845, teaching singing school and holding prayer meetings. He held a second pastorate between 1852-1865.[111]
Melrose, NY	1857	Henry Erben[112]	
Colts Neck, NJ	1857	Melodeon	Church dedicated April 22, 1856.[113]
Flatbush, NY	1857	Pipe organ, (poss. Henry Erben) pictured below.	Gallery erected at east end in 1836-37.[114]

As a rule, it was not until the second quarter of the nineteenth century that churches acquired portable reed instruments and pipe organs. From the table of pipe organ installations above, we see that the First Schenectady Reformed Church was given funds for an organ as early as 1797. However, an instrument was not installed there until 1826. Likewise, although the new edifice of the First Albany Church (North Dutch) was designed in 1798 to accommodate an organ, one was not installed until 1845.[115]

By mid-century, however, the majority of churches seem to have had organs. Newly erected churches, such as the rural Colts Neck

---

[111] David Cole, D.D., *Historical Address Delivered at the Twenty-Fifth Anniversary of the Reformed Church of Yonkers, NY on the Twenty-Third of April, 1868.* (Yonkers: Consistory of the Reformed Church of Yonkers, 1868), 53 and 69.

[112] *Henry Erben & Co., Organ Manufactory,* 1.

[113] *Colonial News,* Freehold, NJ, April 7, 1968, 9.

[114] Cornelius L. Wells, D.D., *Reformed Dutch Church of Flatbush. Celebrated February 9th, 1904, in the Reformed Dutch Church, of Flatbush, N.Y. 1654-1904* (Flatbush: 1904), 40-41.

[115] Alexander, *Albany's First Church,* 247, where he reprints this consistory minute from Nov 26, 1798: "Resolved that the middle tier of pews in the east end of the gallery in the North Church not be sold, but that they be retained as the proper place to fix an organ or other instrumental music when the congregation shall deem it proper to procure it." See also appendix 5 for a photograph of the 1798 architectural rendering of the gallery and another c.1900 photograph of the same space with organ and folding seating for choir.

Figure 2. The interior space of the Flatbush Reformed
Church, Flatbush (Brooklyn), New York, showing the
balcony and organ. The organ was installed in 1857 at a
cost of $2,500.[116]

Reformed Church in New Jersey, were equipped with organs as soon
as possible.[117] This was an especially important development because
a harmonium or melodeon cost as much as $500, equivalent to an
average annual salary for the pastor, and a new pipe organ typically cost
between $1,000 and $4,000.[118]

Organ dedications were heralded events that attracted large
crowds, well-known organists, and an opportunity for a bit of
interchurch organ rivalry.

> **New Organ**.—The organ in the First Reformed Dutch Church,
> Brooklyn, was exhibited on Thursday evening, the 6th inst., to a
> large audience. A number of eminent organists were in attendance,
> who displayed various stops and the combined powers of the
> instrument with much effect. There appeared to be but one
> opinion as to the excellent quality of the organ, which must have

---

[116]   Ibid., 37.
[117]   The church was constructed in 1856. Consistory records indicate that a melodeon
was in use by 1857.
[118]   Organ pricing and pastor salary information taken from church histories, in
which historians had searched deacon record books, and from organ builder and
instrument vendor advertisements in the *Christian Intelligencer*.

been highly gratifying to the artist who constructed it. The points particularly noticed were the voicing of the different stops, and the beauty with which they blended together. The diapasons and pedals were particularly full, round, and mellow tone; the harmonic stops sufficient power to heighten the chorus without producing harshness, and the reed stops, (trumpet, hautboy, and cremona) the character and brilliancy of the instruments they are intended to represent. These points are exceedingly difficult to attain, but in the present instance, we think they are fully accomplished.

The organists who performed were Messrs. Kingsley and Taylor, of Brooklyn, and Messrs. H. Greatoreax, D. R. Harrison, J. Hodges, (son of Dr. Hodges,) S. Jackson, R. Munson, and J. Pound of New York city. The organ is from the manufactory of Mr. Thomas Hall, No. 86 Wooster street, N.Y., who has for many years been distinguished in his profession. – *Brooklyn Daily Adv.*[119]

The above review indicates that the reading audience was familiar with the terminology of pipe organ building and sound principles, a sign that the instrument had become fashionable, if not commonly discussed, by 1845. Furthermore, the review indicates that some organists had become well known, including Mr. Munson, the organist of the Middle Collegiate Dutch Reformed Church, and Henry Wellington Greatorex (1813-58), organist and composer of the popular choral response, *Gloria Patri*.

It is interesting to note that, according to church histories, women's associations often raised the funds to purchase organs through sewing circles, picnics, concerts, bake sales, and other fund-raising activities.[120]

During 1838 the ladies of the church brought forth a project for the purchase of an organ, and with this came into it the only dissension which appeared during the entire period of its work and organization. There was an element of Scotch Presbyterian in the church which was opposed to the instrument from principle. There was another conservative element which regarded the

---

[119] *Christian Intelligencer* 16, no. 19, WN 799 (Nov. 20, 1845), 75.
[120] Onderdonk, *History of the First Reformed Dutch Church of Jamaica*, 106: "The ladies of the Sewing Society had a fair and festival, in the Union Hall Academy, on the same day with the Agricultural Fair, to raise money to pay for the organ. $603 was taken in, being a net profit of $383."

movement as premature from an economic standpoint. The first application for consent to place it in the church was denied by the consistory, but the ladies secured the names of sixty pew holders to a second application, and backed by the enthusiasm of the younger church obtained a reversal of the decision by one vote. This action led to the resignation of one of the elders and two of the deacons and their withdrawal from the church. The two latter after a time returned to its worship, the former transferred the connection to the church of Claverack.[121]

Women had a vested interest in organ installations because learning to play the organ had become part of female domestic upbringing in that era. Furthermore, in many places organs immediately preceded the forming of choirs, for which women's voices were essential. By the end of the century, it was a common sight for a woman to be seated at the organ in a Dutch Reformed church. Clearly, the onset of this musical innovation not only helped bring forth musical change, it also redefined and increased the role and authority of women in the church.

In Summary

By the mid-nineteenth century, the majority of Dutch Reformed churches in the Northeast had implemented one or more of singing schools, Sabbath school choirs, choral societies, or instruments and organ into weekly public worship. However, a progression from one type of choir to another cannot be uniformly observed, nor did the use of instruments or the acquisition of an organ necessarily precipitate choral development. The incorporation of choirs, instruments, and organs into the Dutch Reformed Church was like one ship in the rising tide of American culture that invented and appropriated new forms of music, and that ship sailed into the converging realms of religion, nationalism, and public entertainment. As the prevailing culture lifted up choral music, the ever-Americanizing Dutch church assimilated the choral entities, leaders, and repertoire into its fold as it had English language and customs during its previous two centuries in the New World. Among the choral entities to be found in the Dutch church was the institutional church choir, which will be examined in the next chapter.

---

[121] Gleason, *Semi-Centennial Celebration*, 39. See Table 3. Henry Erben constructed the organ for $1,000 in 1838-39.

CHAPTER 4

The Institutional Church Choir

A distinctive choral organization, one that I will call the institutional church choir, emerged in the Dutch Reformed Church in the early nineteenth century. This ensemble led congregational singing in weekly public worship and, in many cases, offered independently one or more musical selections, called the anthem(s). Sequestered, often in a balcony near an organ, the choir comprised known singers or any willing individuals who read music. In groups as small as a quartet or as large as forty-five or more, they fulfilled a musical desideratum to sing in four-part harmony, a prescription that required singers of both genders.

A professional church musician, with the title of *chorister*, directed the choir in worship, frequently accompanied them on the organ, and rehearsed the choir or individuals during the week. Usually male, although there was at least one early female practitioner, the chorister may have directed the Sunday school choir, run the church or town singing school, given private music lessons, and participated in or led a local choral society. In the Northeast, many choristers embraced the pedagogy and music repertoires of the nineteenth-century church music reform movement led by Lowell Mason, Thomas Hastings, William B. Bradbury, and others.

By the mid-nineteenth century, the reform movement's influence had made a significant mark on the culture of church music by instigating a meteoric rise in the number of institutional church choirs and by prescribing the way the choirs were run by its leaders. Thus, where the singing school graduates had led the "new way" movement in their churches, it was the professional church musician who championed this movement and fashioned the legacies, great and small, that comprise many of the recognizable characteristics of the institutional choir to this day.

The institutional church choir passed through a thirty-year period of rapid transition. It was a new and questionable innovation in the early 1830s, had become a well-accepted feature of worship with a unique repertoire and style by the mid 1840s, but, with the onset of paid quartets, was approaching extinction by 1860. Nevertheless, the unique characteristics, purposes, and social implications of the institutional church choir permanently altered the ecclesiastical culture and worship of the Dutch Reformed Church in America. Dutch Reformed Church choirs helped dispose of antiquated worship traditions and move the denomination squarely into the American Protestant mainstream. Choirs invited the outside world in through a shared musical culture that afforded opportunities for ecumenicity and mission; helped amend unjust social values, such as the disposition toward women in the church; and kept pace with a rapidly changing American culture, thus guaranteeing the church's survival into the twentieth century. The characteristics, purposes, and social implications of institutional church choirs will be examined herein in the following categories: the choir, music leadership, choir location, performance opportunities, choir behavior, and choral sound.

The Choir

Because even the reform movement had moderate and progressive wings, there is no single institutional church choir archetype. The moderate churches admitted choirs to lead and improve congregational singing by adapting the reformer's easily mastered "common tune" repertoire to their worship.[1] While moderate churches may have permitted the choir to sing anthems, they shied away from

---

[1]   "Common tunes" were simple, mostly homophonic, pieces that could be learned with little or no rehearsal.

music that was difficult for the congregation to learn, because the main purpose of the choir singing an anthem would have been to teach it to the congregation. On the other hand, the progressive wing admitted choirs to lead congregational singing and advocated using the choir to "perform" one to several pieces of "cultured" music each week, with the congregation acting as auditors.[2] By the 1850s, a large segment of this group discarded choirs of well-meaning amateurs in favor of paid quartets who could master the more difficult repertoire. On the other end of the spectrum, there were many Dutch Reformed churches not influenced by the church music reform movement, especially those outside of the Northeast and in rural areas, and some churches that refused choirs altogether.[3] Though no strict rules apply to the types and sequence of the measures taken by Dutch Reformed churches in worship music, these four patterns, at least, were observable by the second quarter of the nineteenth century:

- Psalms only led by a precentor, no choir, possibly instrumental accompaniment/organ.

- Psalms/hymns led by a precentor, no choir, likely to have had instrumental accompaniment/organ.

- Psalms/hymns led by chorister/organist-directed institutional choir, organ accompaniment, choir may have sung anthems.

- Psalms/hymns led by chorister/organist-directed institutional choir, organ accompaniment, choir sang anthems, may have hosted choral society and concerts, likely to have replaced choir with quartet at some point.

---

[2]   Western European "cultured" music required greater musical skill and generally exempted the congregation from participation. "Common tune" and "cultured" music types will be discussed in detail in chapter 5.

[3]   In the latter case I refer to the conservative Dutch Reformed churches that continued to sing just the biblical psalms, unaccompanied and led by a precentor. A handful of churches, especially those in Bergen County, New Jersey, continued the practice until about the mid-nineteenth century. In the conservative Midwest, RCA churches did not admit choirs until the last quarter of the nineteenth century. Furthermore, in the Christian Reformed Church, which separated from the RCA in 1857, choirs were not regularly admitted to weekly worship until the second quarter of the twentieth century. See Polman, *Church Music and Liturgy in the Christian Reformed Church of North America*. The evangelical frontier churches were another group that generally eschewed choirs for readily learned congregational music.

The forerunner of the institutional choir was an ensemble composed of young people, from late teenage to mid twenties, who had learned to read music in singing schools or Sunday schools. Its members were radicals. Mounting an assault on the oral tradition still practiced by the older generation, they formed choirs to convert their congregations to the "new way" of singing. Repeatedly, those who clung to the "old way" resisted the fledgling choirs, claiming that choirs had usurped congregational singing, a controversy that first appeared as a rift between generations but later evolved into a contentious and lasting bifurcation within American Protestantism.

Considering the dissuasive effect of these hostilities and the more mundane causes of attrition, such as a loss of interest or relocation, not all singing school graduates progressed to church choir membership. In fact, the general uniformity of age, gender mix, and numbers seen in the singing schools such as in Readington, New Jersey, and Holland, Michigan,[4] could not have been expected to translate to the institutional choir, since singing schools were often composed of students from different churches. A variety of individual church circumstances must have contributed to diverse outcomes in number, age, and gender mix. For instance, in the nineteenth century, proximity to a city generally exposed more people to musical or choral activity than in rural areas. Demographics would have also played a role if there were a cultural or religious predisposition for or against church choirs, possibly based on exposure to a community- or church-sponsored singing school, choral society, or Sunday school choir. Even the capabilities and influence of the chorister, the church's financial resources and space available for a choir, or the happenstance that occurs from one year to the next as good singers come and go could have contributed to diverse outcomes in number, age, and gender mix. Finally, the aforementioned impact of the nineteenth-century church music reform movement had both an increasing and a diminishing effect on church choirs. As will be shown, a radical change in number, age, and gender occurred when professional singers or quartets augmented amateur choirs and were then reseeded with amateurs. Table 4 provides a sample of some Dutch Reformed Church institutional choir sizes,[5] gender distributions, and

---

4   I have included these figures in Table 4 below for comparison purposes.

5   Table 4 includes information on early choirs at the Old Brick Reformed Church; First Church, Albany; and the Readington Reformed Church, though those choirs were probably not institutional choirs. If we use the point at which the church engaged a chorister, not just a singing master, as a benchmark to determine the likely date of the first institutional choir, then such a choir was in operation at the Old Brick Reformed Church in the 1820s, and at First Albany in the 1810s.

approximate ages from a variety of geographical locations listed in a chronological order.[6]

Table 4 Choir Membership
(Chronologically arranged)

Church	Year	Number, Gender, Age, and Other Information
Old Brick Reformed Church, Marlboro, NJ	1785	The consistory minutes imply that younger members of the congregation formed a choir in 1785 to sing psalms and hymns in four-part harmony, precipitating a consistory resolution in their favor in 1787.
	1827	A choir of three men and six women sang at the new sanctuary dedication ceremony, 9/9/1827.
	1877	At the semicentennial celebration on 9/5/1877 the choir consisted of Mrs. John Willis, soprano; Mrs. Minnie Conover, alto; Mr. D. Abeel Statesir, tenor; Mr. Lafayette S. Schanck, bass; and Miss Tille Conover, organist.[7]

At Readington, the exact date of the first chorister is unknown, since it cannot be assumed that Mr. Cocks ever held that position.

[6] The majority of Dutch Americans lived in New York City, the Hudson Valley, upstate New York, north and central New Jersey, and eastern Pennsylvania. A settlement seceding from the Netherlands state church commenced in the Midwest in the 1830s in the states of Illinois, Michigan, Wisconsin, Indiana, and Iowa. In general, in urban areas the Dutch lived among a diverse population, while in suburbs and rural areas they formed ethnic enclaves. The Midwestern Dutch and a smaller group in Bergen County, New Jersey, endeavored to retain their traditional forms of worship, customs, and language. For these churches institutional choirs were not integrated until the last quarter of the nineteenth century. Even more conservative were those Dutch Reformed who seceded to form the Christian Reformed Church. These churches did not admit choirs until the twentieth century. See Polman, *Christian Music and Liturgy*. Presently, only a handful of towns, such as Holland, Michigan, and Pella, Iowa, retain a significant percentage of ethnically Dutch people.

[7] Hammond, *Sing to The Lord!*, 6. See also Brotherton, *History of the Old Brick Reformed Church*, 203-04.

Reformed Church of Readington, NJ	1799	Edward Cock's first singing school class had 14 female and 16 male students. These names appeared on the first contract: Abraham Van Fleet, Derrick Hall, William Van Vleet, John Waldron, Isaac Hall, Patty Hall, Sarah Moorhead, Catherine Kline, Margaret Kasel, Nancy Wychoff, Nancy Hall, Sarah Vlereboom, Isaac Schamp, Elizabeth Probasco, Nathan Hixon, Mary Row, Jacob Mattison, James Emans, John Quick, Margaret Vlereboom, Margaret Stevens, Margaret Hall, Sarah Van Vliedt, Abram Van Vliet, George Hall, Jacob (illegible), Thomas Hall, Henry E. Hall, John J. Meyer, and Elizabeth Demott.[8]
First Church, Albany, NY	1806	The consistory granted permission for "certain young men of the church to sit in front pews in the gallery to assist in the singing."
	1840	Quartet added (2 men and 2 women).
	1845	Two-dozen songbooks ordered for the choir.
	c.1860	Amateur choir disbanded. Only the quartet remained.
	1883	Amateurs reinstated along with quartet.[9]
Reformed Church of Scotia, NY	1822	7/20/1822—The consistory authorized the purchase of two dozen psalm books (possibly for a choir).
	1870	Six or eight chairs placed in the balcony for the choir.[10]

8   Lorena Cole Vincent, *Readington Reformed Church, Readington, New Jersey 1719-1969* (Somerset, NJ: Publ. by the Consistory and Somerset, 1969), 58.
9   Alexander, *Albany's First Church*, 248.
10   Donald A. Keefer, A *History of the Reformed Church of Scotia, NY, 1818-1968* (Scotia: First Reformed Church of Scotia, 1968), 23, 32.

Reformed Church of Warwick, NY	c.1830	Henry Pelton directed a choir of four women and nine men. "Sometimes a dozen or more of the choir would be in their places and the classic old tunes would roll out in a good strong chorus; or it might be a stormy night and except for the scattered voices of the congregation, it would be a solo."[11]
Reformed Church of Interlaken, NY	1832	The consistory permitted the chorister Peter Rappleye to buy eight notebooks for the choir. The choir might have had seven members, if the eighth notebook was for Rappleye.[12]
First Reformed Church of Hudson, NY	1836	"Fortunate in having within it (the church) a large number of young people possessing excellent voices for singing." For the service of dedication, 12/18/1836, the church choir consisted of fifteen women and thirteen men. There were seven pairs of sisters. The women were Caroline and Catharine Morton, Catharine and Alida Miller, Rachel and Mary Jane Gaul, Agnes and Martha Crawford, Jerusha and Mary Miller, Mary and Caroline Shatuck, Margaret and Martha A. Wier, and Emeline Davis. Men included Jonathan Stow, Lawrence Fonda, Robert D. Van Deusen, Norman Miller, Jeremiah Van Rensselaer, Peter S. Wynkoop, Charles Bame, William Sharts, Peter Van Rensselaer, Alexander S. Rowley, John Jordan, Stephen P. Miller, and David I. Gaul. "Miss Caroline Morton, now Mrs. O.M. Hankes, was then the recognized leading soprano singer in Hudson and for many years was the leading voice in the choir."[13]

---

[11] Knox, et al., *1804-1904*, 71-72.
[12] Maurice L. Patterson, et al., eds., *A History of the Interlaken Reformed Church: 1830-1980* (Interlaken, NY: I-T Publishing, 1980), 52.
[13] Gleason, *1836-1886, Semi-Centennial Celebration*, 35-37.

St. John's Reformed Church, St. Johnsville, NY	c.1855	The first organ was installed around 1855. "It is likely that Mrs. William Saltsman was the first organist. Mrs. Saltsman's six sisters sang in the choir during those years and for a long while, their father, Elder George Timmerman, sang with them."[14]
The Van Lente Choir, Holland, MI	c. 1860	The photograph of the Van Lente Choir shows nine male and seven female students who appear to range between teenage and mid twenties.[15]
Lafayette Reformed Church of Jersey City, NJ	1868	"Mr. And Mrs. William Marvin engaged as singers in the choir, $200 per annum." A pipe organ was acquired in 1869. Another consistory minute from June 24, 1873, simply says, "choir organized."[16]
Reformed Church of Yonkers, NY	1868	The morning service, 4/23/1868, 25th anniversary exercises: "The regular choir of the church was a quartet led by Prof. Wm. F. Muller of Yonkers. They augmented the group by two more women and three men 'from the village.'"[17]
Second Reformed Church, Wyckoff, NJ	1869	"The committee on the choir reported that they had engaged Alfred H. Decker as leader, and that he is to furnish an alto singer who, with himself, will serve for $150 a year, and Mr. Zettle, an organist, who is to receive $100 per year. The other two members of the choir to receive each $50 per year."[18]

---

[14] Thomas, *History of St. John's Reformed Church*, 83.

[15] See p. 49.

[16] Consistory minute dated 4/9/1868, Louis Sherwood, *A History of the Lafayette Reformed Church of Jersey City. Prepared for the Fiftieth Anniversary Services, May, 1913* (Jersey City: The Consistory, 1913), 22.

[17] David Cole, D.D., *Historical Address Delivered at the Twenty-fifth Anniversary of the Reformed Church of Yonkers, NY on the Twenty-Third of April, 1868* (Yonkers: Consistory of the Reformed Church of Yonkers, 1868), 5.

[18] Consistory minute dated 7/9/1869, Theo. W. Welles, D.D., *The Pastor and the Church*

Reformed Church of Flatbush, Brooklyn, NY	1901	The first choir listed in the diary consisted of Mrs. Geo. Francis Morse, soprano; Miss A. Tessie Liddell, alto; Chas. R. Osgood, tenor; Wm. J. Richardson, bass (to March 1902); Miss Katharine Walker, 2nd soprano; Mrs. Jas. B. Comstock, 2nd alto; Wm. Crane Andrews, 2nd tenor; B. P. Van Benthuysen, 2nd bass.[19]
Third Reformed Church, Holland, MI	c.1905	Photograph of choir giving an Easter cantata showing 25 women and 22 men. The range of ages appears to be between late teens and early middle age.[20]
First Reformed Church of Bethlehem, NY	1913	A church record from 1913 states that the choir consisted of 10 sopranos, 4 altos, 2 tenors and 5 basses.[21]

The data from Table 4 indicates that an institutional choir of approximately nine to thirty members served many churches in the early to mid-nineteenth century. The gender distribution is not necessarily uniform, as can be seen in the three men and six women in the Marlboro, New Jersey, choir in 1827 and the four women and nine men in the choir in Warwick, New York, c.1830, although it is nearly balanced in the fifteen women and thirteen men in the choir in Hudson, New York, in 1836. Sometimes there are several choir members from a single family, as, for example, the six sisters and their father in St. Johnsville, New York, c.1855 and the seven pairs of sisters in the twenty-eight-voice choir in Hudson, New York. We can suppose

---

or *Rev. John H. Duryea, D.D. and the Second Reformed Church at Paterson, NJ* (New York: Board of Publication of the Reformed Church in America, 1896), 97.

[19] Diary of George Francis Morse, organist and choir director of the Flatbush Reformed Church. The diary, dated Dec. 1, 1901 – April 30, 1911, indicates that Morse began his service at Flatbush in May 1896. The first page lists the names of the choir, beginning with the octet listed above in 1901 and showing additions and deletions until 1910. The choir seems to diminish to a quartet from 1904 to at least 1907, when new names were added either to show additions or replacements to the choir. The diary is courtesy of the Flatbush Reformed Church, Brooklyn, NY.

[20] Courtesy of Dr. Elton J. Bruins and the Third Reformed Church, Holland, MI.

[21] H. S. Van Woert, *History of the First Reformed Church of Bethlehem, NY 1763-1913* (Albany: J.B. Lyon, 1913), 96.

that members were often young from the few photos available, from anecdotal accounts referring to them as younger members, and by the frequent appearance of the "Miss" title in female names.

A development occurred around mid century, when professional quartets were either added to or replaced institutional choirs. The tendency stemmed from a popular perception of the church choir as a performing group, as Americans made few distinctions between the music heard in church, in a sacred music concert, or even at an opera. From Table 5 below we see that a paid quartet was obtained by First Albany, New York, in 1840 to augment the amateur choir. At the Lafayette Reformed Church in Jersey City, New Jersey, the paid members appear to have predated the forming of a choir. However, a common mid-century pattern emerged that the quartet *was* the institutional choir, as in Yonkers, New York, and Wyckoff, New Jersey, shortly before 1870, and in Marlboro, New Jersey, where, in 1877, the nine-member choir of 1827 had diminished to a quartet. Finally, I have included data from the early twentieth century, indicating the resurgence of amateur choirs, often with larger memberships than in the nineteenth century, such as in Holland, Michigan, and the tiny village of Bethlehem, New York, where the choirs had attained impressive sizes of forty-seven and twenty-one members respectively. The data from these churches aligns with the overall patterns of choir membership observed by American church music scholars, who have noted that amateur church choirs were often replaced by paid quartets from the mid to late nineteenth century, but were later regenerated by amateurs through a renewed interest in church volunteerism. This attitude was later given impetus and form by the twentieth-century "graded" choir program movement envisioned by John Finley Williamson (1887-1964).[22]

Music Leadership

I have indicated that it was the professional church musician who transmitted the nineteenth-century reforms to individual churches and who molded many of the characteristics of the institutional church choir; however, this individual did much more. Not only was the chorister the purveyor of musical learning and taste, he was also a link

---

[22] Williamson founded Westminster Choir College (now located in Princeton, New Jersey, and affiliated with Rider University, chiefly located in Lawrenceville, New Jersey). He formed the Westminster Choir in Dayton, Ohio, in 1920 and the school in 1926 to prepare professional "music ministers" for work with amateur church choirs. The way in which many church choirs are organized and function today is largely attributable to the work of Williamson.

to the Americanization of ethnic churches, like the Dutch Reformed. In this role he may have done more to shape the community's worship and artistic culture than any other individual. Consequently, he also may have attained a status that was a bit larger than life. Indeed, the chorister was sometimes in trouble with clergy and consistory for overstepping perceived boundaries, as accusations abounded that worship had become a mere musical spectacle. Moreover, church musicians were often the targets of complaints for unchurchmanlike behavior.[23] This concern was compounded by the fact that with the passing of the *voorzanger* era, there were few choristers of Dutch extraction; thus, aside from the ethnic implications of this trend, Dutch Reformed churches were hiring musicians who did not hold Reformed beliefs. To make matters worse, many choristers were suspected of not even holding to the Christian faith, probably with good reason. Such were the exigencies of the competition to remain in the Protestant mainstream for churches that had chosen to use the institutional choir and organ as a precarious vehicle of survivability against an onslaught of churches in a free society.

In the Dutch Reformed Church, the authority of the consistory and its president (the pastor) to regulate worship and church culture gradually became shared with music leaders. The admittance of women into this arena, not just as volunteer choir members but as organists, choristers, and paid choir members, is an important development in this transitioning culture of the Dutch Reformed Church, for women were not able to be pastors or hold consistory positions at this time. Moreover, women's groups gained considerable power through the appropriation of separately held funds raised through constant and lucrative fundraising activities. Thus, they were able to circumvent or overturn the decisions of the consistory by virtue of having the money to purchase what the male consistory would not support. For instance, when the consistory refused to install an organ at the First Reformed Church in Hudson, New York, in 1838, the women and "younger members" of the congregation obtained a petition with sixty names to reverse the decision. Within a year the church owned a Henry Erben manufactured pipe organ valued at $1,000.[24] The data from Table 5 supports this transfer of influence and can be aligned in the following

---

23 Alexander, *Albany's First Church*, 256-57, where the author recounts that the choir's paid bass soloist, William H. Newton, was fired by the consistory in 1896 for rehearsing his role in the Gilbert and Sullivan opera, *The Mikado*, in a local theater on a Sunday evening. After reconsideration, the consistory reinstated Newton with a censure.

24 Gleason, *1836-1886, Semi-Centennial Celebration*, 39-40.

four categories: changes in worship traditions; changes in the role and gender of the chorister; ecumenism and expenditures; and new construction, renovations, and granting space for music.

Table 5
A Timeline of Musical Innovations
(Alphabetically arranged by location in New York and New Jersey churches)

Church	Year	Names and Other Information
First Church, Albany, NY	1798	Hooker plan for sanctuary provides for organ and choir in balcony.[25]
	1803	September 10—consistory given petition to improve sacred music by forming a singing school.
	1806	Young men ask consistory to sit together to lead congregational singing.
	1809	April 4—invitation to a member to lead the bass singing in the gallery.
	1813	"Committee of Sacred Music" formed by the consistory. Solomon St. John made "singing master." St. John was given use of the consistory room for holding singing school. By opening up the singing school to anyone with church affiliation, the church hoped that tuitions would help retain the permanent services of the chorister.
	1818	April 7—Elis Roberts appointed as chorister for Sundays and mid-week lectures and to teach singing school at a salary of $450 per year for three years.
	1820	Roberts vacates post when church can only afford $150 to renew his contract.
	1830s	Sacred music concerts held to help defray costs of paying chorister.
	1840	Paid quartet hired to augment the volunteer choir.
	1845	E.G.G. Hook pipe organ acquired for $2,275.
	1855	Many members of the music committee resign when a fiscal crisis threatens music expenditures and consistory refuses to raise pew rentals.

[25] Alexander, *Albany's First Church*, 245-57. The second Dutch Reformed Church in Albany, known as the Middle Reformed, hired a chorister in 1833 and instituted an instrumental ensemble to accompany singing in 1836, consisting of two flutes

First Church, Albany, NY (continued)	1868	Mrs. Shaffer, who was reputed to be the most gifted soprano singer in Albany, frequently requested a pay increase. The board of trustees granted the music committee $1,000 per year to negotiate the quartet's salaries since individual negotiations were becoming annoying.
	1883	An amateur choir supplemented the quartet when difficulties in managing and affording a dependable quartet became intolerable.[26]
First Reformed Church of Hudson, NY	c.1836	Enoch Hubbard hired as chorister and singing school master at a salary of $150. "Mr. Hubbard was a man of very small stature, who sang in an unmusical voice, made so by the inveterate habit of snuff taking, played an unmusical violin and invariably beat time noisily with his foot, but he was regarded as an excellent teacher and leader. So thoroughly trained was his choir that it was equal to the rendering on the Sabbath of any music in use, without previous rehearsal. It gave frequent concerts, and was for years the basis of all movements pertaining to sacred music in the city and had a wide notoriety. Thomas Hastings, the eminent composer and leader, at one time, and at another, Prof. Stewart, a well known leader in New York city, visited and led it."

and a cello. The congregation acquired a pipe organ in 1839. The consistory banned preludes shortly after the organ was installed, but when the matter was elevated to the classis the response was, "In regard to the singing of concerted pieces of music by the choir introductory to the regular and customary order of worship; that the same may be tolerated without infringing the Synodical rules on the subject," 251. Later a complaint was lodged that "the present mode of singing is too scientific and various to be performed by those who have not studied or who do not continue to study music," 251. As a result, the chorister was directed to lead hymn singing from the precentor's desk in front of the pulpit without organ accompaniment. Additionally, the hymn tunes were to be selected by a committee of the consistory's choosing. The chorister resigned, and a chorister with little musical or theological training was appointed from the congregation. In 1850 the present organist was asked to fulfill the roles of chorister and organist at twice the previous compensation.

[26] *Our Two Hundred and Fifty Years. A Historical Sketch of the First Reformed Church, Albany, N.Y.* (Publ. by the Officers of the Church, 1899), 39.

First Reformed Church of Hudson, NY (continued)	c.1838	A concert was given in order to raise money for the Henry Erben organ installed by 1839. "At the concert Mr. Hubbard, accompanying himself upon the violin, sang the solo entitled 'Consider the Lilies,' quite well-known today, but then heard for the first time in Hudson."
	1840	Mr. Hubbard retired and Miss Mary Miller and Julia A. Shufelt, later Mrs. Alexander S. Rowley, shared the position of organist without pay until Prof. Francis S. Blanchard hired in November 1840.
	1844	Sanctuary interior remodeled. "A platform in height level with the tops of the pews, upon which the organ was placed, was erected at the front end of the church occupying the space upon the floor between the aisles. This platform was surmounted with a heavy mahogany railing and contained comfortable appointments for a numerous choir."
	1859	"An increased attendance demanded the space which was occupied by the organ and choir. For these a spacious gallery was built in the front end of the church, and the side galleries were removed."[27]
The Reformed Church of New Hackensack, NY	1840	June 18—Special Sunday collection taken for the chorister.
	1841	Consistory resolved to continue Daniel Bishop as chorister and sexton for one year from May 1, 1841.
	1844-45	Daniel Bishop paid from the poor chest. "Resolved that Mr. Bishop remain the coming year the same as he has, on the condition that he thoroughly sweeps and dusts the church once in four weeks, and that H. D. Platt notify Mr. Bishop to that effect."

[27] Gleason, *1836-1886, Semi-Centennial Celebration*, 32-41.

The Reformed Church of New Hackensack, NY (continued)	1847	"Whereas Mr. Daniel Bishop did of his own accord offer to the consistory that he would lead the singing on the Sabbath for what they could collect for him from the Congregation provided He might remain in their house with the privilege of Sexton and Whereas He has without giving them timely notice and while they were in good faith making their annual appeal to the people in His behalf, broken his engagement not only by abandoning his post as chorister but by demanding from the Consistory that which they never agreed to do and were not able to do if disposed on account of the unwillingness of the people to contribute or His being in debt to so many Whereas He might have resigned his office in an honorable manner therefore Resolved That this Consistory cannot but consider the contract of Mr. Bishop in violating an engagement of his own seeking not only dishonourable(sic) but as designed to make a false impression Also Resolved That he be notified to vacate the premises he occupies at the end of thirty days also that His office of Sexton expires on this day. Resolved that the Clerk furnish Mr. Bishop with a Copy of the above preamble and resolutions. Dated February 1, 1847."
	1847	March 12—Samuel Gomer replaced Bishop as sexton.
	1848	Consistory approved adding an organ as long as no cost to the church was incurred.
	1849	John C. Pudney chorister. He held the position until at least 1858. In May 1849 Pudney was paid from the poor chest. Another resolution November 30th gave Pudney permission to use the church every Saturday evening in the winter "to give instruction to the choir and to all in the Congregation that wished to be instructed in Sacred Musick."[28]

---

[28] Tower, *Records of the Reformed Church of New Hackensack*, 174-236.

Brick Church, Waldwick, NY	1845	Henry Sherwood resigned from his position as chorister and undertaker but later reconsidered to remain as chorister if he could "stop undertaking."[29]
Reformed Church of Warwick, NY	1820s	James Hoyt, chorister.
	1830s	Henry Pelton "acting as chorister to a good-sized choir."
	1837	Edward Colton succeeds Pelton. Led singing with flute. Cello added, played by Jeremiah Pelton, son of the former leader.
	1838	William Hoyt, son of the first leader became chorister. He played violin and sang tenor. J. Pelton continued as cellist.
	1843	J. M. Pelton became the chorister by playing cello and singing bass. A melodeon was purchased at some point during his tenure. He taught singing school in Warwick and was one of the organizers of the Orange County Musical Association. In 1857 he went to NYC to "engage in the piano and organ business. From then until 1865 the choir did not have a regular leader.
	1865	Robert Wheat became chorister in October of 1865 and remained 26 years. Wheat had a reed organ purchased and later a pipe organ.[30]
Lafayette Reformed Church, Jersey City, NJ	1865	John Atwood hired as melodeonist and to lead singing for $80 per year.
	1867	Mr. B. Westervelt hired as melodeonist for $40 per year.
	1868	Mr. and Mrs. William Marvin hired as singers for $200 per year. Mr. Westervelt's salary increased to $80.
	1869	Pipe organ costing $1,650 installed. Mr. Westervelt's salary increased to $200.
	1873	June 24—choir organized.[31]

---

[29]   Martha Erickson and Leonard Neil, *200 Years of Brick Church History* (Waldwick, NY: Waldwick Printing, 1974), 26.
[30]   Knox, et al. *1804-1904*, 71-73.
[31]   Sherwood, *History of the Lafayette Reformed Church*, 11.

Old Brick Reformed Church, Marlboro, NJ	1840	23 May—Daniel Polhemus Smock appointed second chorister to assist his uncle Garret H. Smock.
	1850	Cello and violin introduced.
	1853	Melodeon added. Mrs. Sarah Marcellus Smock was melodeonist.
	1858	Chorister receives first salary of $75, raised through subscription.
	1863	Mr. Hickock replaced Smock as organist and choir director. [32]
Second Reformed Church, New Brunswick, NJ	1866-1878	Dr. Chester D. Hartranft pastor from 1866-78. Conducted the choir himself. Had a gallery built across the front of the church behind the pulpit for a fifty-voice choir and, in 1874, the organ moved up to the front of the sanctuary. After giving a prayer or sermon he would turn to the choir and direct with baton. Organized a choral society in New Brunswick. Rutgers awarded him a Doctor of Music degree in 1871 and a Doctor of Divinity degree in 1876. He became president of Hartford Theological Seminary in 1876 and founded the Hart School of Music.[33]
Pompton Lakes Reformed, Pompton Lakes, NJ	c.1851	Squire Aaron Garrison led the choir beginning in 1851 for 25 years. "He stood at the front of the choir loft and struck a tuning fork and held it to the woodwork in front of him. He sang do, mi, sol, do and started the hymn which the choir joined immediately without any other instrumental accompaniment." [34]

[32] Brotherton, *History of the Old Brick Reformed Church*, 201-29.

[33] *(The) One-Hundredth Anniversary of the Second Reformed Church, New Brunswick, N.J., 1843-1943* (New Brunswick: Publ. by the Consistory and Thatcher-Anderson, 1943), 22-27.

[34] H. G. McNomee, *The Church on the Ponds. A History with Reminiscences 1710-1935. In Commemoration of the 225th Anniversary, November 10th to December 1st 1935* (Pompton Lakes, NJ: The Bulletin, 1935), 50 (based on the recollections of Dr. Peter Edward Demarest).

Preakness Reformed Church, Passaic County, NJ	1830s	Major Isaac Van Saun, chorister and church sexton.
	1837	John Stagg, Jr. appointed chorister and sexton.
	1847	David Demarest Jr. chorister and sexton.
	1850	Demarest asked consistory for a salary of $20 for his three positions of chorister, sexton, and singing teacher to the youth of the congregation.
	1853	Position of chorister and sexton separated when David Tompkins hired as sexton and undertaker. The undertaker position required transporting the corpse from the house to the place of interment. [35]
Reformed Church of Readington, NJ	1857	Melodeon purchased for $150.
	1862	Elia Vosseller hired to play melodeon, lead the choir, and conduct a weekly singing class.
	1863	Professor A. J. Abbey led a "musical convention" in the church between March 30-April 3 ending in a concert.
	1864	Voseller's salary set at $150. Two consistory men and members of the choir were charged to find the funds for her salary.
	1865	The consistory permitted a congregational singing school "for instruction in Sacred Music" to be held in the church basement.[36]
Second Reformed Church, Wyckoff, NJ	1840	March 7, 1840, Cornelius Van Gieson, music leader.
	1863	Melodeon purchased, Miss Elizabeth A. Goetschius (Mrs. Angelo Zabriskie) melodeonist.
	1866	Abraham Post and John L. Stagg music leaders.
	1867	June 1—John L Stagg organist and chorister to be paid $200 a year.[37]

[35] George Warne Labaw, *Preakness and the Preakness Reformed Church, Passaic County, New Jersey. A History. 1695-1902. With Genealogical Notes, the Records of the Church and Tombstone Inscriptions* (New York: Board of Publication of the Reformed Church in America, 1902), 182.

[36] Vincent, Readington Reformed Church, 71.

[37] Welles, *The Pastor and the Church*, 96.

From this data we can see how varied the patterns of Dutch Reformed musical innovation were. Some churches, such as First Albany, were very intentional about making musical improvements. That congregation took steps such as having its new sanctuary designed to accommodate an organ and choir, forming a committee on sacred music, hiring at least one well known and costly chorister, building an expensive pipe organ, and hiring a professional quartet to supplement its amateur choir. Other churches took more moderate steps, such as Pompton Lakes, New Jersey, where Squire Garrison led the singing of the choir and congregation for twenty-five years, aided only by a tuning fork. The innovations were most likely driven by available church finances and the prevailing musical and religious culture. It is not safe to say, however, that large churches or urban churches were more likely to embrace musical innovation. Indeed, each church seemed to do as much as it could with what funds and personnel it could obtain.

The catalyst for the innovations began when congregations first admitted choirs to weekly public worship. Subsequent change resulted from a kind of springboard effect, gathering momentum by the second quarter of the nineteenth century as choirs became firmly imbedded in the fabric of worship and church culture, and the voices of its members and leaders began to sway consistories. The transfer of influence was likewise visible on Sunday mornings, for pastors no longer dominated but shared responsibility for leading worship. This can be measured in time allotted, since the amount of music offered during worship increased; in liturgical space, since many sanctuaries were redesigned to accommodate and even display choirs and organs; in expenditure, as churches spent more on organs and music than anything else save construction and salaries; in ecumenism, where churches combined choirs on special occasions for public worship; and in changing social values, with women admitted to leadership positions and the general public adopting the attitude that a well-trained choir offered a better form of praise to God.

Throughout the period 1820-1860, the chorister gained in influence and assumed an expanded role in many congregations. As the need for able keyboard players grew, churches admitted women to the role of chorister in at least a few congregations. Early choristers inherited the job descriptions of their predecessors, the precentors of the prechoir era, who had often been charged with the duties of sexton and undertaker. But the position of chorister required unique skills and training, advancing its status from a working-class occupation to one that encompassed musicianship, teaching, and administration. Table 5 shows three circumstances in which tensions must have mounted to separate the positions of chorister and sexton, the most contentious being in New Hackensack, New York, where Daniel Bishop, who had been reminded by the consistory to sweep and dust the sanctuary, later abandoned his post when he was not granted a fixed salary.

In the nineteenth century, the women of the church banded together in women's circles, in mission activities, and, indeed, in church choirs, where they influenced policy through their combined voices and where their fundraising activities could dwarf the income obtained through pew rentals. As previously stated, it was often the women who raised significant sums of money to procure church organs, but these were the same groups who sponsored missionaries and spearheaded church building programs. In Table 5 we see that women also infiltrated the realm of church music professional as organist, paid singer, and—in the earliest case that I have discovered, at Fort Edward, New York—as chorister, with the appointment of Mrs. Whiting in December 1844.[38]

Outreach and increased church expenditures go hand in hand, for the receipts of such outreach activities as concerts and conventions, along with bake sales, picnics, and sewing circle sales, often funded purchases for the church music program. Astounding amounts were raised and spent, organs aside, such as the $450 annual salary provided Elis Roberts as chorister in 1818 at the First Church in Albany, an amount equivalent to the highest pastors' salaries of the day. More importantly, contracts like this are a harbinger of the move away from choristers being paid through subscription—or the poor box—to fixed salaries established by the consistory. This consideration elevated the church musician to the same financial arrangement as the pastor. When paid singers and quartets were admitted, along with costs for printed music and organ maintenance, it becomes apparent that a sizable amount of the church's resources were being spent on music. The $1,000 stipend for the quartet at First, Albany, in 1868, for example, seems grandiose even by today's reckoning.

While the next portion of this chapter and appendix 5 address church architecture and choir accommodations, Table 5 has already provided details of how several churches renovated liturgical space, often with musical considerations in mind, at what must have been substantial cost. The table also reveals a subtle but critical fact about the use of space, for consistories were and still are charged to approve all requests for the use of church property. Therefore, when the elders at First Church, Albany, permitted Solomon St. John the use of the consistory room for choir rehearsals in 1813, as did the consistory at Fort Edward, New York, for Mrs. Whiting (providing her rehearsals

[38] Gifford, *Phoenix of the North,* 32.

were chaperoned), and when the consistory of the Readington, New Jersey, Reformed Church permitted the chorister to run a singing school in the church basement in 1865, they were casting significant votes of confidence in these activities. In fact, of all the concessions made for choirs, there is surely nothing more significant and lasting than affording and renovating space for their activities.

Choir Location

To gain a better appreciation of how revolutionary and controversial choir seating was, it is helpful to become familiar with the history of Dutch Reformed church architecture in America.[39] The earliest churches had seating on one floor. Men and women sat separately, and the precentor sat in the front of the church near the pastor and elders. By the mid-eighteenth century, oblong meetinghouse style churches with balconies were in vogue, with second-floor seating on three sides. When choirs were introduced they were remanded to balcony seating. Reformed theology held that the choir's primary, if not sole, purpose was to lead congregational singing. Therefore, it was understood, although not necessarily true, that the choir should be located behind the congregation where, for acoustic reasons, the singing was best supported. A more practical reason for installing them in the balcony was, quite simply, that there was more available space there than in any other part of the church.[40]

A church renovation trend toward appointing church interiors in the style of theaters began in the second quarter of the nineteenth century, brought on in part by the evangelical movement.[41] Plush seats, draperies, carpeting, and fanciful choir enclosures, along with a marked increase in pipe organ acquisitions, mark this period. Most choirs remained balconied, although many more were singing anthems. A Glen Reformed Church member offers a vivid depiction of the choir location and worship practice in his church in the 1830s:

[39] See appendix 5 for a brief outline and discussion of the styles and implications of Dutch Reformed church design in America during the period studied.

[40] Whether or not choirs were seated in the balcony by gender division remains to me a mystery. A reprinted photograph in Pinel, "Henry Erben: New York Organ Builder," 436, depicts a finely dressed, young-looking choir of seven from a Congregationalist church in Belfast, Maine, c.1835. Standing in a row across the front of the church balcony, with a female figure (probably the organist/chorister) standing in an elevated position behind and center of the group, are from left to right two women, a man, two more women, and two men.

[41] Jeanne Halgren Kilde, *When Church Became Theatre: The Transformation of Evangelical Architecture and Worship in Nineteenth-Century America* (Oxford: Oxford Univ. Press, 2002).

But the wonder of the great gallery was to be seen on the South side, where an enclosure was built with wainscoting all around, with a rod in front, on which bright scarlet curtains were displayed. Behind these curtains, which were open during all parts of the service, except when the Psalm or Hymn was announced, the chorister and members of the choirs were stationed. When the time for singing approached, the curtains were drawn together and eager consultation was held attended with the rustling of the leaves of hymn books and tunebooks, for these were separate volumes then—all preparation for the coming service of praise.[42]

The pew system also affected choir location.[43] The following passage demonstrates the inherent connection between pew rentals and employee salaries:

The pews were rented on October 2, 1869, those in the middle aisle for $28 each, those on the side aisles, with the exception of four on each corner, for $22 each, the first four at $16 each and the second four at $20 each. The Gallery pews were rented for $6 each. On November 6, 1869, every seat in the church was rented. Preference was given to families wishing to select pews corresponding to former sittings. On May 26, 1870 Mrs. Soops salary as organist was raised to $100. In 1878 pew prices were reduced and the pastor's salary cut by 20%.[44]

One can imagine the resistance that some consistories must have raised when surrendering a sizable portion of rented seating to the choir.[45] To make matters worse, the choir enclosures obscured the view of the choir from the congregation, but not the congregation from the choir, giving the ensemble a privileged vantage point and, as some had feared, an opportunity to misbehave.[46] The photograph below shows a similar

---

[42]   Van Dyke, *One Hundred Fifty Years*, 44.

[43]   Annual pew rental revenues offset church operating costs, especially the salaries of the pastor, chorister or organist, paid singers, and sexton. Prices were determined by comparing the relative distance and view of the pulpit of all church seating. The pledge system replaced this hierarchal economy in the twentieth century.

[44]   Van Woert, *History of the First Reformed Church of Bethlehem*, 64-66.

[45]   During the nineteenth century some churches began suspending pew rents in all or parts of balconies to provide free seating for servants, the youth of the church, indigents, Native Americans, or visitors, as a measure of outreach and hospitality. Still, affording space for the choir would have necessitated redistributing seating throughout the church, which may have ultimately reduced the number of rented pews. There is no indication that choir members paid rent for the places that they occupied in the balcony. However, it is quite possible that a choir member may have continued to pay rent on a family pew that he or she was no longer using.

[46]   A later portion of this chapter will present evidence of complaints about choir conduct.

Figure 3.
Organ and choir seating in the
balcony of First Church, Albany
*(First Church, Albany, archives,
curator Dr. James Folts)*

location for the choir and organ, in a balcony above the main entrance and opposite the pulpit platform, at the First Church, Albany, around 1880. Notice the adjustable seating for the choir by the organ console.

A fourth development occurred in the second half of the nineteenth century, when numerous architectural styles, including neo-Gothic, appeared. Many choirs were relocated to a front platform behind the pulpit, making clear that their role had shifted dramatically from leading congregational singing to something that also encompassed performance values.[47] Table 6 below provides a sample of choir and organ placement[48] from the mid to late nineteenth century, along with related information on church interior renovations.

Table 6. Choir and Organ Placement
(Alphabetically arranged by location in New York and New Jersey churches)

Church	Year	Location of Choir and Other Information
Flatbush Reformed Church, Brooklyn, NY	1836-37	Pews remodeled, gallery built on east end.
	1857	Organ placed in gallery.
	1862	Pews replaced. Pulpit elevated above open platform.
	1887	Extension to rear of the church, organ rebuilt and transferred to the back of pulpit platform.[49]
Glen Reformed Church, Glen, NY	c.1840	"The entrance faced the highway, and in the vestibule were stairs leading to the galleries, extending round the three sides of the auditorium. The west gallery was for the older youth of the church. In the eastern gallery were reservations for the colored folks. In the west gallery behind parted scarlet curtains were the choir and chorister."[50]

[47] In the last quarter of the nineteenth century, some RCA choirs began to wear vestments.
[48] Organ location is generally indicative of choir location.
[49] Wells, *Quarter Millennial Anniversary*, 39-41.
[50] Van Dyke, *One Hundred Fifty Years of Service*, 44.

Reformed, Low Dutch Church, Harlem, NY	1850 1865	Organ placed in church. Organ enlarged and moved to rear of pulpit.[51]
First Reformed Church, Jamaica, NY	1851 1852 1857 1857 1859	Organ installed in the gallery. Gallery extended four feet to allow the choir to stand in front of the organ. Gas introduced, pews, pulpit, and organ painted in wood-grain finish, closed pulpit replaced by an open platform. Fire destroyed the church. New brick and slate (English Gothic with two towers) church dedicated.[52]
Second Reformed Church, Schenectady, NY	1855	"...the pews were arranged in a circular fashion about the pulpit, back of which the organ pipes and choir stalls."[53]
First Reformed Church, Bayone, NJ	1866	Organ installed in rear gallery at the time of church construction in 1866.[54]
Reformed Church, Closter, NJ	1860s-70s	Mason and Hamlin organ added in 1866. Choir and organ seated behind the pulpit in the 1870s.[55]
Old North Reformed Church, Dumont, NJ	1852	The first organ was installed in the back of the gallery. [56]

[51] Edgar Tilton, Jr., *The Reformed Low Dutch Church of Harlem, Organized in 1660, Historical Sketch* (Harlem: The Consistory, 1910), 72.

[52] Onderdonk, *History of the First Reformed Church of Jamaica,* 105-17.

[53] W. N. P. Dailey, *The History of the Montgomery Classis, R.C.A.* (Amsterdam, NY: Recorder Press, c.1915), 107.

[54] Stanley R. Woodruff, et al., *The First Reformed Church, Bayonne, NJ, On the Occasion of the One Hundredth Anniversary, 1828-1928* (Bayonne: 1928), 32.

[55] Walter L. McCain, *The First Hundred Years: A History of the Reformed Church of Closter, 1862-1962* (Closter, NJ: The Consistory, 1962), 4.

[56] *1724-1975. The Story of The Old North Reformed Church* (Dumont, NJ: The Old North Reformed Church, 1976), 20.

First Reformed Church, Jersey City, NJ	1853	English Gothic brownstone church dedicated. "The organ loft, by an arrangement novel in this country, is on the main floor, at the end of one of the aisles, and by the side of the pulpit."[57]
First Reformed Church, New Brunswick, NJ	1866	Odell pipe organ installed in the gallery.[58]
Second Reformed Church, New Brunswick, NJ	1866-78	Dr. Chester D. Hartranft, pastor from 1866-1878, conducted the choir. He had a gallery large enough for a fifty-voice choir built across the front of the church behind the pulpit. In 1874 the organ was moved to the front of the church. After giving a prayer or sermon he would turn to the choir and direct with baton.[59]

The data reflects the mid-nineteenth century tendency to remodel churches to appear more like theaters of the day, including carpeting, cushioned seats, window treatments, wall stenciling, and enclosed spaces for the choir in the balcony.[60] Undoubtedly, the interiors reflected a changing theology of worship, in which congregational participation had nearly diminished to spectatorship. The choir's value as a performing group increased, which led to more elaborate settings in the balcony and the subsequent movement of many choirs and organs to platforms behind the pulpit, so that they could also be viewed by the congregation.

Performance Opportunities

The *Constitutional Liturgy* of 1793 remained little changed until 1906, when it was completely reorganized and revised.[61] Prior to

[59]   *One-Hundredth Anniversary of the Second Reformed Church*, 27.
[60]   Kilde, *When Church Became Theatre*.
[57]   *Christian Intelligencer* 24, no. 13, WN 1209 (Sept. 29, 1853), 50.
[58]   David J. Muyskens, *"The Town Clock" History of the First Reformed Church of New Brunswick, NJ* (New Brunswick: The Consistory, 1991), 47.
[61]   Meeter, *Meeting Each Other*, 155-56. A few unofficial changes were introduced in subsequent editions of the liturgy, mostly by additions and omissions to the baptism and marriage forms. Several motions for revision of the liturgy were put

the twentieth century, the forms did not specify the exact amount and location of music in worship, bowing more to tradition than to prescription. Therefore, pastors, consistories, and music leaders of individual churches, who either cooperated or vied individually for control, determined the choice and location of music in worship.[62] Only when disputes had reached an impasse did executive bodies enter into the fray, as at the Middle Church, Albany, when the regional classis was obliged to rule on the choir's practice of performing preservice music.[63]

By the second quarter of the nineteenth century, choirs in general began to enjoy a favored status in American culture. These perceptions contributed to an increased use of church choirs, and to the number of times pastors and choristers programmed music in weekly worship and during worship on other church occasions.[64] Naturally, the worship occasion had much to do with determining the formula for music. This c.1829 *Service of the Word* from the Niskayuna Reformed Church near Albany, New York, indicates the usual number and location of music elements found in period liturgies. Of the eleven liturgical elements, three specifically require music:[65]

---

before the General Synod in the second and third quarters of the nineteenth century. However, it was only the order for marriage that received a majority support of the classes in 1876.

[62] Disagreements between the pastor and music leader about who selected the hymns for worship are cited in church histories and appear in editorial discourses in the *Christian Intelligencer.*

[63] See note 25.

[64] We shall see that not everyone was pleased with this development, for complaints that the choir had begun to monopolize worship and that music-related expenditures had drawn away valuable resources from the church were commonly raised.

[65] In this and in other orders of worship in the era, when the word "singing" is used it could indicate psalms, hymns, or even an anthem by the choir. In earlier orders of worship, or in churches where hymns and choirs were not admitted, the specific psalm would be listed. It is also important to note that weekly bulletins listing the order of worship were almost unheard of at this time (these did not become common until the turn of the twentieth century). As a rule, worship orders were printed only during special occasions such as important funerals, installations, church dedications, or anniversaries.

Order of Worship According to the Constitution

1st   After a space for private devotion the minister shall introduce the public worship in the morning by invoking the Divine presence and blessing

2nd   salutation

3rd   reading the Ten Commandments or some other portion of scripture or both

4th   singing

5th   prayer

6th   singing

7th   sermon

8th   prayer

9th   collection of alms

10th   singing

11th   pronouncing the Apostolic benediction

This comment was appended to the order:

The order of the afternoon and evening services shall be the same as the morning, excepting the reading of the Ten Commandments. The last service of the Lord's Day shall conclude with the Christian Doxology.[66]

Aside from the specified places for music, the liturgy afforded an opportunity for the choir to sing one or more anthems during the preservice gathering time and the collection of alms, later the offertory.[67] Additionally, many churches had organ music played during one or more of the prelude, offertory, and postlude parts of worship.[68] There

[66]   Scott Haefner, et al. *A Serving People, a History of the Niskayuna Reformed Church 1750-2000* (Niskayuna, NY: Publ. by the Consistory, 2000), 112. Many congregations sang the Doxology, for which the 1812 edition of *Psalms and Hymns* contains a good selection of doxological texts.

[67]   Throughout most of mainline Protestantism, the collection of alms for the poor was later replaced by the offertory, a similar act of giving but interpreted theologically as an *offering* back to God in thanksgiving for the many blessings received by God's people.

[68]   Accounts from the *Christian Intelligencer* verify that this was common practice. In fact, a few commentators criticized organists for choosing inappropriate types of music and for playing in an ostentatious manner. One auditor commented,

is reason to believe that music was more restrained on Sundays when Holy Communion was offered, as suggested by the curtailing of organ music at the South Reformed Church in New York during Communion Sundays in the eighteenth century. However, I have found no additional corroborative evidence to support or refute this point.[69]

Opportunities outside of weekly worship often produced more occasions for singing. At a daily prayer service held June 4, 1834, during a meeting of the General Synod in New York, singing alternated with prayers given by the different delegates:

> Wednesday Afternoon.—The Synod met at the Consistory Room of the Franklin Street Church. Agreeably to the report of the committee appointed at the close of the morning session, the religious exercises were conducted in the following order.
>
> Singing.
>
> Prayer, by the Rev. Dr. Ferris.
>
> Singing.
>
> Prayer, by the Rev. Henry Heermance.
>
> Singing.
>
> Prayer by the Rev. J.D. Fonda
>
> Singing the Doxology

Choirs were welcomed at such special church gatherings as a church anniversary, cornerstone laying ceremony or church building dedication, an important funeral, a national observance, or a pastor's installation service, from which this January 7, 1851, order of installation of the Reverend John Allinger at the First Reformed Church of Jamaica, New York, came. Although it is likely that the choir's role was augmented for the occasion, three of the eleven elements were devoted to music for which hymn and anthem titles are included:

"One Sunday evening, not long since, we heard a very solemn sermon followed by a 'fandango' as one of the audience called it, more like a march than anything else, and would hardly been out of place in an Ethiopian concert room," *Christian Intelligencer* 24, no. 41, WN 1237 (April 13, 1854), 162.

[69] Church records indicate that Holy Communion was offered as infrequently as quarterly in some churches and as often as monthly and on special feast days, like Christmas, Easter, and Pentecost, in other churches.

Order of exercises:

1. Prayer by the Rev. John W. Ward, of Greenpoint.

2. Anthem, sung by the choir from the 52d Chapter of Isaiah, 7 to 10th verses Inclusive; "How beautiful upon the mountains are the feet of him that Bringeth good tidings, that published peace: that bringeth good tidings of good, that published salvation: that saith unto Zion, Thy God reigneth."

3. Prayer by the Rev. Talbot W. Chambers, of New York.

4. Singing of 154th Hymn 2d book: "Let Zion's Watchmen all awake."[70]

5. Sermon by the Rev. Dr. Jacob Broadhead of Brooklyn.

6. Installation of the Pastor by the Rev. D. Schoonmaker, late the pastor.

7. Charge to the Pastor by the Rev. E.S. Porter, of Williamsburgh.

8. Charge to the Congregation by Rev. Thomas C. Strong, of Newtown, President of Classis.

9. Concluding Prayer, by Rev, Mr. Porter.

10. Singing of 153d Hymn of 2d book: "Come as a *Shepherd*; guard and keep."

11. Apostolic Benediction by the Pastor, the Rev. John b. Allinger.[71]

As the century drew on, occasions for church choirs increased. In some churches, the choir may have enhanced nearly every service, commemoration, or event in the life of the church. In cities and towns the church choir participated in or hosted Bible society meetings, temperance meetings, town picnics, or almost any gathering. The outreach provided an ambassadorial link from the church to the outside community that, during a national holiday, tragedy, or local grange fundraiser, brought choirs together from several churches into a combined service. Thus was the more connected church and community life of yesteryear, as indicated in the table below showing

---

[70]   I was unable to determine the hymnal used for this installation service. The text for "Let Zion's Watchman All Awake" appears in the 1846 (1850 printing) and 1860 editions of *Psalms and Hymns*. However, the text for "Come as a Shepherd Guard and Keep" does not appear in the hymnals above, nor does either text appear in the only other denominational hymnal of the era, *Sabbath School and Social Hymns* (1843).

[71]   Onderdonk, *History of the First Reformed Dutch Church of Jamaica*, 105.

the involvement of the church choir at the then suburban New York First Reformed Church of Jamaica, Long Island (now Queens), in all the ways mentioned above and more.

Table 7
Occasions for Choirs at the First Reformed Church of Jamaica, Long Island, New York
(Chronologically arranged)

Date	Event	Other Information
11/4/1835	Singing School	"The singing school of the Dutch Church is now in successful operation. There is, however, an opportunity for the enlistment of a few more pupils." [72]
2/10/1836	Singing School Performance	"The closing performances of the school of singers, taught by Mr. John March, of Newtown, assisted by some members of the Jamaica Sacred Music Society, took place in Rev. Dr. Schoonmaker's church, yesterday afternoon, and evinced a constant improvement going on among us in the delightful science."[73]
7/4/1836	July 4th service	"...was celebrated in the church. Wessell S. Smith was the reader, and John Mills the orator. Dr. Schoonmaker made the opening prayer, and the exercises were closed by Rev. Crane, with prayer and benediction. The Choir sang the 712 and 930th hymn of the present hymnal." [74]

---

[72] Onderdonk, *History of the First Reformed Dutch Church of Jamaica,* 96. The author assembled many of the entries from notices in the *Long Island Farmer,* a regional newspaper of the era.

[73] Ibid., 96.

[74] Ibid., 9. From a consistory minute.

3/23/1840	Jamaica Sacred Music Society	"The regular meeting, the first Tuesday evening in April, the 7th, at 7 o'clock, at the house of Rev. Dr. Schoonmaker. Per order N.W. Conklin, Secretary."[75]
7/4/1842	July 4th service	"...celebrated on temperance principles...The performances of the Sacred Music Society elicited the warmest approbation. The Jamaica Volunteers made an imposing military appearance, and the Flushing Band were much admired for their musical performances."[76]
1/7/1851	Installation of Rev. John B. Allinger	"Anthem, sung by the choir from the 52d Chapter of Isaiah, 7 to 10th verses inclusive: "How beautiful upon the mountains are the feet of him that bringeth good tidings, that publisheth peace: that bringeth good tidings of good, that publisheth salvation: that saith unto Zion, Thy God reigneth."[77]
10/2/1851	Queens County Agricultural Society Address	"...1500 present...A voluntary on the organ, by Miss M.E. Brinckerhoff, opened the proceedings....An anthem and ode were sung by Thos. Bradlee and the choir." [78]
4/13/1852	Funeral service for former pastor Jacob Schoon-maker	The choir sang an anthem titled, "How blest the Righteous, when he dies," and a hymn, "Unveil thy bosom, faithful tomb."[79]

---

[75]   Ibid., 96.
[76]   Ibid., 98.
[77]   Ibid., 105. Full order of worship cited above.
[78]   Ibid., 105-06.
[79]   Ibid., 107-08.

9/28/1854	Queens County Fair	"C. Lyon gave the address in the church. Voluntary on the organ by Jos. T. Duryea, invocation by Rev. P. D. Oakley, singing by the choir. The Audience were dismissed with the benediction."[80]
11/8/1855	Long Island Bible Society Meeting	"...at 2 p.m. the members of the choirs of the different churches led by Abm. Duryea, conducted the music."[81]
9/14/1858	Laying of corner-stone of new church	"Large gathering of ladies mostly, a stage erected for the speakers.... The choir sat on a bench by the stage, and sang first 'Let Zion and her sons rejoice,' and at the close of the addresses sang: 'Behold the sure foundation Stone.'"[82]
10/6/1859	Dedication of new church building	"The choir of the church added to the interest of the occasion by their singing, which was in good taste and well executed, Geo. C. Kissam, M.D., and Benj. Duryea, presiding at the organ."[83]
8/16/1860	Church outing and picnic	"Nearly 100 wagons, after a parade through the main street, accompanied by a brass band from Brooklyn, set out, about 9 o'clock, for a picnic to St. Ronan's Well, Flushing. There were near 1,000 persons on the ground. The children, led by J. Henrie Young, chorister of the church, sang sweetly" [84]
9/22/1861	Jamaica Bible Society Meeting	"The choir of the church led music in their usually effective manner."[85]

[80]   Ibid, 114.
[81]   Ibid., 115.
[82]   Ibid., 172. A fire destroyed the first church building Nov. 19, 1857.
[83]   Ibid., 125.
[84]   Ibid., 127.
[85]   Ibid., 129.

4/10/1862	Response to a Presidential Proclamation	"President Lincoln issued a proclamation, recommending to the people of the United States, that at their next weekly assemblies, they especially acknowledge and render thanks to our Heavenly Father, who has vouchsafed signal victories to the land and naval forces engaged in suppressing an internal rebellion. On the following Sunday (Apr. 13) Mr. Allinger noticed the proclamation in appropriate words, and a Te Deum was sung by the choir."[86]
10/3/1862	Funeral for a soldier	"John M. Johnson, of Duryea's Zouaves, died Sept 7, in hospital from wounds received at Manassas, Aug 3, in his 22d year. His remains were brought to Jamaica, and the funeral appointed at the church. Oct. 3, 11 A.M., Rev. J.B. Allinger officiating, assisted by Rev. Messrs. Oakley and Huntting. It partook of a civic and military funeral. The firemen turned out in large numbers, and after the solemn service in the church, led the procession to the grave. Fifty of the Ironsides Regiment and twenty of Duryea's Zouaves were the especial escort and the latter, in two files of ten each, marched close behind the bier, acting in the capacity of pall-bearers. An unusually large audience was present though it was stormy. In the church, everything was solemn and appropriate. The coffin was placed before the pulpit, covered with a pall and American flag. The music upon the organ and by the choir was exquisitely sweet, solemn

10/3/1862 continued		and appropriate; and this young soldier received a fit testimony of regard and honor. The village stores were closed during the services."[87]
3/1/1863	Sunday School Anniversary	"Sunday evening. On the anniversary of the Sunday School, the large church was nearly filled, the scholars occupied twenty pews. Four hymns were sung. Jas. Phraner player on the melodeon, Miss Luc J. Ham led the music. Mr. Pardee, of New York, and Carlos A. Butler, of Jamaica, addressed the scholars."[88]
4/19/1864	Funeral service for President Lincoln	"Bells tolled at 7 a.m. Businesses closed at 9 a.m., service for whole town at Reformed Church at noon, bell tolled for a half hour before sunset. Present at the service were ministers from the following denominations: Episcopal, RC [Roman Catholic], Methodist, Presbyterian. United members of different church choirs."[89]
5/18/1870	Sacred Music Concert	1870 May 18, Wednesday evening.—a concert of sacred music in the church, Wm. Tillinghast, conductor. Mrs. Spader, Armstong, Story, H.U. Rider, Ella Hendrickson, Miss Matti E. Phraner, Mr. Jas Phraner and Mr. G.W. Allen were among the singers."[90]

---

[87] Ibid., 132-33.
[88] Ibid., 132.
[89] Ibid., 136.
[90] Ibid., 143-44.

4/9/1871	Choir assists congregation in learning new hymns	"Consistory agree to adopt the "Hymns of the Church." When it was first introduced (April 9) it was intended that the choir should come down stairs and spread themselves among the people and so have congregational singing. The change had no success."[91]

The data reveals just how "Americanized" the congregation of the First Jamaica Reformed Church had become and how connections between ecclesiastical and public life were cemented by the church choir's participation. Especially important were the occasions when the choir participated in the celebration of national holidays and town celebrations where intermixing of members of different denominations was assured. As there was no American state church (as had often been the case in Europe) but a host of competing Protestant denominations, the opportunities for interdenominational socializing and idea sharing through joint services were great. Furthermore, as in choral festivals in our time, the chance to share a new choral repertoire was also great.

Choir Behavior

The articles and editorials that appeared in the *Christian Intelligencer* between 1830-60 mirrored an ongoing and widely held debate on church music in the period. This material is particularly valuable because the editorial staff and many of the publication's contributors reflected on the Dutch Reformed Church experience. Items have been selected to represent the major issues of the debate, along with specific complaints levied at choirs and leaders. The correspondence on church choirs is especially interesting, since the debate shifts from whether or not choirs should be permitted to form in the early 1830s to a critical review of choir participation in worship, the selection and performance of music, and the modes of conduct of choir members and leaders once choirs became accepted in the next decade.

One article, "On the Use of Organ in Worship," signed *Germanicus*, adopts the propaganda style of the church music reform movement

---

[91]   Ibid., 172. *Hymns of the Church* was published in 1869. It was the first denominational hymnal that included words and music interposed on the same page since the Hopkinson Psalter in 1767. The hymnal in style and content very much resembled the Church of England's contemporaneous hymnal, *Hymns Ancient and Modern*.

that combined biblical exegesis, historical precedent, and enlightened reasoning to fashion an imperative for its mission. It begins:

> At the present day it is the custom in most of our churches for the people to sing, though they are but little skilled in vocal music; every other branch of study which promotes their worldly interest is carefully attended to, while they expect that the Lord would be satisfied with such an imperfect tribute of praise which requires neither money nor labor.[92]

This passage from 1830 berates the music of American tunesmiths and the unschooled way in which congregations sing, the two primary charges against the status quo that helped make way for choirs:

> I take the present occasion to express my deep regret, that most Christian communities are indifferent to the improvement of psalmody. They seem contented if the customs a century back are retained. It appears to matter very little with them what the quality is, provided the usual quantity be afforded them. It gives them no pain to hear good poetry murdered with the scrannel ditties of spurious composers. They sit without emotion while noble sentiments are mangled by uncouth singing. So long as such apathy prevails in relation to the music of the church, talent and skill will be excluded.[93]

In the same year, Thomas Hastings moved to New York City, commencing his lengthy crusade to reform church music. He quickly became the regional movement leader through a wide lecturing circuit and by publishing several tunebooks with partner William B. Bradbury. Hastings's well orchestrated campaign was partly responsible for church choirs in New York and its vicinity becoming a generally accepted and welcomed part of ecclesiastical life by the mid-1840s. Nevertheless, the Reverend David D. Demarest memorialized this often-expressed complaint about church choirs in his popular 1856 church history:

> It is worthy of notice, that in the Church of the Netherlands singing has ever been regarded the duty of the whole worshiping assembly. It was long regarded so in this country, and even at this day the choir is in theory the leader in the praises of the

---

[92] *Christian Intelligencer* 2, no. 9, WN 61 (Oct. 1, 1831), 34.
[93] *Christian Intelligencer* 1, no. 16, WN 16 (Nov. 20, 1830), 61. The article's byline read, "From an address on Psalmody delivered at a Sacred Concert, by the Editor of the Star and Index."

congregation, but in practice, alas! A committee delegated with full powers to attend to that part of worship.[94]

If choirs had usurped congregational singing, then an important precept of Reformed worship elucidated by Calvin would have been compromised. Demarest's comment must have been an overgeneralization, since ample evidence exists that Hastings, Mason, and their followers trained many choirs to improve congregational singing—not to monopolize it. What's more, it is interesting that Demarest established a historical continuity not with the Reformation, but with the Netherlands, as Dutch ethnicity and worship traditions were for some still very much entwined. On the opposing side of the argument, this correspondent offers a different assessment of the value and impact of church choirs:

> It is, in my humble opinion, sufficient for our purpose, that almost all Christians recognize its (church choir's) utility, and it only remains for us to use without abusing it. The spirit of the age in which we live demands its use, and the few who oppose it ought to learn wisdom by experience. What is the relative position which our Dutch church now occupies, in comparison with other denominations, and to what is it owing that she now covers so small a space of ground, although the first established? Is it not because she has been so stubborn in her adherence to old usages, when by a more yielding course she could have satisfied the wishes of the people, without sacrificing a tittle of doctrine or principle, and thus maintained her ascendancy? [95]

Although acknowledging that the choir still needed careful supervision, this correspondent went so far as to attribute some of the cause of the Dutch Reformed Church's slow growth to the denomination's reluctant reception of choirs. The American marketplace demanded choirs so, in contrast to Demarest's desire for historical continuity with the Netherlands, those individuals who had fully assumed an American identity argued in favor of choirs.

The chief criticisms of church choirs were that they had broken with the Reformed tradition by usurping congregational singing and, more importantly, that they had strayed from the central purpose of Christian assembly by focusing on aspects of musical performance instead of worshiping God.

---

94   Demarest, *History and Characteristics*, 173.
95   *Christian Intelligencer* 17, no. 37, WN 869 (March 25, 1847), 145.

It is greatly lamented that singing should be confined in public worship to so few. Singing should be the work of the congregation, to the extent of their ability. It is well for those who can sing with greater facility than others, to form themselves into a choir and lead, though not to the exclusion of any in the congregation whose singing is in any degree tolerable. The choir should be taught, while learning to sing, that the worship of God is to be a leading consideration, rather than any degree of refinement in mere singing. If thus impressed, they will not be fastidious and out of humor, if the older people strike in with their old familiar notions....[96]

Occasionally articles with the same aim were collected in one issue. This passage from a second editorial appends the list of complaints with the costs associated with church choirs:

Organs and choirs have become substitutes and no longer aids.... The interest on a cost of an organ, and the expense of a leader, with all the paraphernalia, equal the amount necessary to support a pastor in some of our largest country village congregations.[97]

Apparently, only a few churches attempted Lowell Mason's method of placing strong singers within the congregation to bolster singing, thus having no choir at all. While the response to this idea was often favorable at first, it appears that the desire to have a separate choir overcame the practicality of this measure:

The gentleman, who is the Organist of the German Mission Church in Houston Street, has the credit of showing what can be done in six months towards improving a congregation in the science of sacred music. If each of our churches had the same number of singers scattered through the audience we should hear no more complaints about the choir monopolizing the performance of an important and delightful part of public worship.[98]

The most common complaints about choirs were, however, directed at the repertoire and style of music performance in worship. Especially in the 1850s, issue upon issue of the *Christian Intelligencer*

[96] *Christian Intelligencer* 17, no. 27, WN 859 (Jan. 14, 1847), 108. Reprinted from the *Utica Baptist Register*.
[97] Ibid, 106.
[98] *Christian Intelligencer* 24, no. 21, WN 1217 (Nov. 24, 1853), 82.

carried a spate of reprinted or newly crafted articles and editorials condemning the infiltration of operatic music into weekly worship. The following quotation comes from an article written for the *Musical World & Times*, a popular New York-based music periodical of the period, edited and published by the influential music critic, Richard Storrs Willis (1819-1900):[99]

> SACRED MUSIC AS IT IS.
> ...Socially, music as an art, with all its humanizing influences is advancing; its progress, it must be confessed, is onward. The New World is the scene where fresh laurels are daily won by foreign artists, and where native talent is encouraged and appreciated. But this is not the case with sacred music! Its legitimate sphere is invaded, either by operatic influences *directly*, or by those who ape operatic airs in the house of God. Operatic taste, under female guidance, is now moulding what *should be* congregational singing, led by an effective choir of men, into contemptible solos, in which we are at a loss whether to despise the display of vanity, or to pity the deluded victim of popular applause! City churches are mostly to be blamed for the commencement and continuance of this outrage on sacred music, as an element of devotion in the house of God. What is the result? Country churches in every direction are imitating the sin. Where are those who should resist this continued prostitution of sacred music? Where are the willing hands to engage in this needed work of reformation.[100]

The writer of this article undertook a particularly venomous attack. It is, however, a classic mid-century negative view of the state of church music. It assumed that truly great art music was being composed outside of the United States, and that sacred music operated under a different "sphere," which was being ruined by the incorporation of operatic music. Since the author views operatic music as somewhat effete, he argues for a greater role for choirs of men. Further, he names the common American split between urban and rural churches in his diatribe, blaming the operatic tastes on urban culture.

The above article left the subject of choir deportment to this editorialist, who points out that many choir members are young outsiders who do not know or observe proper conduct during worship:

---

[99] Willis was a personal friend of Felix Mendelssohn and the music critic for the *New York Tribune*, the *Albion*, and the *Music World & Times*, where he served as editor from 1852-64.

[100] *Christian Intelligencer* 25, no. 2, WN 1250 (July 13, 1854), 6 [italics in original].

While it sometimes happens that some in the choir are consistent members of the church, this is not a general fact. *In the main*, they are young persons, and they occupy the place because of their musical abilities. I aver, without the fear of contradiction, that in very many cases the organ loft, or choir seats, are the centers of inattention, whispering and levity, if they are to be found at all within the walls of that particular congregation.[101]

This correspondent shares the opinion of the former, but adds "shameful rustling of leaves" and novel perusal to the list of complaints:

The conduct of some choirs is disreputable and disgraceful. Incessant whispering and laughing fills up the space between verses occupied by the voluntary; a shameful rustling of leaves disturbs the minister in prayer; and a zealous perusal of the last novel helps to fill up the lagging twenty minutes or interminable half hour which the minister occupies with his sermon.[102]

Leaders were targeted with harsh criticisms, not so much for their deportment, but for violating the sanctity of worship by incorporating performance values into their work. It seemed that a fine line had been drawn between the musical excellence that the reformers cultivated to praise God and a particular collection of ephemeral characteristics of public performance that were identifiable in secular entertainments.

The stress is laid on musical performance, and *effective execution* is the point aimed at. Gross abuses of the sanctity of that part of the service exist also in the *person of the leader, or hired performer*. Will any one deny that there are persons who get their living by public singing, mere ministers to public amusement, who are recognized leaders in the praises of the blood-bought Church of Jesus Christ? That those whom the theatres applaud in the week, the assembly of saints must succumb to on the Sabbath, and be insulted by this elevation of the unholy and the unclean—lepers, conducting "the priests unto God," when they bring their spiritual sacrifices?[103]

The organist's repertoire and playing was under constant surveillance and received a steady stream of critique in the period:

---

[101] *Christian Intelligencer* 17, no. 36, WN 868 (March 18, 1847), 143.
[102] *Christian Intelligencer* 13, no. 13, WN 1157 (Sept. 30, 1852), 52. Reprinted from the *Christian Inquirer*.
[103] *Christian Intelligencer* 17, no. 36, WN 868 (March 18, 1847), 143.

Between the verses, you very often hear the organist, in a too light and secular movement, play fragments of opera pieces, and every kind of music, in fact, except solemn organ music; thereby displaying his vanity, and forgetting that the contents of each verse are in close connection, and that, therefore, the interludes—according to every idea of rhetoric—ought to be in full harmony with the sentiments of the words. You may easily imagine how the closing voluntary in most case—is performed. The organist sometimes draws out every stop in his organ, and, quite forgetting the place where he is playing, and only thinking of displaying the dexterity of his fingers, performs overtures, grand marches, etc.; and it has sometimes seemed to me as though he aimed to drown the impression made by a solemn sermon, or as though he wished to express his joy that the sermon was ended.[104]

Concerns that organists played inappropriate pieces of music and in an ostentatious manner were frequently raised. Like the earlier cited reference to a "fandango," accounts suggest that organists often played transcriptions of orchestra, band, and opera music. Organ music, such as the collections published by Charles Zeuner (1795-1857), must have been quite limited. Readily available, however, were single sheets of music arranged for piano and voice that the organist could adapt to a solo piece for organ. The researcher would benefit from further investigation of this repertoire, especially by comparing the material to patterns of organ building in the era.

Church member correspondents produced the most scathing reviews of paid singers because the salaried outsiders had replaced amateur church choirs, taken over congregational singing, performed operatic literature in an operatic style in church, and did not show the kind of personal piety that many churchgoers expected.

We have attended service in a church in your city, where this practice has been adopted—a church, let us say, whose pastor and officers are not often accused of a haste in seizing upon novelties—and must state, that we were not conscious that the *Quartette* was delegated to do all of the singing for the congregation, on the contrary, thought more voices were united in the exercise among

---

[104] *Christian Intelligencer* 23, no. 15, WN 1159 (Oct. 14, 1852), 60. Reprinted from an article previously published in the *Music World*, "Church Music in New-York," by Prof. Julius Erikson.

the body of the assembly than we have usually observed in other churches; but as we ourselves joined in the audible utterance of the Psalms and Hymns, perhaps our attention was so preoccupied as to render us unable to form a correct opinion; however, we do not believe that many Christians in the congregation alluded to, will be willing to own that they design to relinquish all their share of the singing to the Quartette, and thus satisfy their consciences with praise to God by proxy; nor do we conceive such to be legitimate fruits of the "innovation" if you will.[105]

To many auditors, church music by mid century had fallen into a lamentable state brought about by the introduction of professional musicians and marked by music and performance styles of secular entertainments. In fact, many of the reforms of the early part of the century had vanished. The following "good old days" comment recalls the high point of amateur choirs.

There was a time when hymns were *sung* in our churches. Now they are torn to tatters by shrieks, or shaken to pieces by trilling, or their necks broken by sudden leaps down lofty precipices.... The large choir, with which no small portion of the congregation joined, has grown small, and would that we could say "beautifully less," till two or three at most "do the hymns," while not a soul is permitted to lift up his voice, hardly his heart, in the whole congregation. The singing in our churches is becoming an occasion for the display of musical talent. It is a show, a scene, a mere display, oftentimes: where persons without principle or character, entirely unknown to the worshippers, tare to tatters the beautiful devotional hymns of our churches, "and the people delight to have it so....In many churches, the proportion of voluntary on the organ to singing by the choir is unpardonably excessive. In some instances we have thought that the hymn was considered as affording opportunity for the organist to show his skill, and not the occasion to sing praise unto the Lord, and give thanks unto the name of the Most High....We would have a choir, a large, old-fashioned choir, composed of the best singers in the congregation.[106]

---

[105] *Christian Intelligencer* 17, no. 45, WN 877 (May 20, 1847), 177.
[106] *Christian Intelligencer* 13, no. 13 WN 1157 (Sept. 30, 1852), 52.

It is left to see how this bias affected the reports of how choirs sounded, for it appeared that amateur church choirs had been issued the untenable expectation of sounding professional, but without implementing the performance practice associated with the formal and informal secular schools of music. The closest evolution of a sacred style was forwarded by the church music reformers in the first half of the century, yet, the more chaste music accompanying that style had surrendered to a variety of styles ranging from European art music, to opera and theater music, to a simple and emotional sacred style that was associated with the evangelical movement.

Choral Sound

Church choirs can receive the kindest and most heartfelt praise and, alternately, the most scathing criticism for their singing and behavior. The uniqueness and visibility of the choir's service to the church as worship leaders and as a performing ensemble attracts a degree of attention and scrutiny that those who serve in "quiet" ways do not usually enjoy or endure. To this heightened visibility is added the nature of choir members and leaders, who often chose to participate either because they are musically talented or believe they are, and who can be prone to demonstrations that justify some of the negative attention that they receive.

Children's choirs tend to earn only praise for their efforts, though musical expectations are appropriately lessened. Such was the tone of this observer at the twenty-eighth anniversary exercises of the Market Street Church Sunday school in Manhattan, New York:

> ...it will be seen from the list of pieces sung, which we give below, that the pupils were to be the principal actors in the scene, and they acquitted themselves well. More than this, the singing in parts was thrilling, the duets very fine; and the infant class, of some ninety dear little creatures under six years of age, who could warble more sweetly? We may ask with confidence, when did our friends present hear the anthem "Praise ye the Lord" executed with a finer combination of sweetness and skill?[107]

Adult choirs can receive high marks, especially on joyful occasions when perhaps a new anthem is offered after much preparation. On these occasions, the choir's presence and participation add significant

---

[107] *Christian Intelligencer* 20, no. 17, WN 1,005 (Nov. 1, 1849), 66.

value to the event, as was observed during a new church dedication in Belleville, New Jersey, on December 8, 1853:

> We are not accustomed to indulge in laudation of the music furnished on such occasions. But we cannot withhold an expression of the pleasure with which we joined in the various praises of the sanctuary as they were led by the voices of the choir on this occasion. All was done unostentatiously, yet with great effect and heartiness.[108]

Likewise, the correspondent covering the ceremony for laying the cornerstone at the Second Reformed Dutch Church in Philadelphia, Pennsylvania, April 21, 1853, had this to say about the choir:

> The services of an excellent and well-timed choir led the several hymns of praise in an admirable manner, and further interspersed the services with music of a pleasing character; concluding with the long metre doxology "Praise God, from whom all blessings flow," to the world-wide favorite tune, Old Hundred, in the singing of which a majority of the vast assembly united.[109]

Since a church member usually relayed the occasions to the *Christian Intelligencer,* high approbation was normally given, as in even this brief report of the laying of the cornerstone of the Reformed Dutch Church in Branchville, New Jersey, July 25, 1850:

> Abraham Ammerman's well-trained choir led the people in praise after each address, and threw a solemnizing influence over the minds of all.[110]

A more musically erudite evaluation of choral singing can be found in reviews from a variety of music magazines that flourished from the second quarter of the nineteenth century on and produced an early group of American music critics.[111] Many critics were themselves musicians who spoke the "language" of music and studied its schools and trends. Their reviews of choral singing offer useful information

---

[108] *Christian Intelligencer* 24, no. 24, WN 1220 (Dec., 15, 1853), 94.
[109] *Christian Intelligencer* 23, no. 44, WN 1188 (May 5, 1853), 174.
[110] *Christian Intelligencer* 21, no. 6, WN 1046 (Aug. 15, 1850), 22.
[111] Two respected music critics of the era were Richard Storrs Willis, composer, educator, and music critic for the *New York Tribune,* the *Albion* and the *Music World & Times,* where he served as editor from 1852-64 and John Sullivan Dwight (1812-1893), founder of the very influential music magazine, *Dwight's Journal of Music,* which he published for thirty years.

for modern music scholars who wish to know how choirs sounded in the era and who compare the techniques, concerns, and goals of choral directors with those in our time.

The critics generally agreed with the goals that leaders of the church music reform movement had set for choirs.[112] Therefore, they applauded balance among choral parts, unified tone color, breath control and phrasing, proper articulation, and clear but unaffected diction. The critics found singing styles inconsistent with their idea of church music offensive, such as the capricious vocal stylizations one might employ in a Jacques Offenbach (1819-1880) operetta, or the more weighted and dramatic vocal style used in the operas of Richard Wagner (1813-1883). This standard is rehearsed in an editorial signed M.W.T. Notice also that the writer does not resist the opportunity to elucidate his moral reserve for church choir members.

> In the choir of a church choir great judgment should be used. There are certain requisites absolutely necessary in those who are to lead this important part of Christian worship....First. The persons performing, if not decidedly pious, should be of moral principles with at least enough piety to make them serious while singing the praises of God, who "will not be mocked by solemn sounds upon a thoughtless tongue." Secondly. They should have good and well-cultivated voices, with confidence sufficient to perform their parts with well-ordered grace and modesty, free from a bold and offensive display of the strength of their vocal powers. Thirdly. The several parts of the choir should be judiciously arranged, the voices *compared*, and proportionately numbered, so as to give perfect harmony to the whole, that each part, though performed by several, should be so timed and modulated as to appear *one* on each part, like the *unison strings* of a well-tuned instrument—the *music* and the tune being suitably adapted to the subject, or words sung. And here we would suggest, that as the selection of the hymns is left to the *minister*, so also should the *tunes* to be sung be left to the choice and discretion of chorister or leader of the choir, and with *rare* exceptions should his responsibility in this matter be interfered with.[113]

---

[112]   For instance: Thomas Hastings, *Dissertation on Musical Taste* (Albany: Websters and Skinner, 1822); Hastings, *The History of Forty Choirs*; and Lowell Mason, *Letters from Abroad* (New York: Mason Brothers, 1854). This edition with a new introduction by Elwyn A. Wienandt (New York: Da Capo, 1967). See also Richard Storrs Willis, *Church Chorals and Choir Studies* (New York: Clark, Austin & Smith, 1850).

[113]   *Christian Intelligencer* 18, no. 12, WN 896 (Sept. 30, 1847), 46.

The second and third instructions appear to have been directed at soloists or quartet members within the choir. Both instructions stressed the need to maintain a unified ensemble sound and to avoid the possibility of individual voices being heard above others. The requirement for a "proportionately numbered" choir in the third instruction anticipated the reduction of many choirs to a quartet and countered the popular movement with a reminder of how effective well-balanced choral sound can be. It is interesting to observe the final recommendation that the chorister be allowed to select the tunes, since a number of accounts from the period indicate a controversy had developed over this task. The debate over selecting tunes is one more sign of the power struggle that ensued between clerical leaders and music leaders. This King Solomon-like suggestion to allow the minister to select the texts and the chorister to select the tunes offered a compromise that many churches still observe today.

Even the venerable Thomas Hastings was not safe from critical review. This reviewer accused the master of having taken his choral techniques to an extreme at the Presbyterian Church in Washington Square, Manhattan.

> The choir, which is a large one, is under the direction of Mr. Hastings. They exhibit the fruits of much careful drilling, which is particularly evinced by their time, and in the prolonging and swelling of the individual notes, which they do with great precision and unity: too much perhaps, for the general effect, as the attention of the auditor being strongly attracted to this uniform and mechanical process, is proportionately robbed of the aggregate result to which this as a detail is intended only to contribute.[114]

Professional quartets, or quintets, as in the case below, were not exempt from the scrutiny of music critics. All the more, their status subjected them to the type of analysis that accompanies those on any professional stage. The following concert review is from the Middle Collegiate Reformed Church in Manhattan, where, just four years earlier, the church had installed a Hall and Labagh pipe organ with much fanfare. The review renders a remarkable opinion of choral music at this prestigious Dutch Reformed Church at mid century:

> The music is under the direction of the Basso, Mr. Black, who possesses a strong and deep voice,—quite musical, though not

---

[114] "Choirs of New York and Brooklyn," seventh notice, *Message Bird* 50:294 (New York: May 1, 1850), 314.

always accurately intoned; the result of no deficiency of ear, but rather of inattention, combined with imperfect vocal schooling. Besides Mr. Black, the choir consists of two sopranos, a contralto of excellent quality, and a tenor, remarkable for its sweet, even, and blending quality of tone. Considering the power and steadiness of this latter voice, we have been somewhat surprised to learn that it is contributed by the organist, Mr. Munson. The united effect of this band are in many respects deserving of all praise. Especially in this case, when the sopranos, urged by an access of loudness of organ, are impelled to bring up their voices to a balancing degree of power. There is, however, "a worm i' bud," with this choir, which is making sad ravages with the beauty of their performance. We allude to a certain disconnected staccato manner of *syllabising*—to coin a term for the occasion. It is needless to say that such a method is destructive of unity, subversive of all intelligent expression, and utterly at variance with that smoothly flowing and *legato* manner, which should ever be observed in the practice of psalmody. We suspect the importation of this evil in the present instance to be charged to the organist, who, we perceive, is not always careful to preserve that distinctive touch which belongs exclusively to the organ. Yet, let us in justice to Mr. Munson, add, that we noticed nothing of this illiterate manner in his singing, which, so far, as the occasion demanded, was on the contrary chaste and artistic. We may therefore conclude that the defect we have described may in the present instance be easily removed—on the part of the choir, by frequent practice without the instrument, using tunes written in equal time and with open notes, which should be sustained to their utmost length, being careful to take breath only where the sense of the words will permit; and on the part of the Organist, by more careful attention to what belongs, as he is aware, to the mechanical details of the instrument. Would the latter gentleman permit us, we would respectfully urge upon him the less frequent use of the *Twelfth*, *Fifteenth*, and *Principal*, as accompanying stops, especially where these are based on the *Open Diapason*.[115]

The passage offers a fine description of the state of music-making in a Dutch Reformed Church in 1850. Even more, it demonstrates the degree to which the public had become conversant with music terminology and the extent to which capable reviewers adjudicated

---

[115] "Choirs of New York and Brooklyn," fifth notice, *Message Bird* 50:222R (New York: Apr. 1, 1850), 279.

these venues. The terminology employed regarding choral sound and execution points to the successful campaign of the church music reformers in New York City in just twenty years. Their techniques had become "state of the art" ways to prepare a choir and the criterion for which choirs would be critiqued. Organs, too, had become firmly established in church and concert music, as builders were increasing both the size and tonal capabilities of the instrument to foster or align with the growing perception of the organ as orchestra. Organists gained in stature as concert artists, at least in part, for playing orchestral transcriptions.

Conclusion

In the twenty years between Thomas Hastings's arrival in New York City and the review quoted above, a massive transformation had occurred. Choirs had become firmly rooted in American culture, and institutional church choirs and professional music leaders had secured an important place within the worship of Protestant America. In the Dutch Reformed Church, choirs sang hymns and anthems and were afforded a space of their own in the balcony. Instruments first, then organs, infiltrated this scene by adding more and more performance values to public worship as American culture blurred, if not erased, the lines between sacred and secular music-making as well as those between denominations. Women seized the opportunity to make and lead music by providing the means for organs to be acquired.

An industry had grown up around choirs for concerts, instruments, and printed music. Especially important in this vane was the tunebook, the all-in-one pedagogical tool and ecumenical music collection that kept pace with America's musical taste. Surely, nothing else had a more direct impact on each church, and, therefore, on the growth of choirs than the music book choir members held.

CHAPTER 5

Tunebooks and the Dutch Reformed Church

From the mid-eighteenth century until the late nineteenth century the tunebook was the primary source of music for singing schools, Sabbath school choirs, choral societies, public school music education, and institutional church choirs. Numbering in the thousands of publications, American tunebooks broadcast a vast repertoire of arranged or newly composed music that kept pace with the changing currents and tastes in American musical culture, music education, and religion.[1] One might ask how Dutch Reformed churches came to use tunebooks when the General Synod had defined the denomination's musical repertoire by publishing a psalter/hymnal. While it was true that approved poetic texts were published in these books, no printed music was contained in the psalter/hymnals commencing with the *Psalms*

---

[1] For general treatments on the subject of tunebooks, see Allen Perdue Britton and Irving Lowens, completed by Richard Crawford, *American Sacred Music Imprints 1698-1810*; Elwyn Wienandt and Robert H. Young, *The Anthem in England and America* (New York: Free Press, 1970); Gilbert Chase, *America's Music from Pilgrims to Present*; and Irving Lowens, *Music and Musicians in Early America*.

and Hymns (1789) until the *Book of Praise* (1866).[2] In fact, the majority of Protestant hymnals in America at this time did not contain music. Therefore, during this period of tuneless psalter/hymnals, choirs—or at least the church's song leader or organist—found it necessary to obtain one or more separate music collections, or tunebooks, to coincide with the poetic meters of their psalter/hymnal.[3]

The earliest tunebook I encountered with Dutch Reformed provenance was the *New-York Selection of Sacred Music containing a great number of plain tunes, carefully arranged, and particularly designed for church worship, and generally suited to the several metres [sic] in the Psalms and Hymns used in the Dutch Church...* The collection was compiled by F.D. Allen (identified in the tunebook's preface as a teacher of sacred music and promoter of sacred music concerts) and published by him in New York in 1818. The 106-page collection is in two parts. The first and largest part contains eighty-one metrical tunes grouped by short meter, common meter, long meter, and particular meter. The tunes are designed for congregational use as they employ simple meters and melodies and are arranged in four-part homophonic (note against note) musical texture. The second part of the book, the appendix, is more curious because it offers fifty-eight metrical tunes adapted to the most popular hymn texts of the day, especially the hymns of Isaac Watts, Timothy Dwight (1752-1817), John Dobell (1752-1840), and John Rippon (1751-1836). These more complicated settings, mostly from the English parish music of composers like William Tans'ur (1700-83), Martin Madan (1726-90), Thomas Clark (1775-1859), and Isaac Tucker (1761-1825), require greater musicianship to perform. They contain more complicated rhythms, elaborate or ornamented melodic lines, and polyphonic (independent melodies or melodic imitation between vocal parts) musical textures. There is no indication in the preface that some of these tunes were intended to be sung as choral anthems; however,

---

[2]   The *Book of Praise* (1866) was arranged in split pages so that texts and tunes of the same meter could be matched. *Hymns of the Church* (1869) was the denomination's first hymnal to wed text with tune on the same page.

[3]   Britton and Lowens, *American Sacred Music Imprints 1698-1810: A Bibliography*, identified 545 collections published by 1810. After 1810 the number of new tunebooks published accelerated through the rest of the century. The leading compilers, Thomas Hastings, William B. Bradbury, Lowell Mason, George James Webb (1803-1887), and Isaac Baker Woodbury (1819-1858), together account for well over a hundred tunebooks published in America. Some volumes sold particularly well. In *America's Music: From the Pilgrims to the Present*, Gilbert Chase records on p. 131 that Lowell Mason's *Carmina Sacra* (Boston and New York, 1841) sold 500,000 copies between 1841-58 and that *The Hallelujah* (Boston and New York, 1854) sold 150,000 copies in just five years.

since the pieces are more difficult than those grouped in the first part of the book, one suspects that they were included for that reason. Based on his assessment of the state of church music in the preface, F.D. Allen surely counted himself among the church music reformers of his age. Accordingly, the pieces in this collection represent the more "cultured" music introduced in the period. It then stands to reason that choirs would have been at least occasionally needed to teach this "new" music to the congregation and perhaps offer some of the pieces as anthems.

From the mid 1830s through 1860, at least a dozen tunebooks were endorsed or advertised for sale in the *Christian Intelligencer*.[4] Evidence that the Dutch Reformed Church used tunebooks was also found in the denomination's magazine, where particular collections used on such special occasions as a Sunday school anniversary and a music convention held by Thomas Hastings were indicated.[5] Herein two representative collections will be discussed: *The New Brunswick Collection of Sacred Music*, 7th edition (1835), which had eight editions between 1817 and 1841 and was the most successful music collection published in New Jersey in its time;[6] and the *Handel and Haydn Collection of Sacred Music* (1827),[7] a volume of choir anthems used by the First Church,

---

[4] Those advertised included Wm. B. Bradbury, *The Jubilee: An Extensive Collection of Church Music for the Choir, the Congregation, and the Singing-School. New Edition, Containing Additional Anthems, Opening and Closing and Closing Pieces, Etc.* (New York: Mason Brothers; Boston: Mason and Hamlin, 1858); Wm. B. Bradbury and George F. Root, *The Shawm* (New York: Mason Brothers, 1853); Thomas Hastings and Wm. B. Bradbury, *The Psalmodist* (New York: Mark H. Newman, 1844), *The New York Choralist* (New York: Mark H. Newman, 1847), *The Mendelssohn Collection* (New York: Mark E. Newman; Cincinnati: Wm. H. Moore, 1849), and *Psalmista* (New York: Mark H. Newman, 1851); Thomas Hastings and Solomon Warriner, *Musica Sacra, or the Utica and Springfield Collection United*, 10th rev. ed. with appendix (Utica: William Williams, 1835); Lowell Mason, *The Hallelujah* (New York: Mason Brothers, 1854); Lowell Mason and George James Webb, *The National Psalmist* (Boston: Tappan, Whittemore, and Mason; New York: Geo. F. Cooledge, 1848), and *Cantica Laudis* (New York: Mason and Law; Boston: Tappan, Whittemore, and Mason, 1850); Cornelius Van Deventer, *The New Brunswick Collection of Sacred Music*, 7th ed. (New Brunswick: Terhune & Letson, 1835); I.B. Woodbury, *The Dulcimer: or The New York Collection of Sacred Music* (New York: F.J. Huntington, Mason Brothers, 1850).

[5] Citations from these occasions were given in chapter 3 (pp. 70, 71, and 76). The specific tunebooks mentioned were *The New York Choralist* (1847), *The Psalmodist* (1844), *The S.S. Lyre* (New York: Mark H. Newman, 1848), and the *Psalmista* (1851).

[6] See Charles H. Kaufman, *Music in New Jersey, 1655-1860: A Study of Musical Activity and Musicians in New Jersey from Its First Settlement to the Civil War* (Rutherford, NJ: Fairleigh Dickinson Univ. Press, 1981) for an analysis of each of the eight editions of the *New Brunswick Collection of Sacred Music*.

[7] See George Heller and Carol Pemberton, "The Boston Handel and Haydn Society Collection of Church Music (1822): Its Context, Content, and Significance," *Hymn* 47: 4 (Oct., 1996), 26-39, for a thorough study of the tunebook publications of the society.

Albany, New York, in the 1820s.[8] Both collections provide valuable information about tunebook use and the institutional choir repertoire in the Dutch Reformed Church.

A Closer Look at Tunebooks:
A Brief Historiography and an Analytical Method

Most of the tunebooks studied exhibited signs of the extensive movement to reform sacred music by virtually dismissing the indigenous music of colonial America and replacing it with two distinctive patterns of repertoire: music that found inspiration in the simple "common tunes" of American composers like Lowell Mason and Thomas Hastings, and pieces selected or adapted largely from Western European composers.[9] A blending of these two patterns can be found in the *New Brunswick Collection of Sacred Music*, essentially a provincial tunebook from the 1810s. The latter pattern is found in the *Boston Handel and Haydn Collection of Sacred Music*, a widely circulated 1820s anthem book encompassing the "cultured" repertoire disseminated by the Handel and Haydn Society.

In this chapter I have made general observations about tunebooks from several collections. Additionally, guided by the two particular collections studies cited above, I have surveyed the contents of the *New Brunswick Collection of Sacred Music* and the *Boston Handel and Haydn Collection of Sacred Music*. Since my research has focused solely on choirs, I have limited the material examined in each book to pieces most likely performed by a choir—that is, those listed in the tunebook indexes under the titles "anthems, set-pieces," etc. Still, my aim was not a comprehensive analysis of this material. Rather, I extracted and analyzed musically the compositions found in the *New Brunswick Collection of Sacred Music* and discussed more generally the repertoire and mode of performance at the First Church, Albany, of the *Boston Handel and Haydn Collection of Sacred Music*. Through these findings I have drawn conclusions about the types and styles of music used, the manner in which the repertoire was performed, and the impact of this music on church choirs, worship, and the religious culture of the Dutch Reformed Church.

---

[8]   I am indebted to Dr. Elton Bruins for alerting me to the existence of this tunebook and to the kind staff of the Van Raalte Institute at the Theil Center, Hope College, Holland, Michigan, for allowing me to examine this book.

[9]   Richard Crawford, "Psalmody," in H. Wiley Hitchcock and Stanley Sadie, eds., *The New Grove Dictionary of American Music*, 4 vols. (New York: Grove's Dictionaries of Music, 1986).

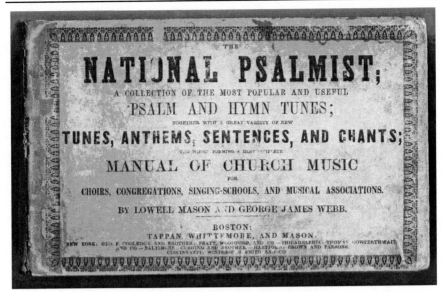

Figure 4. Lowell Mason and George James Webb's *The National Psalmist* (1848), front cover

General Characteristics of the Tunebooks

The tunebook has long since vanished from the gamut of published music. Since there is little in contemporary music publishing with which to make a comparison, a general description seems advisable. The two books I selected are typical in form, appearance, and general content of the hundred or so I have examined. They are oblong and bound on the shorter side in what booksellers call "boards" (wood, or what we now called cardboard). The boards are connected end to end with a piece of leather or fabric. The leaves are sewn together and the boards attached to the contents through an interior paper laminate. Book sizes vary but are typically about nine inches wide by six inches high. Anthem collections tend to be larger, have larger print, and include keyboard accompaniments.

By the 1840s tunebooks had acquired a market-sensitive appearance and size. The geographically based titles of the 1830s, like *The New-Brunswick Collection of Sacred Music*, gave way to titles that depicted such musical or religious images as *The Shawm* (1853), *The Psalmista* (1851), *The Hallelujah* (1854), and *The Jubilee* (1858), and titles that would have attracted a wider audience, like the *National Psalmist* (1848). Cover designs became more decorative too, with the full title page information displayed in a variety of fonts within a border. As the century drew on, collections appear to have increased in content size from *The New Brunswick Collection of Sacred Music's* relatively meager 160 pages to 322 pages in the *Musica Sacra* or the *Utica and Springfield Collections United*, 352 pages in *The Dulcimer*, and 400 pages in the *Mendelssohn Collection*.[10]

The interior layout and general content of the books are remarkably similar. Each contains a preface describing the merits and innovations of the volume or edition. The preface was also a place for editorializing about the state of church music in general or to debate particular issues with other tunebook compilers. This was the case in the preface to Mason and Webb's *The National Psalmist*, where a lengthy discourse on church music was followed by this statement intended to quiet an ongoing dispute about the role of church choirs:

> It may be thought that we are disposed to attach undue importance to congregational singing; but let it be remembered that while we would urge this as an essential form of church music, we would urge with equal earnestness the importance of choirs and of the choral style.

At first, Mason had promoted using church choirs primarily to aid and improve congregational singing. However, by the time of this 1848 tunebook, the "science" of choral singing had been well propagated, choral societies abounded, and anthem-singing institutional choirs had become normative. There was a vast market for choral repertoire judging from the number and variety of tunebooks published in the period. Indeed, while the metrical tune sections of tunebooks continued to expand, so did the number of choral responses and anthems printed in each volume.

Most of the tunebooks contained an opening didactic section. *The New Brunswick Collection of Sacred Music* adopted an earlier shape-note approach widely disseminated in William Little and William Smith's *Easy Instructor*.[11] Tunebooks from the 1830s on typically based their instructional sections on a musically adapted Pestalozzian educational model, applying a "scientific" approach through an elemental

---

10   For instance, announcements for Hastings and Bradbury's *The New York Choralist* proudly declared that the tunebook contained more than one thousand musical compositions.

11   A study of the *Easy Instructor* was made by Irving Lowens in "The Easy Instructor (1798-1831): A History and Bibliography of the First Shape-Note Tune Book," *Journal of Research in Music Education* 1 (1953): 1-26, and *Music and Musicians in Early America* (New York: Norton, 1964), 115-38.

breakdown of music such as rhythm, pitch, dynamics, and tempo.[12] Practical exercises were included with each element discussed, followed by aspects of music theory and *solfeggio* covering intervals, scales, keys, and music terminology. These pedagogical sections frequently required twenty to thirty pages and seemed obligatory, if not redundant, in the wake of a mission promoting music education in schools and churches.

Following the didactic section was the bulk of each collection, containing the psalms and hymns, tune and text intertwined,[13] arranged by meter.[14] This material filled the need for tunes to match poetic texts found in hymnbooks. By the mid 1840s, each new collection was represented as the most current compendium of wide-ranging and best resources known from European and American composers old and new. While a standard corpus of texts and tunes were maintained in early tunebooks, this became less the case after 1840, with an ever-increasing demand for newly discovered or composed material.[15] Most of the books included musical compositions penned by the editor or editors. While some tunebooks included figures for keyboard accompaniment in the 1830s (i.e., the *Musica Sacra* or *Utica and Springfield Collection United*), the *New Brunswick Collection* did not. However, all of the books I examined after 1840 included figures or musical notation for keyboard accompaniment, and the *Dulcimer* included a two-page "Instructions for Playing the Organ, Piano-forte, Melodeon and Seraphine by Figures."[16]

---

12   Shortly after 1830, the inductive reasoning school of Swiss educator Johann Heinrich Pestalozzi (1746-1827) significantly affected the emerging educational method in the United States. Thomas Hastings and Lowell Mason were much indebted to Pestalozzian methods, such that they occasionally paid tribute to this educator in their tunebook prefaces and even included a few pieces of music by Swiss composers in their collections.

13   Since the psalter/hymnal contained the full poetic texts, typically only one or two stanzas were intertwined with the music in tunebooks.

14   When we refer to meter here we mean the poetic meter of the text, not the time signature of the music. Generally, the number of syllables of text per poetic line determines the meter of a text. Each line of text then figures in the overall designation of the meter. For instance, if all of the lines of text contain eight syllables, then the poetry is in Long Meter (L.M.). If the lines alternate between eight syllables and six syllables, then the poetry is in Common Meter (C.M.).

15   Lowell Mason, George James Webb, Thomas Hastings, and William B. Bradbury amassed vast collections of tunes. In the late 1840s their collections fueled a lasting interest in German church music in America, expanding the interest of the American public past its previous affinity for English and American music.

16   Devised during the Baroque era of music (1600-1750), a musical *figure* is a numerical indication of a musical interval to be played above a written bass line. The number(s) permit the keyboardist to *realize* the intended harmony for the given passage, while affording the player the opportunity to add improvisatory material.

The *New Brunswick Collection of Sacred Music* had only eleven works designated as anthems. *Musica Sacra,* its tenth edition contemporary with the seventh edition of the *New Brunswick Collection,* had fifty-seven compositions in the index titled "Anthems, etc." The *Mendelssohn Collection* had fifty-seven pieces in its "Anthems, Choruses, Motets, Hymns Introits, and Sentences" index, filling about one-third of its pages. Finally, the *Dulcimer* had an impressive ninety-two pieces in the section titled "Anthems, Quartetts, Choruses, Chants, Set Pieces, Etc. Etc.," along with an oratorio by Woodbury titled *Absalom,* its components derived from a multitude of sources, including simplified choruses of master composers.

Each book contained an alphabetical and a metrical index, and the books became more consumer oriented throughout the 1840s, adding first-line tables and, in the *Dulcimer,* a "Chorister's Index—Comprising all the Odd Metres in common use, with appropriate music." The back covers served as advertising billboards for the publisher's other tunebooks currently for sale. Tunebooks sold for about sixty cents a copy, or less if purchased by the dozen.

The New Brunswick Collection of Sacred Music

The *New Brunswick Collection of Sacred Music* was a quirky little book and a smaller collection than is usually found, expanding to only 255 pieces in its eighth (1841) and final edition. Its circulation was apparently limited to New Jersey and eastern Pennsylvania. Its quirkiness came from contradictory impulses—to remain very conservative, yet survive in multiple editions amid a rapidly changing market. As a sign of its conservatism, the collection perpetuated the soon outmoded *Easy Instructor* didactic section and used *shape-note* musical orthography. It also perpetuated two soon-to-be obsolete notions about musical terminology: one, that time signatures also connoted tempo; and, two, that sharp keys were associated with major scales and flat keys with minor.

Of its three editors, the Dutch Reformed Cornelius Van Deventer (1767-1849) held sway throughout each of the tunebook's editions. Yet, curiously unnamed outsiders pulled more weight in the editing process.[17] According to Kaufman, writing in 1981, "For the first time

---

[17]   Barstow's (New York and Richmond) 3rd ed. editors deleted 42 and added 74 compositions from the previous edition. New Jersey publisher Peter A. Johnson's 4th edition editor added 31 pieces from early sources, arriving at a tunebook that Kaufman assessed as having "had no claim on modernity."

the *NBC* was brought into the mainstream of contemporary sacred music," with the seventh-edition inclusion of twelve new tunes from the *Handel and Haydn Society Collection*, seven of which were by Lowell Mason.[18]

The Anthems in *The New Brunswick Collection of Sacred Music*

The seventh edition (1835) had eleven anthems or set-pieces, a quantity lagging well behind its peers in accommodating the rising need for choral repertoire. As will be seen, the pieces it included, excepting the few from Lowell Mason, were already a generation old. The following table compares anthem types, forms, textures, and voice parts:

Table 8
Anthems in *The New Brunswick Collection of Sacred Music* (7th ed., 1835)

Title	Attribution	Type/ Form	Texture/Voice Parts
Come ye Disconsolate	Samuel Webbe	Anthem/ Strophic	Melody and bass line, optional harmonizing part included for second half of strophe/one and two parts
*Daughter of Zion	Lowell Mason	Anthem/ Strophic	Homophonic/ Four parts, except when two parts in the first four bars of each "B" section
Denmark	Martin Madan	Set-piece/ Through-composed	Homophonic/ Four parts except for a trio in the second section
Dying Christian	Edward Harwood	Set-piece/ Through-composed	Homophonic with one brief fuguing passage /Three parts

---

[18]   Charles H. Kaufman, *Music in New Jersey, 1655-1860* (Rutherford, NJ: Associated Univ. Press, 1981), 140.

*From Greenland's Icy Mountains (Vesper Hymn)	Lowell Mason	Anthem/ Strophic	Homophonic/ Three parts
Hark! The Vesper Hymn, &c.	Russian Air	Anthem/ Strophic	Homophonic/ Solo melody with two descant parts beginning at measure four
Hark! The Song of Jubilee	R. Latimer Cooke	Anthem/ AB	Homophonic/ Three parts
*O Praise God in His Holiness	Lowell Mason	Anthem/ Through-composed	Homophonic, with one brief fuguing passage/ Four parts
The Parting	W. F. Miller	Anthem/ AB	Melody and bass line/One part
Thou Art Gone to the Grave	Dr. Clark	Anthem/ Strophic	Melody and bass line/ One part
*The Voice of Free Grace	Dr. Clark	Anthem/ AB	Homophonic/ Four parts

*1st time in this edition

Of the eleven compositions designated "anthem" in the index only "Denmark" and "Dying Christian" are *set-pieces*.[19] Both pieces were immensely popular, appearing in numerous earlier American sources commencing with Andrew Law's (1749-1821) *A Collection of Hymn Tunes* in the 1780s.[20] From the early to mid-nineteenth century, newly

[19]   According to Richard Crawford, in Stanley Sadie, ed., *New Grove Dictionary of Music* (London: Macmillan, 1980), s.v. "Set-piece," the form is a through-composed (the music continually changes to fit a changing text, versus strophic forms where the same musical material is repeated to successive "strophes" of text) musical composition using a metrical text and frequently containing several verses. The set-piece often features word repetitions, melismas, texture changes, mood shifts, and climactic conclusions.

[20]   Britton and Lowens (Crawford completed), *American Sacred Music Imprints 1698-1810: A Bibliography* (1990).

composed set-pieces like these became increasingly rare, and, while the term, *set-piece*, is retained into the third quarter of the nineteenth century, it came to mean almost any through-composed form.[21]

"Denmark," from Martin Madan's highly acclaimed *Lock Hospital Collection* (London, 1769), is a through-composed (set-piece) anthem in four sections (the third section repeated), set in alternating meters of 2/4 and 3/8 and in D major. The texture is homophonic but varied from four voice parts in the first section, to three (marked trio) in the second, and back to four voices for the third and forth strophes (marked chorus). Known for his elaborate melodies, Madan's very popular church music did not arise from either country church music or the cathedral tradition but from the stage.[22] In this style he used varying rhythmic figures, melodic ornamentation, sequences, and melismas to increase the dramatic effect of the piece in each subsequent section. A distinctive feature of this piece is the brief section of repeated measures that alternate between the dynamics of *piano* (soft) and *forte* (loud), a technique derived from the era's instrumental art music.

Edward Harwood's "Dying Christian" (CD track 9) remains essentially in three voices, changes meters with each new section, and modulates once from F minor to F major. Its ever-changing and unembellished melody assists in it maintaining clear text declamation throughout the piece's relatively lengthy eighty-six measures.[23] The charming aspects of this composition are its rhythmic variety and melodic adaptability, as it aims to depict musically a Christian's emotional concourse from death to resurrection. It is likely that "Dying Christian" was a staple at funerals, a frequent occasion to gather a choir.

The other nine pieces are anthems or hymns arranged or intended to be used as anthems. Lowell Mason's "Daughter of Zion" (CD track 8), in B-flat major and set in 3/4 time, consists of three eight-bar periods comprising a twenty-four-measure ABA form (once repeated) and a six bar *coda*.[24] Each period has two equal four-bar phrases in an antecedent/ consequent style of melodic contour. The work uses the rhythmic motive of a dotted quarter and an eighth note to begin each phrase of

---

[21] For instance, Hastings and Bradbury, *The New York Choralist* (1847).

[22] Wienandt and Young, *Anthem in England and America*, 158.

[23] Anthems found in tunebooks were relatively short in duration, the majority being from 30-70 measures. Set-pieces, by design, were generally a bit longer, but still quite short when compared to much of the standard historic anthem repertoire.

[24] The *coda* (literally "tail" in Italian) is any concluding passage that exists outside the basic form of a composition and is used to reach or build upon the impression of finality. Favored by Lowell Mason, the coda was one of many techniques borrowed by the sacred music reformers from European instrumental art music.

Figure 5. A shape-note page of the anthem, "Daughter of Zion," from Cornelius Van Deventer, *The New Brunswick Collection of Sacred Music*

the "A" period. It is harmonized in four parts (the melody in the tenor), except for the first four bars of each "B" section that are in two parts, the first time pairing the soprano/tenor and the second time the alto/tenor. The alternating *soli* (solo, or small group in this case) and *tutti* (full choir), the *soli* in the first "A" and the "B" periods, and the *tutti* in the second "A" period, solidifies the text and tune refrain of the final "A" section.[25] The piece is characteristic of the reform movement's simple and straightforward musical imperative, using symmetrical forms and phrases and a note against note homophonic setting.[26]

Another Mason tune, the popular "From Greenland's Icy Mountains" (CD track 2), found in the *Boston Handel and Haydn Collection of Church Music*, is a sixteen-bar strophic form in three voice parts, in F major and in the *slowest* duple meter of "C." The middle voice carries the simple but charming folk-like tune, its melodic contour rising and falling in tonic and dominant-seventh triads, depicting both the mountains found in its text and the arduous path of the Christian missionary. The harmonic language, limited to tonic and dominant-

[25]   This technique, sometimes called the *concertato principle*, originated in the Baroque era of music and applied equally to instrumental and choral genres as a compositional device for musical expansion and as a means for varying tone color and dynamics.

[26]   This type of setting, called "common tune" or "syllabic," was the pattern evidenced in metrical psalmody, whereby close to or exactly one note only was supplied for each syllable of text.

seventh chords along with a mid-point half cadence (the dominant chord of the key, in this case a C chord) approached by secondary dominant (V/V or G) chord, and the triadic melody exudes a sense of spaciousness and adventure that was commensurate with the depiction of the text's remote and exotic places.

The third Mason anthem, "O Praise God in his Holiness," a setting of Psalm 150 in F major, is set in 3/2 meter and voiced in four parts. Except for a brief imitative passage near the end, it is strictly homophonic (note against note), with some variety obtained by alternating between two-, three-, and four-voice parts. The piece achieves unity through the arrangement of consequent/antecedent four-measure blocks, followed by an imitative eighth-bar repeated episode and a four-bar coda. Its simple melody, located in the tenor voice, rises and falls in conjunct (stepwise) motion. The text is syllabically set in four-bar phrases of eight syllables that obtain rhythmic continuity through a one-measure long-short rhythmic motive. The harmonic language and (harmonic) rhythm is simple, using only plagal, half cadences, and perfect cadences, briefly passing through D major (V/ii) then a C major (V) sequence before arriving at a perfect cadence in the third four-bar phrase.[27] The same four-bar progressions are repeated throughout the piece, although in differing order.[28]

"Hark! The Song of Jubilee," set in 3/8 time and in F major, is arranged almost strictly in three homophonic voice parts. Its two sixteen-bar sections consist of a verse and refrain, the refrain containing "hallelujahs."[29] Because many of these earlier works were arranged in two, three, or four parts, this three-part version is marked "air" on the middle voice to call attention to the tune. This line also bears the marking, *con spirito* ("with spirit" or "lively"), at the point of the refrain. The first sixteen bars are set metrically into two verses, each containing two seven-syllable phrases. The sixteen-bar "hallelujah" refrain is set in irregular eleven-, seven-, seven-, and six-syllable per four-bar phrases.

---

27   A plagal cadence is a chord progression of IV to I. A half cadence ends on V. A perfect cadence is a progression from V to I.

28   It is significant that the *New Brunswick Collection of Sacred Music* included three anthems composed by Lowell Mason, since Mason's common-tune style of music was quickly becoming standard in the repertoire of the Protestant mainstream. That this volume included both the earlier English parish style music and Mason's newer style music marks a midpoint in the transition away from the former repertoire to the American common-tune music popularized by Mason and Hastings.

29   Perhaps filling the void left after the sacred music reform movement's wholesale curtailing of fuguing tunes, "hallelujah" refrains, often executed in brief passages of imitative counterpoint and appended to metrical tunes and anthems, gained popularity in American psalmody.

No doubt the metrical sevens and the irregular "hallelujah" refrain help maintain an interest in this piece as a departure from the wealth of meters arranged in eight- and six-syllable phrases.

Much the same can be said of "The Parting," a melody with a bass line, consisting of a sixteen-bar verse in 6/8 time and an equal length refrain in common time. The connotations of 6/8 time as a *fast* time and of common time as the *slowest* duple time are further obfuscated by the Italian tempo markings that accompany each section, for the 6/8 time is coupled with the term *largetto* ("relatively slow"), and the common time with the word *allegretto* ("relatively fast"). We are left to wonder without the help of a metronome marking or some other key to tempo equivalence whether the composer wished to keep the value of the eighth note the same in each section.[30] In G major, the piece carries the tune in the upper voice and is a good example of the early "ditties" that were purged from tunebooks toward the middle of the nineteenth century and, in some cases, replaced with newer "ditties." This one may have survived as long as it did because of its niche-filling liturgical function as a parting hymn or benediction response.

Samuel Webbe's (1740-1816) well-known hymn tune, "Come, Ye Disconsolate," is reprinted here in a two-verse strophic form. In D major, it is scored with a melody and bass line and an optional harmonizing part for the last eight measures.

The perennial favorite, "Hark! The Vesper Hymn" (CD track 10), its melodic pattern depicting the tolling of bells, is set here in F major with two descant voices above the melody, depicting slower tolling bells. The "Russian Air" appeared in a number of earlier collections, including *Templi Carmina: Songs of the Temple, or the Bridgewater Collection of Sacred Music* (1802).

"Thou Art Gone to the Grave," an F major melody and bass line in a common time metrical setting of eight alternating thirteen and eleven syllable phrases, and "The Voice of Free Grace," a verse/refrain piece in four voice parts, keyed in B-flat major and set in the meter of 3/8, are typical of the simple imported English syllabic song/anthems and present no further remarkable characteristics.

In summary, *The New Brunswick Collection of Sacred Music* (7th ed.) is an example of an early provincial shape-note tunebook. Its meager

---

30   *The Boston Handel and Haydn Society Collection of Church Music* (1822) included metronome and tempo markings for each tune, along with an explanation and endorsement of Johann Nepomuk Maelzel's (1772-1838) invention in the preface: "But the machine most recently invented, and which now deservedly possess the greatest celebrity is Maelzel's Metronome, or Musical Time-Keeper."

collection of 11 anthems and 199 metrical tunes in 29 different meters is representative of early nineteenth-century American tunebooks that encompass a repertoire of almost entirely English and American origin. One cannot be sure if the anthem collection was to be used by the choir in weekly worship or just for special occasions. Several of the anthems are suited for funerals, such as "Dying Christian," "The Voice of Free Grace," "Thou Art Gone to the Grave," "Daughter of Zion," and "The Parting." "From Greenland's Icy Mountains" would have been an appropriate anthem for a missionary meeting. "Hark! The Vesper Hymn" would have been suitable for an evening service or meeting, and "O Praise God in His Holiness" for almost any occasion, but especially as an opening hymn for a church dedication or anniversary. It is possible that the collection, in addition to marking a midpoint between English parish music and common-tune music, also marked a midpoint between choirs that were assembled for special occasions and the institutional choir that sang in weekly worship.

The Boston Handel and Haydn Collection of Sacred Music

In the early 1820s, the Boston Handel and Haydn Society published two similarly titled tunebooks. Prepared by Lowell Mason, *The Boston Handel and Haydn Society Collection of Church Music* was first published by the society in 1822 and survived twenty-two editions through 1858, selling more than fifty thousand copies. The revenue from the tunebook secured the financial future of the society, and the book's immediate success launched Lowell Mason's illustrious career. While the tunebook's appearance and general contents were much the same as any other tunebook of the era, its unparalleled collection "set forth an aesthetic that became standard in many American churches."[31]

The tunebook that I examined in Holland, Michigan, was also produced by the society, but with the title, *The Boston Handel and Haydn Collection of Sacred Music*. It was first published one year before Mason's involvement in the society in 1821. A second volume was published in 1823 and a third in 1827, the one I examined. Also intended as a fundraising tool, this collection was unique because its contents were selected anthems and oratorio extractions that the society had

---

[31] Heller and Pemberton, "Boston Handel and Haydn Society Collection" (1822), 26. The volume includes a pedagogical section, a large number of metrical tunes, and a section of anthems, motets, and set-pieces. Making the collection unique were the many pieces culled from the oratorios, sacred music, and art music of such composers as Handel, Haydn, Mozart, and Beethoven.

performed in sacred music concerts. Therefore, unlike most tunebooks, this collection did not include the pedagogical or metrical tune sections.

The volume's dimensions were 14 inches wide by 9 ¾ inches high, quite a bit larger than the usual tunebook size. The binding was also customized, including a border design, an engraved number six on the side of the binding, and a pasted front cover paper label that read, "Choir of the R.P. Dutch Church" and "Albany." On the inside title page was scrawled in pencil "#11," possibly indicating a renumbering of the books at some time.

The full title page and index information are given below: (Title page: #11)

> The Boston Handel and Haydn Society Collection
> Of
> Sacred Music
> Consisting of
> Songs, Duetts, Trios, Chorusses, Anthems, & c.
> Selected for the Works of the Most Celebrated Authors.
>
> Arranged for the Organ or Piano Forte,
> By the
> Handel and Haydn Society.
> Vol. III.
> Boston:
> Published by the Handel and Haydn Society.
> Printed by James Loring,
> No. 132, Washington-street
> 1827.
>
> Index:
> To Volume Three

Air	Angel of Charity	Handel
Chorus	Swell, Swell the Chorus	
Recitative	And Saul was very wroth	
Air & Chorus	O mighty King	Haydn
Chorus	Break forth into Joy	W. Jackson
Air	Come ye Disconsolate	German*
Quartette	Come ye Disconsolate	Harmonized by Stevenson

*   CD track 7

Air	For Ever Blessed	Handel
Solo & chorus	Go Forth to the Mount	Stevenson**
Doxology	Glory Be to the Father	W. Jackson
Chorus	Glory to God in the Highest	Pergolese [sic]
Chorus	God is our King	Gardiner
Semi-Chorus & Chorus	Sons of Zion	Nauman
Solo & Chorus	Glorify the Great Jehovah	Haydn
Chorus	Hallelujah to the God of Israel	Haydn
Quartette or Chorus	Hark! Tis the Breeze	Air by Rousseau Harmonized by Stevenson
Air	How can I on thee repose	Beethoven
Chorus	Hosanna	Handel
Chorus	He broke the Idols	Handel
Motetto	He was like a Morning Star	
Chorus	Lo he cometh	Haydn
Quartette or Semi chorus	Lo my shepherd is Divine	Haydn
Air	Lord thou has been my refuge	
Recitative	Now Israel Worshipped the Idols	
Chorus	He broke the Idols	Haydn
Recitative	Now Samuel Anointed Saul	
Quartette or Semi-chorus	Lo My Shepherd is Divine	Haydn
Recitative	Now the Philistines	Haydn
Chorus	Lo He Cometh	

** CD track 6

Recitative Motetto	Now the Philistines Fought He was like a Morning Star	From the Oratorio of Judah
Chorus & Duet	O God when thou appearest	Mozart
Sestetto	O How Beautiful	Haydn
Chorus	O Judah Boast	Handel
Anthem	O Lord Our Governor	Stevenson
Air & Chorus	O mighty King	Haydn
Anthem	O Rejoice in God our King	Beethoven
Chorus	Praise him in Judah	Mozart
Chorus	Praise Him Sun and Moon	Staunton
Solo & Chorus	Sing unto God	From the Oratorio Judas Maccabeus, Handel
Chorus	Solyma, O happy Solyma	Mozart
Semi-chorus & Chorus	Sons of Zion	Nauman
Chorus	Sound aloud Jehovah's name	Haydn
Chorus	Swell, Swell the full Chorus	Handel
Recitative	Then Jesus Went up to Jerusalem	Boyce
Chorus	Hosanna	Handel
Anthem Duett	The Lord Shall comfort Zion	W. Jackson
Chorus	Break Forth into Joy	W. Jackson
Solo & Chorus	The Sun Ascends	Haydn
Air	To Thee in God	Mozart
Recitative	The Wolf and the Lamb	Haydn

Sestetto	O How Beautiful	
Chorus	Sound aloud Jehovah's name	
Te Deum	We praise thee, O God	W. Jackson
Recitative	When God is in His Wrath Revealed	
Air	When Storms the proud Terrors doom	Handel
Chorus	O Judah Boast	
Recitative	When rosy steps young day appears From the Seasons	Haydn

Solo & Chorus The Sun Ascends

Much of the material published in this volume is extracted from the sacred oratorios of important Western European composers. Included with each score is a keyboard reduction of the instrumental accompaniment complete with Italian tempi and dynamic markings. The recitatives and arias are scored in a single staff with the accompaniment below and indicate the soloed voice part, or character in the case of oratorios, within the staff. Chorus parts are scored with a staff to each voice part and are marked "chorus," or "semi-chorus" at the onset of each new section requiring the chorus. Thus, the music orthography and score layout are the same as in modern editions.

Whereas the preface indicates that the collection was intended for sacred music societies and churches, even a cursory evaluation of this book's texts reveals the publisher's intention to assemble a fairly wide selection of theological topics. Interestingly, this makes sense from either the sacred concert or worship perspective, since sacred concerts took on some of the characteristics of worship and worship took on some of the characteristics of sacred concerts.

It is interesting that the publisher grouped some pieces in this index topically and according to the recitative, aria, and chorus pattern found in many oratorios, but did not necessarily group pieces from the same larger work or even by the same composer. Naturally, the grouping relays the publisher's intention for a contiguous performance of the material. But, in this particular tunebook there are many added pencil markings, presumably from a member or leader of First Church's choir, that give us more information about how the pieces were performed.

For instance, in the piece, "Lo My Shepherd is Divine" by Haydn, two fanciful pencil marks delete a "B" section in two places. Another marking appears between the recitative, "With Rosy Steps Young Day

Appears," and the chorus, "The Sun Ascends," as a reminder to move immediately from the recitative to chorus, a "segue" in modern musical terminology. Later in the composition a marking appears, changing a portion of the chorus to a two-bar solo, followed by a marking to resume the chorus. In "Glory to God in the highest" by Pergolese [*sic*], a marking calling attention to the *da capo* repeat sign is circled, and there are markings in the music from time to time to align rhythms between vocal parts. Finally, in "Glorify the Great Jehovah" by Haydn, the names of two soloists are entered: "Little John" and "Flagh [*sic*]."

In summary, *The Boston Handel and Haydn Collection of Sacred Music* was a product of the church music reform movement. Its contents were representative of the "cultured" music endorsed by the society, a repertoire unlike the English parish music and "common tunes" found in the *New Brunswick Collection of Sacred Music*. Although we cannot be entirely sure whether First Albany used this tunebook during weekly Sunday worship or just for special occasions, it seems probable that the book was used in worship, since First Albany's music history demonstrates a forward-looking attitude generally. Having provided balcony space for a choir in the 1798 plans of its new sanctuary, allowed a choir to form in 1806, instituted a music committee in 1813, installed a professional quartet in 1840, and added a large pipe organ in 1845, it seems likely that this affluent and influential church would have tapped into the well-regarded "science" of music and *cultured* forms of music emanating from New England in the 1820s. First Albany may have been instructed as well by the manner in which church choirs in New England had served their congregations, for Richard Crawford informs us that Congregationalist church choirs had sung anthems during worship as early as the 1750s.[32] Finally, the markings in the book, especially those indicating abridgements, indicate usage more consistent with a worship service than a concert setting. In the former a composition may need to be tailored, but in the latter compositions are more often performed intact.

A Few Summary Words on Tunebooks

Even with numerous inferences of tunebook use by Dutch Reformed churches and the more specific allusions to certain collections, one can only speculate exactly how and to what extent tunebook contents influenced worship and church life. While the collections continued to add more anthems and choral responses as the century

---

[32]   Crawford, "Psalmody," 635-42.

drew on, aside from the evidence obtained from First Albany, it is still unknown exactly how much, if at all, the tunebooks were actually used in public worship. It cannot be overlooked that many churches may have acquired the tunebooks for their singing schools and Sunday schools but never intended to use them in a worship setting. Furthermore, it's entirely possible that some or all of the anthems in any given collection were not used, but just the collection's metrical tunes as a supplement to the psalter/hymnal.

It is, however, probable that tunebooks had some measurable impact on church choirs and the musical life of this tradition. First, the instructional portion of the book, at the very least, allowed many children to become musically literate and to develop the aesthetic skills and sensitivities that engender the desire to make music. Second, tunebook compilers went to great lengths to supply a wide compendium of music that was culled from European or American sources or newly composed. It is truly remarkable how eclectic these collections were. A single volume might contain, for instance, portions of or complete short oratorios, English cathedral music, "common tune" style anthems, music of colonial American tunesmiths, German chorales, Anglican chants, and secular tunes—even opera arias—with sacred texts. By 1850 chorally active Americans would have become acquainted with a wide range of choral music literature and, through exposure, likely become more accepting of different types of music, especially worship music.[33] Thus, it is not going too far to say that the American tunebook of this era was a most ecumenical tool, as it scaled denominational walls through the democratization of worship music.

Finally, the tunebook was very much a tool for social interaction and change. As the primary tool for choral organizations of all types, the possession of a tunebook afforded the owner entrée into a new social situation, the choir rehearsal. During the choir rehearsal the genders could mingle in a commendable activity, and, in particular, women were empowered as full participants and leaders. As people from different churches gathered to sing together, a common musical taste developed. The ubiquitous tunebook had domesticated choral music. In time, the gender scales were rebalanced, as not only did women's voices account for half or more of each choir, but also through the related means of organ study women began to assume leadership roles in church music.

---

[33] The *Mendelssohn Collection* preface alerts the reader that the German chorales it includes are not "heavy and dull...decayed melodies of antiquity," as the reader might have assumed, but could be readily enjoyed by American choirs.

CHAPTER 6

A Brief Case Study, Conclusion, and Further Thoughts

A Brief Case Study

By analyzing one church's choral history against the backdrop of its congregational history, a more detailed and integrated picture emerges of the impact of the institutional choir on the worship and ecclesiastical culture of the Dutch Reformed Church. For this case study I have selected the First Church in Albany, New York, for which a very fine church history exists.[1] Dr. James D. Folts, First Church's historian, also assisted me in locating relevant documentation during my visit to its archive last June. Moreover, the tunebook discussed in chapter 5 has provided information useful to this study.

For several reasons First Albany was a good case study candidate. It was the second Dutch Reformed Church established in America, having called its first minister, Johannes Megapolensis (1601-1670) in 1642. Thus its history is long and rich, as is its musical history. The church existed in a smaller and less culturally diverse habitat than New York City; therefore, First Albany was the proverbial "big fish in a small

---

[1] Alexander, *Albany's First Church*.

pond." Furthermore, the city of Albany's influence on the church and the church's influence on the city can be observed. For instance, when the city suffered a financial crisis in 1855, so did its leading church, and the music budget was drastically slashed. A final reason for selecting First Albany to study was that it has a "flagship" status in its denomination. First Albany has always been aware of its standard-bearer role and has acted prudently and with circumspection in maintaining historic traditions and in forging new ones. Other churches have scrutinized the actions and decisions of First Albany. Therefore, it is fair to assume that other churches in the denomination have at one time or another come under its influence.

By 1800 First Albany had already been worshiping in English for twenty years and had been keeping consistory records in English for several years. In 1803 a petition was signed by leading church members to improve congregational singing, and in 1806 a grassroots choir was started by some of the young men. In 1813 a chorister was hired and a singing school commenced.

First Albany experienced the pressures of competition and financial hardships. For instance, in 1816 the church advertised that its singing school was free of charge to any member of a Christian fellowship. There is no doubt that the measure was taken to compete with another church-run singing school that had siphoned off some of First Albany's youth. Throughout this period the church struggled to figure out how to pay the chorister. In 1818 it hired Elis Roberts at an astounding $450 per year for a three-year contract but were then unable to pay him his full rate in the third year. He vacated the post in 1820. The church had hoped that tuitions from the singing school would supplement the chorister's salary, for the chorister ran the singing school too. In the 1830s sacred music concerts were held for this reason. Nevertheless, salary concerns and music budget issues continued to plague First Albany periodically, including the aforementioned severe cutback in 1855.

However, a series of printed Sunday school anniversary programs offer evidence of a successful Sunday school choir in the 1830s and 40s. These programs list the hymns sung by the children. A designated copy of the *Boston Handel and Haydn Society Collection of Sacred Music* tunebook supplies evidence that First Albany had a capable institutional choir as early as the 1820s. The tunebook contained excerpted portions of oratorios, mostly from the works of Handel, Haydn, Mozart, and Beethoven; included no metrical tunes; and had only a few easier English or American anthems. The contents of this tunebook suggested that there was a well-trained choir at the church; only such a choir could perform the relatively difficult works compiled from the Boston Handel and Haydn Society sacred music concert repertoire. Handwritten notes in the margins identified which pieces First Albany's choir performed, in what combinations and in what manner, naming soloists and sections to be repeated or deleted. The notes indicated that the church choir used the book extensively, combined pieces in a miniature oratorio fashion, had soloists capable of singing the recitatives and arias, and probably had some instrumental accompaniment to play the keyboard part included in this book.

A period of prosperity permitted hiring a professional quartet in 1840 and the purchase of a Henry Erben pipe organ in 1845 for $2,650. Yet by 1855, a fiscal crisis required the music committee to curtail expenses and more carefully monitor even the money spent on printed music. One would think that at this time amateur (free) musicians would have been the answer to some of the financial woes at First Albany. Yet fashion must have held sway, because it was at about this time that the amateurs in the choir fell away and the paid quartet assumed the full duties of choir support in worship. When finances improved in the 1860s, extravagant amounts were spent on the quartet and particularly on one singer who could command the bulk of $1,000 appropriated to the music committee for this purpose. Finally, we know that although amateurs were again incorporated into the choir in 1883, the practice of using a paid quartet as section leaders remained until at least the turn of the twentieth century.

Conclusion

The case study of First Albany demonstrates the impact of financial, cultural, and individual conditions on the conduct of church music programs. Worship trends often make an appearance with little fanfare, then leave as they entered. As a result, the growth and development of choirs at First Albany was not an orderly process. In chronological sequence, the congregation formed a choir, established a singing school and a Sunday school choir under the direction of a professional musician, established an institutional choir under the influence of the northeastern church music reform movement, hired a professional quartet, bought an expensive pipe organ, allowed amateur singers to disperse, then reunited amateurs with the quartet again in the 1880s. But this was surely not the only nor the prototypical pattern for choral development in the denomination, despite First Albany's alleged influence. In fact, I found no instance of this pattern being replicated exactly in any other church. What we do see at First Albany, however, is a nearly complete list of what happened to a lesser extent in many of the denomination's churches. For instance, some churches never implemented quartets. Other churches used the choir to lead congregational singing only. Some churches acquired large pipe organs. Other churches made due with a melodeon.

This leads us to consider the institutional choir as a very real reflection of a particular congregation's religious life. For this we are assisted by Clifford Geertz's definition of religion as a "dynamic system of symbolic expressions and behaviors" and Stephen Marini's synopsis of Geertz's four major components of a religious culture as systematic beliefs, institutional structures, ritual behaviors, and spiritual or moral practices.[2] It is through these lenses that we can assess the transforming impact of institutional choirs on the worship and culture of the Reformed Church in America.

Regarding systematic beliefs, the incorporation of choirs eschewed John Calvin's music prescription. While children's choirs were employed in Calvin's time to lead the congregation in the psalms, and indeed, many Dutch Reformed church choirs in nineteenth-century America were employed for the same reason, the majority of choirs appear to have sung anthems separately from the congregation. In fact, under the direction of a competent chorister, choirs would have been expected to cultivate greater musical capability and a different sound and repertoire than the rest of the congregation. Whereas Calvin insisted that the congregation participate in all singing, the singing of anthems and responses by the choir often relegated the congregation to an auditor role. Naturally, the increased performance role of choirs coincided with the pattern of redesign of churches in the mid-nineteenth century as auditoriums, including moving choirs and organs to a forward platform. The onset of choirs also introduced a new and wide-ranging sacred music repertoire to the congregation, with both texts and music that reflected American mainstream Protestantism.

The incorporation of institutional choirs affected institutional structures by placing some of the decision-making regarding worship in the hands of the chorister/organist and choir. Whereas the consistory, and particularly the pastor, had been responsible previously for the conduct of worship, the paid chorister was typically given authority to select some or all of the music used in worship. An indication that

---

2   Clifford Geertz, "Religion as a Cultural System," in *The Interpretation of Cultures* (New York: Basic Books, 1973), 90, and Marini, *Sacred Song in America*, 10.

institutional structures were being tested can be seen in disputes that arose over whether or not church organists should play preludes, whether or not the organist or the pastor should select the hymns, or even if the music that the choir was singing was "too cultured" for the congregation. Not only did choirs and their leaders gain a voice in such matters. I contend that choirs helped unravel the autonomy of male-dominated consistories by instigating a pattern of democratic decision-making. Indeed, the power that women's guilds wielded to finance any project, such as the organ at First Hudson in the 1830s, was evidence of the Dutch Reformed Church's movement toward democratization.

The effect of choirs on ritual behavior has been central to my thesis. Worship was transformed by the incorporation of choirs, organs, and their music. But another way to assess the impact of choirs on ritual behavior is to look at the monumental amounts of money spent on space for choirs, organs, chorister's salaries, and printed music. As Richard Crawford contended, economics played an essential role in understanding America's music.[3] A pipe organ could cost four to five times the annual salary of the pastor. The chorister and sexton were often the only other paid employees of the church, with some part-time choristers earning half or more what the pastor earned. And as we have seen at First Albany, where $1,000 was appropriated to pay the quartet in 1868, lavish expenditures knew almost no bounds when it came to providing the best music possible for weekly worship. These expenditures flew directly in the face of the iconoclastic Reformed tradition, which once happily stuck to its ancient liturgy and unaccompanied psalms in especially humble buildings.

Especially important, and I believe heretofore underestimated, is the effect of choirs on the moral or spiritual practices of the church. As we have seen, choirs could forge ecumenical relationships with other denominations. Truly, more than music was shared at times when churches came together, for missions and matters of social justice provided a just cause for uniting. The democratization that elevated women to a greater status and role in the church may have contributed to the elimination of the pew system and other preferential forms of seating, such as placing servants in the balcony. Returning to the status and role of women, it was the foothold that women achieved through their guilds, choir membership, and the positions of organist and chorister that again must have contributed to the easing of restrictions

[3]   Crawford, *An Introduction to America's Music*. That economics was the guiding force in American music beginning in the nineteenth century was the central thesis of the book.

against women serving on consistories or as pastors in the twentieth century.

In as much as other mainline denominations opted for this same scenario, I can hope for parallel studies in other American denominations and the more complete rendering of a picture that is complex and diverse. Indeed, such an image is far more significant to the understanding of the history and culture of church life, liturgy, music, and certainly the very theologies operating in this relatively understudied topic and era than was previously thought.

One final point about the Dutch Reformed Church seems indicated. It is especially well made by Howard Hageman:

> If anyone speaks of *the* Reformed way of worship, he is talking nonsense. There can be no such thing. The historical pattern which has emerged can be scrapped tomorrow if we find ourselves better instructed from the Word of God. This fact is important. Not only does it account for the great variety of beginnings, the extreme fluidity of our liturgical history, but it also reminds us of the encouraging openness of our present liturgical situation. Let others lament the lack of any fixed liturgical norm or the fact that Calvin's *Liturgy* did not become our *Book of Common Prayer*. If we are Reformed we shall *glory* in it not because we believe in unbridled license but because of our conviction that our liturgical life has always been and still must be under the judgment and corrective of the living Word.[4]

The Dutch Reformed have always been and are still reforming people. They were reforming from at least the time of the *Devotio Moderna* in the late Middle Ages. The founder of their new faith, John Calvin, was a reformer who continued to reform his understanding of the role of music in worship throughout his life. Their first minister in America, Jonas Michaelius, was a reformer who understood that the privations of the New World meant that they could dispense with the usual documentation needed to prove membership, thus admitting all who confessed their faith to the Sacrament of Communion. Their American patriarch, John Livingston, was a reformer whose vision recast the church in an entirely American direction. The Consistory of the Old Brick Church in Marlboro was a reformer when it admitted new tunes to be sung in English by a choir in 1785. The Consistory at First Albany was a reformer when it instructed architect Phillip Hooker to

4   Hageman, *Pulpit and Table*, 16.

design a space that would accommodate organ and choir in 1798. The evangelical outpost of Fort Miller Reformed Church in Fort Edward, New York, was a reforming church, whether out of necessity or design, when it hired Mrs. Whiting, a woman, as its chorister in 1844.

Further Thoughts

Paul Allwardt and Richard Crawford correctly argue that tunebook studies would greatly repay research effort. The contents of tunebooks offer a detailed view of prevailing trends in music culture, education, worship, and entertainment. Much could be learned about music performance practice and especially the relationship of the tunebook to musical life and education, language studies, music consumerism, social life and customs, and attitudes about church and American life. In effect, the tunebook offers the kind of resources that researchers will probably be gleaning from the iPod in a century or so. It is no small thing, for instance, that the choir at First Albany grouped and performed pieces in its tunebook into cohesive sets, like a miniature oratorio. From sacred concert programs in the era we know that this quasi oratorio arrangement was prevalent. It was surprising to discover, however, that the pattern appears to have been replicated in weekly public worship at First Albany. Additional repertoire and similar case studies could substantiate this practice in other churches and help identify other ways in which repertoire was used in worship.

Other repertoire studies might undertake an examination of the contents of nonauthorized hymnals in the denomination, as many have turned up in church archives with member names inscribed in front cover. What hymns were included in these books that were not available in the ever-increasing hymnody of new editions of the denominational psalter/hymnal? What theological topics did the hymns present that church leaders found offensive? Why were there frequent disputes between clergy and choristers about who chose the hymns for worship? How and in what ways did these hymns really shape the beliefs and attitudes of Dutch Reformed congregations about worship and music? Furthermore, what pictures of church life and music do the many original hymn texts of the denomination's clergy and laity reprinted in the *Christian Intelligencer* give us? Finally, regarding repertoire studies, what did organists play as solo music and how did they accompany hymns? Was the *Zangtrant,* or song style, mentioned in appendix 4 observed in any particular way? How did accompaniments, interludes, and even organ registrations affect the way in which hymns and anthems were sung?

A further investigation of the social and cultural implications of church choirs on worship and church life is also needed, perhaps commencing with an examination of the early to mid-nineteenth century debate over choirs, detailing the concerns over choir performance and behavior. As revealed through editorials in the *Christian Intelligencer*, was it Hastings's campaign that caused a favorable turning point in the attitudes toward church choirs in the mid 1840s, and in the Dutch Reformed Church in particular? Will demographic or geographical studies reveal any patterns in choir acceptance—the makeup of its personnel, worship style, and repertoire—or any particular adopted pattern from any preexisting musical condition, such as a singing school, Sunday school choir, or choral society? Finally, how did women choristers, organists, and singers influence choir formation, repertoire, social patterns, and overall attitudes about choirs? And how did women gain a significant voice in church music decision making by their fundraising activities and by studying the organ? *Soli Deo Gloria.*

APPENDIX 1

A Timeline of Dutch Reformed
Liturgy and Music

1536   *Institutes of the Christian Religion* published by John Calvin.

1539   *Souterliedekens* published (a metrical version of the psalms in Dutch set to secular melodies).

1562   *Genevan Psalter* completed.

1563   Heidelberg Catechism prepared by Caspar Olevianus and Zacharius Ursinus.

1566   Belgic Confession (Guido de Bres) and Heidelberg Catechism adopted by Synod of Antwerp.

       Genevan Psalter translated from French to Dutch by Peter Datheen.

1568   Datheen Psalter authorized for the Dutch Reformed Church at Synod of Wezel.

1574   Synod of Dort requires the use of only authorized liturgical prayers and bans use of organ during worship.

163

1618   Great Synod of Dort commences.

1624   Thirty families arrive to colonize New Netherland.

1628   Jonas Michaelius (first ordained Dutch Reformed minister) arrives in New Amsterdam.

1633   Adam Roelantsen (schoolmaster and *voorzanger*) arrives in New Amsterdam. Frame wooden church, parsonage and stable built at tip of lower Manhattan in New Amsterdam.

1640   Constantin Huygens's book, *Gebruyck of Ongebruyck van't Orgel inde Kerchen der Vereenighde Nederlanden*, restores organ use in Netherlands Reformed worship.

1642   Stone church replaces wooden church in Fort at New Amsterdam.

1696   Nahum Tate and Nicholas Brady Psalter ("New Version") published.

1707   *Hymns* published by Isaac Watts.

1719   *Psalms of David* published by Isaac Watts.

1720   Theodorus Jacobus Frelinghuysen controversy with Henricus Boel begins Great Awakening.

1727   First organ installed in New York Dutch Reformed church, but not used when Lord's Supper administered. Organist Hendrick Michael Kock receives two-year contract.

1733   Frelinghuysen's sermons published.

1757   Tate and Brady, *A New Version of the Psalms of David...Together with Some Hymns...as used in the English established Church in Amsterdam*, published.

1764   Archibald Laidlie, first RCA minister to preach in English, installed in New York.

1767   Francis Hopkinson's *The Psalms of David...For Use of the Reformed Protestant Dutch Church of the City of New York* published by the New York Consistory.

1774 *A collection of the psalm and hymn-tunes, used by the Reformed Protestant Dutch Church of the City of New York...in four parts, viz. tenor, bass, treble and cantor...*published in New York.

1785 Consistory of Old Brick Church, Marlboro, NJ, rules in favor of young members who had formed a choir and wished to sing new psalm and hymn tunes in harmony.

1788 Belgic Confession translated into English.

1789 *The Psalms and Hymns of the Reformed Protestant Dutch Church in North America.*

1790 Middle Collegiate Reformed Church installs a pipe organ possibly manufactured by John Geib.

1790s The Second Great Awakening begins, launching an Arminian evangelical agenda.

1793 Official liturgy translated into English. Constitution's preface allows freedom to choose worship forms.

1794 First General Synod held.

Singing school established at the First Reformed Church, Schenectady, NY.

1798 Phillip Hooker building design for First Church, Albany, includes balcony space for organ and choir.

1799 Sarah Van Doren starts first Sunday school at First Reformed Church, New Brunswick, NJ.

Singing school established at the Reformed Church in Readington, NJ.

1803 Petition to improve music put forth at First Church, Albany.

1806 Young men organize choir at First Church, Albany.

1813 *The Psalms and Hymns of the Reformed Protestant Dutch Church in North America* published.

Earliest known sacred music concert at a Dutch Reformed church takes place at Middle Dutch Reformed Church, Nassau Street, NYC.

Committee of Sacred Music formed at First Church, Albany.

1815   Boston Handel and Haydn Society formed.

1816   First complete performance of Franz Joseph Haydn's *Creation*, King's Chapel, Boston.

General Synod makes English official worship language.

1817   *The New Brunswick Collection of Sacred Music* first published.

1818   *The New York Collection of Sacred Music containing a great number of plain tunes, carefully arranged, and particularly designed for church worship, and generally suited to the several metres [sic] in the Psalms and Hymns used in the Dutch Church* published.

1820   Organ of unknown manufacturer installed at Reformed Church in Katsbaan, New York.

1820s Flute and cello added at Rotterdam, NY (Earliest known use of instruments to accompany congregational singing in an American Dutch Reformed Church).

1822   True Reformed Dutch Church secedes from the Reformed Church.

Thomas Hastings's *Dissertation on Musical Taste* published.

The Boston Handel and Haydn Collection of Church Music published (Handel and Haydn Society's first tunebook).

1824   American Sunday School Union established.

New York Choral Society established.

Hall and Erben pipe organ partnership founded.

1826   *Magazine of the Reformed Dutch Church* begins publication.

Erben organs installed in New York City Dutch Reformed churches on Garden Street, Franklin Street, and Greene Street, and in Schenectady, New York.

1827   Choir of three men and six women sings at church dedication ceremony at Old Brick Reformed Church, Marlboro, NJ.

The third volume of *Handel and Haydn Society Collection of Sacred Music*—used by First Church, Albany, choir—published.

1828 Sabbath School Union of the Reformed Dutch Church formed.

1830 *Christian Intelligencer* begins publication as a weekly from the *Magazine of the Reformed Dutch Church.*

General Synod orders subcommittee to develop the first of several sets of additional hymns.

Lowell Mason introduces music education to Boston public schools.

Thomas Hastings delivers lecture on choirs at the Middle Dutch Reformed Church.

1831 *Additional Hymns* published by the Reformed Protestant Dutch Reformed Church in America.

1832 Thomas Hastings moves to New York City.

Peter Rappleye permitted to buy eight notebooks for the choir at Interlaken, NY.

1833 Lowell Mason founds the Boston Academy of Music.

1834 Hendrick De Cock and H.B. Scholte secede from the church in the Netherlands during the *Reveil* ("Awakening").

1835 New York Musical Academy organized.

1836 Choir at Reformed Church in Hudson, NY, contains 15 women and 13 men.

1838 Brooklyn Academy of Music opens February 20.

1840 William Batchelder Bradbury arrives in Brooklyn as organist.

Paid quartet added at First Church, Albany.

1843 *Sabbath School and Social hymns of the Reformed Protestant Dutch Church in the United States of America* published.

1844 Mrs. Whiting permitted to hold singing school at Fort Miller Reformed Church.

1848   *Psalms and Hymns* published by the Protestant Dutch Reformed Church in America.

1850   Holland, Michigan, immigrants unite with Synod of Albany, joining the Reformed Protestant Church in America.

1851   Thomas Hastings leads two-day music convention at the Reformed Church in Somerville, NJ.

1856   Immigrants in Pella, Iowa, unite with the Reformed Protestant Dutch Church in America.

Frederick J. Van Lente starts a singing school in Holland, Michigan.

1857   Christian Reformed Church founded with the secession of Graafschap and Polkton churches.

APPENDIX 2

General Synod Resolution of June 1831 on Hymns

ADDITIONAL HYMNS—adopted by the General Synod of the Reformed Dutch Church in North America, at their Session, June, 1831, and authorized to be used in the churches under their care. Rutgers Press—New York.

The introduction of sacred songs into the public and private worship of God is one of the most important subjects for the consideration and application of those who are placed over the Household of Faith. The church should exercise great wisdom and discretion in its selection, not only as it relates to the style of music, to the principles of taste, and the effect it produces, but much more as to the subject-matter of the hymns, for it must be remembered that sacred music is designed not only to excite emotions, but also to instruct, exhort and admonish. This latter design is of such great importance, and its effects so powerful, that some one has well said "Let me make the songs of a church, and I do not care, who makes their creed."

It is on this account that our church has ever been cautious in its selection of Hymns, and has disapproved of the introduction into public and social assemblies any other than those which have been duly authorized.

It has become very fashionable of late to introduce private and unauthorized selections into the weekly lectures, and particular meetings for worship and prayer, with the design of creating greater interest and giving more powerful excitement to the passions.

We say nothing at present against the injury produced by exalting particular ordinances proposed by expediency over the stated and ordinary divine institutions, but we would direct the attention of the churches, to the mischief that may finally result from the indiscriminate use of unauthorized versions of the psalms, and unauthorized collections of sacred songs.

With a view to prevent such mischief as well as to gratify the wishes of ministers and members of the church, the General Synod of 1830,

"*Resolved.* That the Rev. Thomas De Witt, D.D., William McMurray, D.D., Isaac Ferris; and the Elders Peter D. Vroom, Jr. and John D. Keese, be a committee to select from the different collections now published, Hymns on a variety of subjects, to constitute a second book of Hymns, to be added to these now in use, in all future editions of our Psalm and Hymn Book, and that said committee report such selection to the next General Synod, for their approbation.

The Committee reported the selection they had made to the General Synod on June 1831. Whereupon the following resolutions were adopted.

1 *Resolved,* That the said Additional Hymns, reported by the committee appointed by the general Synod in 1830, be accepted, ordered to be published as a second Book of Hymns, and authorized to be used in the same manner, as the Psalms and Hymns now in use.

2 *Resolved,* That all future editions of the Psalm Book shall contain the additional Hymns, together with the canons of the church, as soon as the Board of Direction of the Corporation shall be able to make necessary arrangements with the publisher.

3 *Resolved,* That a separate edition of the Additional Hymns be published.

4 *Resolved,* That the Board of Direction of the Corporation be directed to take out separate Copy-rights for each of the books, and authorize their publication; and that they superintend the publication of each book."

The Hymns are 172 in number, together with 17 Doxologies. These, with those already in use, will afford the church a copious selection of interesting subjects, and a variety of metres to aid in devotional exercises, and to improve sacred music. This selection, with a few exceptions, is judiciously made. The exceptions relate to a few imitations of popular songs, to an improper choice of figures in some of the hymns, and to the too great number of peculiar metres. But these exceptions obtain to a greater degree and extent, in almost every other collection of hymns, and we intend not by allusion to them to derogate from the merits of this production.

Being contained in a small volume, these additional Hymns may be readily carried with us in our pockets, and will be a convenient Manual of devotion in our retirement as well as in our occasional attendance at select social meetings at private houses, or the Lecture-rooms. We owe the respected Committee who compiled these hymns, and superintended the press, and their publication, a debt of gratitude for their assiduity and care.

It will be well for the different classes to call the attention of their congregations, to the introduction and use of these hymns, and to discountenance the use of any other, than those already duly authorized. In this way the publisher will be encouraged in getting up a neat edition of our Psalms and Hymns, and the churches will be protected against the introduction of error by means of unauthorized collections." [1]

---

1   *Christian Intelligencer* 2, no. 13, WN 65 (Oct. 29, 1831), 50. While announcements of new hymnal editions are to be found in the *Christian Intelligencer*, this is the only announcement published along with the General Synod Resolutions for the adoption of the hymnal, as well as admonitions to ministers to discontinue the use of unauthorized hymnals or other music collections.

Sacred Music Concert Notices, Programs, and Reviews

The following concert notices, programs, and reviews were collected mostly from issues of the *Christian Intelligencer*, the weekly magazine of the Reformed Church in America, first published in 1830. The collection reflects some of the sacred music concerts that occurred in New York City, either in Dutch Reformed churches or in churches where participation or attendance by Dutch Reformed people was likely. Although I have deleted the long lists of ticket distributor addresses found at the bottom of each concert listing, I have otherwise included all of the information given in each advertisement. Additionally, I have attempted to recreate the advertisement's layout appearance in these transcriptions, perpetuating even the misspellings or antiquated spellings of names and words, such as "Hayden" for the composer Franz Joseph Haydn and "Pergolese" for Giovanni Battista Pergolesi, "Duett," "Quartette," etc.

ACADEMY OF MUSIC

"The New York Academy of Sacred Music," held its anniversary performance in the Tabernacle on Friday evening, May 12th. The house was scarcely large enough to accommodate the multitudes who flocked to this feast of music. On no other occasion during the week, except the Bible Anniversary was there a more overflowing auditory.

We are not fully qualified to judge of the performances, and therefore may err, but the following it struck us, were more admirably executed than the rest, viz:—*The Anthems,* "Why lament the Christian dying?" and "Oh thou who dry'st the mourner's tear." *The chorus,* "To thee, Cherubim and Seraphim continually do cry." *The Motet,* "By the rivers of Babylon, there we sat down;" and the *Anthem* (in chanting style) "The earth is the Lord's, and the fullness thereof." We may be mistaken, but it appeared to us that the "solos" were not done so well. On the whole, we believe the pieces gave pretty general satisfaction, and cannot but hope the cause of sacred music has been promoted thereby.[1]

(The following concert took place October 25 and November 29, 1838, at the Ninth Street Dutch Reformed Church.)[2]

Part I

> Overture – Messiah
> Handel
>
> Chorus: Now elevate the sign of Judah
> Haydn
>
> Duett and Chorus: Hail Judea (Judas Maccabeus)
> Handel
>
> Air: But thou didst not leave
> Handel
>
> Chorus: Lift up your heads
> Handel

[1]   *Christian Intelligencer* 7, no. 43, WN 355 (May 20, 1837), 171.
[2]   *Redway, Notices, Announcements, etc., on Music from the Commercial Advertiser, 1838.* Cited in Allwardt, *Sacred Music in New York City, 1800-1850,* 223a.

Duett: The Lord is a man of War
Handel

Thanksgiving Day Anthem: The Lord is King
Chapple

Recit. And Chorus: Behold a Virgin, and O thou That tellest good
   tidings to Zion
Handel

Part II

Marche Religieuse
Swindells

Chorus: The Lord Gave the Word (Messiah)
Handel

Air: The people that walked in darkness
Handel

Chorus: The last day
Whitaker

Trio: Disdainful of danger (Judas)
Handel

Chorus: O Father, whose almighty power (Judas)
Handel

Solo: Sound the Trumpet in Jerusalem (trumpet obbligato)
Himmel

Chorus: Then round about the starry throne
Handel

Hallelujah
Handel

CONCERT OF SACRED MUSIC IN THE REFORMED DUTCH CHURCH, NINTH STREET, NEAR BROADWAY.—Mr. I. B. Price begs leave to announce that, at the request of several gentlemen who were present at the Concert of Sacred Music, given in the Reformed Dutch Church, Ninth street, near Broadway, on the evening of the 25th October last, he will repeat the performance, with some little variations, in the same Church, on the evening of Thursday, the 29th last. This evening was fixed upon previous to its being known that the 29th had been appointed as a day of public Thanksgiving; but he hopes that the circumstances will be rather favorable than otherwise. In addition to the bountiful selection formerly announced, Mr. Price will sing the favorite sacred song, "O Thou that Tellest," from the Messiah, and Messrs. Rogers and Massett will sing the splendid Bass Duett, "The Lord is a Man of War," from Israel in Egypt. The Orchestra will be numerous and effective. The performance to commence at half past seven o'clock. Tickets of admission 50 cents each. Children half price; may be obtained at the following music stores; Atwill's, 291 Broadway, Mitlet's, 375 Broadway, Firth and Halls's, 1 Franklin Square, Neely's 221 Bleeker street, and Price's, 302 Hudson street, also of the sexton of the Church.[3]

---

[3]   *Christian Intelligencer* 9, no. 17, WN 433 (Nov. 17, 1838), 67.

ANNIVERSARY PERFORMANCE OF SACRED MUSIC—The New York Academy of Sacred Music, will give their 4th Anniversary performance in the Broadway Tabernacle, on Friday evening May 10th, commencing at a quarter before 8 o'clock. The pieces selected are of a devotional character and consist of Solos, Duetts, Trios, Quartettes, Semi-Choruses and Full Choruses. The Orchestra will be strong and effective.

Vocal Leader,	Mr. Geo. Andrews
First Violin,	Professor U. C. Hill
Flute,	Professor J. L. Downe

ORDER OF EXERCISES

Part First

1. Tune – Kings – H.M.	Bost.
Prayer	
2. Tune – Winchester	German
3. Motette – O what beauty, Lord, appears	Mozart
4. Solo,	
5. Quartette – I would not live alway,	Kingsley
6. Installation Anthem,	Hastings
7. Mottete – O how lovely is Zion	Mozart
8. Duett and Chorus – Time is winging us away,	Zeuner
9. Recitative and Chorus – The multitude of angels	M. P. King
Address.	

Part Second

1. Chorus – Hosanna	Zeuner
2. Solo,	
3. Anthem from Psalm 104 – Bless the Lord,	Hastings
4. Solo	
5. Anthem – Jerusalem, my happy Home	L. Mason
6. Duett and Chorus – There is an Hour,	Hastings
7. Quartette and Chorus, "When shall our Burthened Spirits rest."	Hastings
8. Grand Hallelujah Chorus.	Handel

Tickets 50 cents each.

Clergymen attending the anniversaries will be supplied by applying to Mr. Collier, 148 Nassau St.[4]

---

[4]   Ibid. 9, no. 41, WN 457 (May 4, 1839), 163.

GREAT UNION PERFORMANCE OF SACRED MUSIC.—The Committee of Arrangements of the New York Academy of Sacred Music announce to the citizens of New York and vicinity, that with the aid of various Leaders and their Choirs, who have kindly consented to assist the Academy on the occasion, a Union Performance of Sacred Music will take place in the Broadway Tabernacle on Friday evening, May 24th, commencing at a quarter before eight o'clock. There will be, it is expected, about nine hundred vocal performers, assisted by a powerful and efficient orchestra. The pieces selected are of a devotional character, and the performance, as a whole, it is confidently believed, will be unprecedented in this country.

Vocal Leaders – Mr. George Andrews
            Mr. S. B. Pond
            Mr. C. Holt, Jun.
Leader of the Orchestra – Professor U. C. Hill
Flute – Professor J. L. Downe

ORDER OF PERFORMANCE

PART FIRST

    1. Overture

2. Te Deum – "We Praise thee, O God	W. Jackson

PRAYER

1. Invitation – "Thy Spirit and the Bride may come." (By the Academy,)	E. Collier
2. Tune – "O ville,"	E. Ives, Jr.
3. Tune – "Park Place,"	S. B. Pond
4. Tune – "Harborough,"	Sh(ill.)ubsole.
5. Anthem – "O Praise the Lord,"	Handel
6. Solo – By Mr. Church	
7. Quartette – "When winds breath soft."	
8. Hymn – "Salvation! Oh the joyful sound,"	L. Mason
9. Sanctus and Hosanna	

   ADDRESS

PART SECOND

1. Tune – "Old Hundredth,"	German
2. "What is life?" – (A Response and Chorus)	Hastings
3. Anthem – ""Praise Ye the Lord,"	Pergolese
4. Duett and Chorus – "There is an hour,"	Hastings

Solo by Mr. Oakley – "Sound the Trumpet in Jerusalem,"
>   (with Trumpet accompaniment)   Himmel
>   1. Verse – "Yes, we trust the day is breaking,"   Zeuner
>   2. Quartette and Chorus – "When Shall our
>   burthened spirits rest," (by the Academy)   Hastings
>   3. Solo, by J. O. Flager, Esq., Albany, – "The
>   Sailor's Song,"   Bannister
>   4. Thanksgiving – (a full Anthem)   Hastings
>   5. Anthem – "O Praise God in his Holiness,"   L. Mason
>   6. Grand Hallelujah Chorus   Handel

BENEDICTION

The price of Tickets is fixed at one dollar each, and will admit a
gentleman and lady... Subscriber Tickets will, on this occasion, (it being
an extra performance) admit a gentleman and lady, only.[5]

5   Ibid. 9, no. 43, WN 459 (May 18, 1839), 171.

PUBLIC PERFORMANCE OF SACRED MUSIC—The New York Academy of Sacred Music, will give a public performance in the Broadway Tabernacle, Friday evening, October 11th, commencing at half-past seven o'clock. The pieces selected are of a devotional character, and consist of Solos, Duetts, Quartettes, Semi-Chorus, and full Choruses. The different parts will be sustained by members of the Academy. The orchestra will be effective.

Mr. George Andrews, Vocal Leader
Professor U.C. Hill, First Violin

ORDER OF PERFORMANCE

PART FIRST

1. Tune Chatham – L. M.	Hastings

PRAYER

1. Solos and chorus – O haste, with every gift inspired	
2. Solo – by Mr. Holt	
3. Quartette – O ye mourner cease to languish	Corri
4. Anthem – Praise the Lord ye servants	Chapple
5. Solo – by Mr. Seely	
6. Semi-Chorus and Chorus – When I survey	Teap

PART SECOND

1. Tune, Zephon – L. M. – Stand up my soul	L. Mason
2. Anthem – Duet and Chorus – "Give the Lord the honor due unto his name."	Kent
3. Solo – Mr. Church	
4. Quartette and Chorus – "Where shall our burthened spirits rest"	Hastings
5. Solos and Chorus – Thou art the King of glory, O Christ	Vandel
6. Anthem – Awake put on thy strength, O Zion	W. Jackson

Tickets 50 cents each;
Subscribers are requested to be present.[6]

---

6   Ibid. 10, no. 11, WN 479 (Oct. 5, 1839), 43.

GREAT UNION PERFORMANCE OF SACRED MUSIC, is the Broadway Tabernacle Wednesday evening, October 30th, to commence at half past seven, consisting of Solos, Duetts, Trios, Quartetts, Semi-chorus, and full Choruses. There will take part about

ONE THOUSAND PERFORMERS

> Viz: 20 City Choirs, and the New York Academy of Sacred music,
>> Choir from Williamsburgh
>> do   Bridgeport, Connecticut
>> do   Bloomfield, New Jersey
>> do   Westfield, New Jersey
> and the Harlem Sacred Music Society
> The orchestra will be full and efficient
>> Vocal Leaders – Mr. George Andrews
>> "   "   Mr. C. Holt, Jun.
>> Leader of the Orchestra – Professor U.C. Hill
>> Piano Forte – Mr. Scharfenberg

ORDER OF PERFORMANCE

PART FIRST

1. Anthem – Dedication	Hastings

PRAYER

2. Anthem – Praise the Lord ye servants	Chapple
3. Solo by MR. Holt – The Pilgrim Fathers	
4. Anthem – How beautiful upon the mountains	L. Mason
5. Tune Kimbolton – L.M.	Handel
6. Quintette – When winds breathe soft	Webbe
7. Anthem – How lovely are thy dwellings	
8. Solo, by Mr. W. H. Oakley – Comfort ye my people	Handel
9. Chatham – L. M.	Hastings
10. Solo, E.F. Brigham, of Brooklyn – Not worlds on worlds in phalanx deep	J. C. Andrews
11. Solo and Chorus – O haste, with every gist inspired	Webbe

PART SECOND

1. Duette and Chorus – We seek a rest	Hastings
2. Solo, by Mr. Seely – The Sister's Call	Brown

3. Anthem – Give Thanks	G. J. Web
4. Double quartette – O how lovely is Zion	Mozart
5. Tune, Ariel – C. P. M.	L. Mason
6. Solo, by Mr. Church – Look aloft – music by himself words by Mrs. Sigournev	
7. Sacred Glee – Deep is the Sleep	Hastings
8. Anthem – When the world shall build up Zion	J. P. Cole
9. Recitation – Thou shalt dash them to pieces by Mr. Oakley Grand Hallelujah Chorus	Handel

BENEDICTION

The pieces are diversified in character, and the performance will, it is confidently expected, please the friends of sacred music.

Single ticket, $1.00. Ticket to admit a Gentleman (sp.) and Lady, $1.50, for sale by Gould, Newman & Saxton, corner of Nassau and Fulton. Firth and Hall, No. 1 Franklin square. Atwill, No. 201 Broadway, Edicot, 359 Broadway. Coolidge & Lambert, 57 Wall street.

Subscribers Tickets will admit a Gentleman and a Lady.[7]

7   Ibid. 10, no. 14, WN 482 (Oct. 26, 1839), 55.

PUBLIC PERFORMANCE OF SACRED MUSIC—The New York Academy of Sacred Music, will give a public performance in the Broadway Tabernacle, Friday evening January 24th, commencing at 7 o'clock. The pieces selected consist of Solos, Duetts, Quartetts, Semi-chorus, and full Choruses. The different parts will be sustained by members of the Academy. An address will be delivered by the Rev. E. N. Kirk, and a collection taken up.

ORDER OF PERFORMANCE

PART 1

1. Anthem "Give Thanks"	G. J. Webb
Prayer	
2. Anthem – "Praise the Lord Ye Servants	Chapple
3. Motette – "O what beauty, Lord appears"	Mozart
4. Solo	
5. Recitative and Chorus" Lo! He cometh"	Hayden
6. Quartett – "There is a stream"	
7. Chorus – "To Thee Cherubim"	Handel
Address by Rev. E. N. Kirk	

PART II

1. Tune – Zephon L. M.	L. Mason
2. Anthem – "How beautiful upon the mountains"	"
3. Solo	
4. Tune – Ariel. C. P. M.	
5. Duett and Chorus – "There is an Hour"	
6. Chorus – Awake! Put on thy strength O Zion	W. Jackson
7. Chorus – "Worthy is the Lamb"	Handel

Tickets of admission will be required, and may be obtained gratis....[8]

---

8   Ibid. 10, no. 26, WN 494 (Jan. 18, 1840).

NEW YORK ACADEMY OF SACRED MUSIC—The Anniversary performances of the New York Academy of Sacred Music, will take place in the Pearl street Church, Rev. Mr. Rowland's, near Broadway, on *Wednesday and Friday evenings* May 13th and 15th, commencing at half past 7 o'clock. The pieces selected for these performances are varied in character and consist of Solos, Duets, Trios, Quartettes, Semi-Chorus and full Choruses. The different parts will be sustained by members of the Academy. The orchestra will be select and efficient.

Vocal Leader, Mr. George Andrews
Order of Performance for Wednesday evening April 13th

PART I

1. Tune – "Psalm 148" H. M.	Kolff
PRAYER	
2. Trio and Chorus – "this place is Holy Ground"	Hastings
3. Anthem – "Song of Angels"	"
4. Quartette – "Harp of the Winds"	Mozart
5. Anthem – "Awake put on thy strength, O Zion"	W. Jackson
6. Solo by Mr. Hastings	
7. Chorus – "Gloria in Eccelsis"	Pergolesi
8. Solo by Mr. W.H. Oakley, "Comfort Ye My People	Handel
9. Grand Chorus – "Worthy is the Lamb"	"

PART II

1. Duett and Chorus – "There is an Hour"	Hastings
2. Duett by Messrs. C. D. and J. D. Field, "Who is this that on the tempest rides"	
3. Chorus – "Awake the Harp"	Hayden
4. Solo by Mr. Church "Sweet Day"	
5. Recitative by Mr Holt "In Splendor Bright"	Hayden
6. Grand Chorus "The Heavens are telling"	
7. An Anthem by male voices, under the direction of Mr. W. H. Oakley	
8. Duett and Chorus – "Time is winging us away"	Zeuner
9. Chorus "Glory to God" from Mozart's 12th Mass	
10. Grand chorus – Hallelujah to the Father	Beethoven

BENEDICTION

Tickets 50 cents each;
Clergymen will be supplied with tickets gratis,
Subscribers are requested to be present.
Due notice will be given of the performance on Friday evening.[9]

9   Ibid. 10, No. 42, WN 510 (May 9, 1840), 167.

THE NEW YORK ACADEMY OF SACRED MUSIC, will give a public performance in the Mercer street Church (Rev. Dr. Skinner's) on Friday evening June 5th, commencing at a quarter before 8 o'clock. The pieces selected consist of a few plain pieces of Sacred Music, and Solos, Duetts, Trios, Quartetts, Anthems, and full Choruses. The different parts will be sustained by members of the Academy. The orchestra will be select and efficient.

Vocal Leader,   Mr. George Andrews
First Violin   Professor. E. C. Riley
Professor Munson will preside at the Piano Forte

ORDER OF PERFORMANCE

Part I.

1. Anthem – From all that dwell	Dr. Arnold

PRAYER

2. "Why on the bending Willows"	Nogelli
3. Quartette – "Blessed are they"	Mozart
4. Chorus – Hallelujah to the God of Israel	Hayden
5. Tune – Malden, C.M.	Kolff
6. Chorus – "Now elevate the Sign of Judah,	Hayden
7. Solo by Mr. Munson, "O Thou who dwellest"	Dahlmen
8. Grand Chorus – "Worthy is the Lamb"	Handel

Part II

1. Tune – Queenston. C. L. M.	Hastings
2. Chorus – "Gloria in Eccelsis"	Pergolesi
3. Trio – "The Sky Lark"	
4. Chorus – "Glory to God" from the 12th Mass	Mozart
5. Solo by Mr. Oakley	
6. Chorus – "Grand Hallelujah"	Handel

BENEDICTION

Single tickets, 50 cents,—or a family ticket $1.
Subscribers are requested to be present.[10]

---

[10]   Ibid. 10, No 45, WN 513 (May 30, 1840), 179.

The **ANNIVERSARY OF THE NEW YORK ACADEMY OF SACRED MUSIC** occurring this year on the evening of the day appointed by the President for a National Fast, the music to be performed has been selected mainly with reference to such an important occasion.

The Concert will take place in the Broadway Tabernacle, on Friday evening May 14th (1841), commencing a half past seven o'clock— and the Board of Officers takes pleasure in announcing that

MR. COLBURN,

The distinguished vocalist from Boston, will, on this occasion, sing several popular solos, and the Rev. E. N. Kirk will deliver an eulogy for the occasion, and will be sung by the Academy.

The Orchestra will be full and effective.

Professor Munson will preside at the Piano Forte.

ORDER OF EXERCISES

PART FIRST

1. Overture, by Amateurs of the Academy	
2. Tune "Paran" L. M.	Kubler
3. Prayer	
4. Duett and Chorus – "There is an Hour"	Hastings
5. Solo by Mr. Colburn – The Land of the Blest"	Handel
6. Funeral Dirge – from the Oratorio Saul	Handel
7. "Bright Spirit, Rest" – A Requiem, composed for the occasion	Hastings
8. Solo by Mr. Seely – "The Last Man"	Calcott
9. Anthem – "When the Vale"	Hastings
10. Solo by Mr. Colburn – "Pilgrim Fathers"	Miss Browne
11. Treble Solo, by a Young Lady – "Let the Bright Seraphim"	Handel
Trumpet Obligato by Mr. Wolter	
12. Grand chorus – "Let the Celestial concerts all unite	Handel
13. Eulogy by Rev. E. N. Kirk, on the late President Harrison	

PART SECOND

1. Anthem – "Why lament the Christian dying"	Hastings
2. Solo by Mr. Comes	
3. Solo (by Mr. Colburn) and Chorus "The Marvellous Works"	Handel
4. Solo by Mr. Colburn "Sound the trumpet in Jerusalem"	Himmel

5. Grand Chorus "The Heavens Are Telling"	Haydn
6. Solo by Mr. Colburn – "Battle of the Angels"	Webb
7. Grand Chorus, "Glory to God" from the	
12th Mass	Mozart

BENEDICTION

Tickets 50 cents each.

Clergymen will receive tickets gratis, by applying to Mr. Saxton, corner of Fulton and Nassau streets.[11]

---

[11]   Ibid. 11, no. 42, WN 562 (May 8, 1841), 167.

NEUKOMM'S GRAND ORATORIO OF DAVID—(Last time this season)— Complimentary to Mr. U.C. Hill.—Mr. Hill having for many years given his valuable and efficient services as Leader and Conductor of Concerts, Oratorios &c. for benevolent and other purposes, the New York Sacred Music Society have resolved to perform the Oratorio of David, at the Broadway Tabernacle, on Tuesday evening, the 18th instant, for the benefit of Mr. Hill, their Conductor.

The most eminent talent in the city have graciously tendered their services.

Principal Vocal Solo Performers:

Mrs. Strong	Miss Pearson	Mrs. C. Horn Jr.,
Mr. C. E. Horn	J. Swartz Massett,	Mr. J. Pearson

Principal Instrumental Performers:

Messrs. A. Boucher   Violoncello
James K. Kendall, Leader of the Band at
the West Point Military Academy   Clarionett
J. L. Downe   Flute
Wolter   Trumpet
A. Kendall   Harp
D. R. Harrison Organist of the First Part
Edward Hodges, Mus. Doc., late of
Bristol, (Eng.,) Organistvof the Second Part,

In addition to the above, the Orchestra, Vocal and Instrumental, will be unusually numerous and efficient.

Characters Represented.—Michal, (daughter of Saul,) Mrs. Strong; Sister of David, Miss Pearson; David, (first time,) Mr. C. horn, Jun.; Goliath, Mr. Pearson; Saul, J. Swartz Masset; Jonathan, (for this occasion,) Mr. C. E. Horn; high Priest, Mr. J. Pearson; Messenger, a member. Chorus of Shepherds, Warriors, Levites, Male and Female attendants, by the Society.

Tickets, One Dollar, for sale at the Music Stores and principal Hotels; Hale's News Room, Wall Street; at the Bookstores of Dayton & Saxton, corner of Nassau and Fulton Street; M. W. Dodd, Brick Church Chapel; J. S. Taylor, 145 Nassau street; D. Fanshaw, 148 Nassau street; at the door on the evening of the performance.

Performance to commence at eight o'clock precisely.

Members of the Society, and other friends of Mr. Hill can obtain sale tickets, by applying to the Secretary, No. 111 Nassau street.

May 15, 1841.[12]

---

[12]   Ibid. 11, no. 43, WN 563 (May 15, 1841), 171.

FOR THE BENEFIT OF THE CITY TEMPERANCE SOCIETY.
The NEW YORK ACADEMY OF SACRED MUSIC respectfully announce to the Public, that their next Concert will be given to aid the CITY TEMPERANCE SOCIETY, and will take place in the Broadway Tabernacle, on Friday evening, July 16th, commencing at quarter before 8 o'clock.

The orchestra will be full and efficient.

ORDER OF PERFORMANCE

PART I

1. Overture by amateurs of the Academy	
2. Tune "Beethoven" – L. M.	Beethoven
3. Prayer	
4. Anthem – "Praise waiteth for thee, O God"	Hastings
5. Anthem for Easter or for Sacramental occasion	Hastings
6. Solo by Mr. Bell	
7. Anthem – Duet and Chorus – "Hear my Prayer"	Kent
8. Duet – Messrs. Holt and Comes	
9. Chorus – "O Lord, in thee have I trusted"	Handel
10. Solo by Mr. Comes	
11. Chorus – "Then round about the starry throne"	Handel
12. Chorus – "Gloria in Excellis	Pergolesi

PART II

1. Tune – "Westchester"	Hellendel
2. Anthem – "Sing, O Heavens"	Hastings
3. Solo by Mr. Seely	
4. Solo by Mr. Holt, and Chorus – "Marv'lous Works"	Haydn
5. Duet by two young ladies	
6. The Pledge – A Temperance Ode	Dr. Arnold
7. Solo by Mr. Holt	
8. Grand Chorus – "Glory to God"	Mozart

BENEDICTION

Tickets 50 cents each.....[13]

---

[13]   Ibid. 11, no. 51, WN 571 (July 10, 1841), 203.

ORATORIO OF "THE MOUNT OF OLIVES."

NEW YORK SACRED MUSIC SOCIETY.—The Board of Managers beg leave to announce that their first public performance for the season, will take place on Tuesday evening, November 2d, at the Broadway Tabernacle, upon which occasion will be produced, for the first time in this city, Beethoven's celebrated Oratorio of "The Mount of Olives," with all the original accompaniments.

This sublime Oratorio has been several weeks in rehearsal, and will be given in a style hitherto unsurpassed.

Principal Vocal Performers:

Mrs. Strong,	Mr. J. Pearson
Miss Pearson,	Mr. S. Pearson (by permission of E. Simpson, Esq.)
Leader and Conductor	Mr. U. C. Hill
Organist	Mr. D. R. Harrison

Tickets $1..

Books of the words, may be had free of charge,..

The "Mount of Olives" will be succeeded by Haydn's splendid Oratorio of "The Season," which is now in preparation.[14]

---

[14]   Ibid. 12, no. 15, WN 587 (Oct. 30, 1841), 59.

CONCERT OF SACRED MUSIC

The NEW YORK ACADEMY OF SACRED MUSIC will give their first concert this season, on Friday evening, Nov. 12th, in the Broadway Tabernacle, commencing at half past 7 o'clock.

ORDER OF PERFORMANCE

PART I

1. Tune "Temple"		Arnold
Prayer		
2. "How excellent is thy loving kindness,"		
3. Anthem from Psalm 104		Hastings
4. Hundredth Psalm		
5. Solo by Mr. Bell		
6. Duett and chorus – "Soft Echoes,"		Hastings
7. Solo and chorus – "Sound an Alarm"		Handel
8. Duett by two young ladies		
9. Recit. Chorus – "The multitude of Angels,"		King

PART II

1. Easter Anthem		Hastings
2. Duett by Messrs. Holt and Comes		
3. Anthem – "We will rejoice,"		Arnold
4 Solo by Mr. Comes		
5. Chorus – "Awake, put on thy strength,"		Jackson
6. Solo by Mr. Holt		
7. Grand Double Chorus–"He gave them Hailstones,"		Handel

Tickets 50 cents.....[15]

[15]   Ibid. 12, no. 16, WN 588 (Nov. 6, 1841), 63.

GRAND UNION PERFORMANCE OF SACRED MUSIC.—The New York Academy of Sacred Music, assisted by a select number of Choirs from this city and Brooklyn, will give an Union Performance in the Broadway Tabernacle, Providence permitting, on Friday evening, Feb 11th, commencing at 7 o'clock. The whole number of the singers will be about 500; and the Board of Directors have authorized their Professor of Instrumental Music to engage for this occasion a large and effective Orchestra of instrumental performers.

PROGRAMME

PART I

      1. Introduction – "From all that dwell,"   Dr. Croft
Prayer
      2. "Stand up, my soul, hake off thy fears,"
      3. Chorus – "Salvation, O thou joyful sound,"   Hastings
      4. Solo by Mr. Oakley – "My flock, my friends,"   Neukomm
      5. Semi-Chorus and Trio by the Academy –
         "When I survey, "&c.
         Chorus – "Where the whole realm of nature mine,"
         (Arranged by Dr. Bradbury).
      6. Chorus – "Sovereign of worlds, display thy power," Beethoven
         Solos by Mr. Bell – "Bid the bright morning arise;"
         and 'Speak! And all the world shall hear thy voice."
      7. Chorus – "Jesus shall reign where'er the sun."
         Solo by Miss Wicks – "For Him shall endless prayer
         be made."
         Duett by Miss Wicks and Miss Booth – "And voices," &c.
         Chorus – "Blessings abound," &c.
         Trio by Miss Wicks, Messrs. Comes and Holt–"Where
         he displays," &c.
         Chorus – "Let every creature rise and bring,"   Hastings

PART II

      1. Chorus – "Jerusalem, my happy home,"   L. Mason
         Semi-Chorus by the Academy – "In joy and peace
         in thee," and "O where, thou city of my God."
         Chorus – "Jerusalem, my happy home, " &c.
      2. Duett by Mr. Oakley and Mr. Bennet, from the
         Oratorio of David,"   Neukomm
      3. Chorus – "O give thanks,"   Mozart
      4. Solo by Mr. Holt

5. Chorus – "The marvelous works,"   Haydn
6. Solo by Mr. Comes
7. Duett – "Time is winging us away."
   Chorus – "Youth and vigor soon will flee," &c.
   Duett – "Time is winging," &c.
   Chorus – "But the Christian shall enjoy,"   Zeuner

BENEDICTION

Tickets 20 cents each....[16]

---

[16]   Ibid. 12, no. 29, WN 601 (Feb. 5, 1842), 115.

CONCERT OF SACRED MUSIC—In the Reformed Dutch Church at the corner of Green and Houston streets, under pastoral care of the Rev. I. S. Desmund—in aid of the Church and Sabbath School, on Wednesday evening, March 2d, commencing at half past 7 o'clock—under the direction of R. N. Perlee.

ORDER OF PERFORMANCE

PART I

1. Chorus – "Holy Lord God of Sabaoth,"	Swaffield
Prayer	
2. Chorus – "I will arise."	
3. Solo and Trio – "Jerusalem, my happy home."	
4. Duett, Solo and Chorus – "I waited patiently,"	Chapple
5. Solo by Mr. Johnson – "The Infant's Prayer,"	V. Novello
6. Solo and Chorus – "What of the Night,"	Hastings
7. Solo by Miss Booth – "Lord, I believe,"	Barnett
8. Quintette – "The Voice of Angels,"	Dr. Clark

Address by the Rev. J. M. Macauley, on the subject of "Sacred Music."

PART II

1. Chorus – "Fairhaven."	
2. Quartette – "O thou whose power,"	Whitaker
3. Solo and Chorus – "The marvelous works,"	Haydn
4. Semi-Chorus – "The Night of the Grave."	
5. Chorus – "The Last Day,"	Whitaker
6. Duett – "The Better Land,"	Kingsley
7. Duett and Chorus – "Watchman, onward,"	Hastings
Solo by a Gentleman.	
Chorus – "Blest are the souls."	

BENEDICTION

Single tickets 25 cents – Tickets to admit a Gentleman and two Ladies, 50 cents.[17]

---

[17]   Ibid. 12, no. 32, WN 604 (Feb. 26, 1842), 127.

THE NEW YORK ACADEMY OF SACRED MUSIC will give their first public performance, this season, on Friday evng., 28th inst., at the Broadway Tabernacle.

Leader – Mr. S. B. Pond
Leader of the Orchestra – Mr. Saml. Johnson

Order of Performance:

    1. "When shall the voice of Singing." – Sac. Lyre, 278.
Prayer
    2. Bass Solo. – Mr. Comes. – "Sovereign of Worlds, display thy power," Acad. Anth., 21
    3. "Evening Song at Sea" Messrs. Howe, Johnson, Bell, and Rowell
    4. "Soft and holy is this place," – Sac. Lyre, 254.
    5. Original Song, by Mr. Hastings
    6. "Spirit of Peace, celestial Jove," – Sac. Lyre, 266
    7. Bass Solo. – Mr. Comes – "Thou art the King of Glory," Handel – "Dyer's Chorus, 73.

Address

    8. "Zion will soon in beauty rise – Acad. Anth., 65.
    9. Solo, by Dr. Cuyler, of Hartford
    10. Recit. Mr. Bell, "They sung the song." Sac. Lyre, 344. Chorus. – "Great and Marvelous."
    11. Mr. Howe, of Porland. – "But who shall see that glorious day."
    12. Grand Hallelujah Chorus, (Handel) – Dyer's Chorus, 40.

Benediction

Tickets – fifty cents each admitting a Lady and Gentleman. Clergy will receive theirs, by calling on E. Collier, at 147 Nassau street.[18]

---

[18] Ibid. 12, no. 15, WN 639 (Oct. 29, 1842), 59.

CONCERT—A Concert of Sacred Music will be given in the Ref. Dutch Church, corner of Greene and Houston streets, by the Choir, assisted by several Professors and Amateurs, on Thursday evening, 22d of February 1844, (Washington's Birthday) Messrs. Nash and Bell have volunteered their services. The Rev. I.S. Desmund will deliver and Address - Subject - "Washington." Concert will commence at half past seven o'clock. Tickets $25c.

Programme.

Part 1st.

    1. Chorus – Claremont.

Prayer.

    2. Chorus – "Make a Joyful Noise."
    3. Duett – By Two Young Ladies.
    4. Quartette and Chorus – "Oh! How lovely."
    5. Duett, or solo.
    6. Duett and Quartette – "There is a Stream."
    7. Solo – by Mr. Nash
    8. Quartette, Duetts, and Chorus "Jerusalem," &c.

Address.

Part 2nd

    1. Chorus – "But in the Last Days."
    2. Solo – by Mr. Bell
    3. Solo and Chorus – "Oh! What beauty."
    4. Solo – by Mr. Nash
    5. Chorus "O Give thanks."
    6. Duett – By Messrs. Nash and Bell
    7. Chorus – "Hope in the Lord"

Benediction.

Proceeds for the benefit of the church.[19]

---

[19]   Ibid. 14, no. 31, WN 707 (Feb. 17, 1844), 123.

GRAND CONCERT OF SACRED MUSIC.—The Choir of the Reformed Dutch Church, corner of Fifth Street and Avenue B. Wed, July 31st, 1844, 8 p.m.

Vocal Leader – Russell W. Westcott

Instrumental Leader - Mr. S. Johnson

Mr. F. H. Nash will sing some of his most admired pieces.

Programme.

Part I.

    Overture – Full Orchestra
    Hymn – Let all the earth with cheerful notes – L. Mason
    Prayer – Rev. F. F. Cornell
    Full Chorus – Blest are the souls that hear and know.
    Quartet – My Mother's Bible, ---A. A. Hutchinson.
    Recitative and Solo – Angels ever bright and fair, Miss Booth,
        ---Handel.
    Motet – Glory to God in the Highest ---- Ludwig Hellwig.
    Solo – Pilgrim Fathers.... R. W. Westcott, ---Mrs. Hemans
    Chorus – Salvation to our God.....C. Palina
    Duet – When night comes over the plain....F.H. Nash, Z. Warner,
        ....C. Nelson
    Sentence – Holy is the Lord

Intermission, ten minutes

Part II.

    Chant – the Lord is my Shepherd
    Solo – Christ stilling the tempest...F. H., Nash
    Trio – How holy is this place
    Chorus – Lord, O have loved the place of thine abode.
    Quartet – Hail, smiling morn,....Spofforth
    Anthem – O, Praise the Lord, all ye nations.
    Quartet – Evening Song at Sea....E. Howe, Jr.
    Semi-Chorus – Land of our fathers, ...Webbe.
    Tune – Old Hundred – Doxology

    Benediction

Tickets, twenty-five cents to admit a Lady and Gentleman.[20]

20   Ibid. 15, no. 2, WN 730 (July 27, 1844), 7.

THE MOZART ASSOCIATION,
Assisted by the New York Melodians
Will give a concert of Sacred Music,
In the N.W. Ref. Dutch Church, Franklin St.,
Tuesday, Feb. 11th,
For the Benefit of the Funds of the Church

Leader – F. H. Nash
Organist – H. D. Timm[21]

---

[21]   Ibid. 15, no. 30, WN 757 (Feb. 6, 1845), 119.

"**A CONCERT OF SACRED MUSIC** will be given in the Reformed Dutch Church in Franklin Street, on Tuesday evening, December 30th, in aid of the funds of the MUSIC COMMITTEE; and the committee would observe, that the Conductor of Music in the Church, Mr. F. H. NASH, will be assisted by the following eminent talent, who have in kindest manner, volunteered their services: Miss Booth, Mr. Oakley, Mr. Andrews, Mr. B_____, Mr. Dunning, Mr. Comes, Mr. Bell, Mr. S_____, &c; together with the New York Amateur Quartette Association, and several members of the New York Sacred Music Society.

Director ......Mr. F. H. Nash
Conductor.....Mr. Geo. Andrews
Organist ....Mr. James L. Ensign

Programme

Part First

> 1. Chorus, He Lives, the Everlasting God.
> 2. Duett, Messrs. Oakley and Nash
> 3. Solo, by Mr. Dunning
> 4. Duett, Dear Heavenly Home... Miss Booth and Mr. Nash
> 5. Solo, Mr. Andrews
> 6. Quartette, Amateur Quartette Association

Part Second

> 1. Chorus
> 2. Solo, "Friendship will never fade,"...Mr. Nash
> 3. Quartette, Amateur Quartette Association
> 4. Solo, The Trumpet Shall Sound"...Mr. Bell
> 5. Finale, *Cantata*, "The Morning." First time in this city.

Single tickets, 50 cents; three tickets, admitting two ladies and a gentleman, $1; to be had of the Consistory, of the Sexton, or at the door, on the evening of performance.[22]

---

[22]   Ibid. 16, no. 24, WN 804 (Dec. 25, 1845), 95.

CONCERT OF MISCELLANEOUS MUSIC—a concert of Miscellaneous Music will be given by the Choirs of the Ref. Dutch church corner of Avenue B and Fifth Street, on Thursday evening, February 3, commencing at 7 ½ o'clock, under the direction of Russell W. Westcott. Eminent talent will assist on this occasion, which will make it a rich and chaste performance to all lovers of good music. Tickets 25 cents each, or family tickets, six for $1, can be obtained at Raynor's Bookstore, 76 Bowery, and at the door on the evening of the concert.[23]

---

[23]   Ibid. 18, no. 30, WN 914 (Feb., 3, 1848), 119.

CONCERT OF SACRED MUSIC—At Evangelical Mission Church on Houston Street. Nov 16, at 7 ½ o'clock.

This object in view, a "Union of Sacred Music," (vocal and instrumental) composed of about one hundred ladies and gentlemen, members of the Reformed Dutch, Lutheran, Presbyterian, and other Protestant denominations, has been organized, through the labors of Dr. C. W. Lange, Professor of Music, and Organist of the German Evangelical Mission Church in Houston street.

The friends of sacred music will find an opportunity to form an estimate of the importance and utility of such a Union, by the exhibition of its first fruits in the Concert on the 16th, in which about twelve of the masterpieces (in full choir and in solos) of German composers will be performed, with and without instrumental accompaniment, under the director of Dr. Lange. The names of the authors of the pieces which will be performed are a sufficient warrant for their excellency—such as Handel, Mozart, Haydn, J. A. P. Schultz, Beethoven, Klein, Graun, Mendelssohn, &c., &c., as the programme will show.[24]

(Concert review)

The gentleman, who is the Organist of the German Mission Church in Houston Street, has the credit of showing what can be done in six months towards improving a congregation in the science of sacred music. If each of our churches had the same number of singers scattered through the audience we should hear no more complaints about the choir monopolizing the performance of an important and delightful part of public worship. The pieces were executed in a spirited manner, but a choral from the Oratorio of Paul, The Resurrection, music for male voices; a prayer versified for an Alto voice; Recitative and Air from the Oratorio of Creation; Choir and Choral, Death of Christ; The Shepherd's Sabbath Hymn, for male voices; The solemn Hour, by Mozart, and the Hallelujah Chorus from Handel's Messiah, were rendered with the best effect.
Musica Audiatur.[25]

---

24   Ibid. 24, no. 19, WN 1215 (Nov. 10, 1853), 74.
25   Ibid. 24, no. 21, WN 1217 (Nov., 24, 1853), 82.

CONCERT FOR THE ORGAN FUND
Of the South Dutch Church, Cor. Fifth
Avenue and 21st Street

We do not exactly understand to what particular organ the above announcement refers, whether *vocal* or instrumental.[26] One thing is certain, the programme was excellent, the first part being mainly from Rossini's "Stabat Mater."

Mrs. Westervelt, Miss Gellie, Mr. Cook and Dr. Guillmette, were the vocal artists; Mr. Schreiber, cornet; Messrs. Morgan and Currie, organists; and a "private cornet party," (among whom, if we are not mistaken, were recognized the tones of Mr. Allen Dodworth and Dr. Doremus), and a chorus, were on the programme.

Mrs. Westervelt sang "Fac ut portem" very finely. Her voice is of a delicious quality, and needs only a little more spirit infused in to make her a delightful singer. The constant use of portamento has an unpleasant effect on the hearer, and renders her execution heavy. The same fault exists with Miss Gellie, but her voice being of lighter character, it is less perceptible. Miss Gellie's best effort was the "Inflamatus."

Mr. Cook did not appear to be in voice, for we would not like to think that his voice is really changed, but that it was merely owing to a cold, that he sang in such a forced manner.

Dr. Guilmette gave "Veni Sancte Spiritus," in a superb way. His breadth of style, which some times appears exaggerated in lighter music, had here its proper element.

Dr. Guilmette lends his soul to the music for the time being, and must necessarily delight the hearer, but at the same time it made us still more conscious of the absence of feeling in the other singers who assisted him on this occasion.

In the quartet, "Sancta Maria," which was taken much too fast, and apparently without the slightest regard for the sentiment of the words, this difference of musical feeling was perceptible; the soprano and tenor were continually running away, and the alto kept them

---

[26]   This concert was held to raise funds for an organ installation completed by Thomas Robjohn in the same year.

company, while the basso, with his mighty voice, endeavored in vain to give them a spark of religious feeling that forms the most distinctive feature of this noble work of Rossini. The choruses were very well sung, although at fault sometimes in regard to tone.

Mr. Schreiber's cornet never sounded more sweetly than on this evening, when accompanied by Mr. Morgan on the organ. He is always welcome.

Mr. Morgan performed the fugue in G minor, by Bach, [27] followed by a fantasia, with pedal obligato, on "God save the Queen." It was a splendid performance. Among the audience were some Canadian or English hearts, whose loyal feelings were touched by their national air, as it were, stood up till the anthem was finished.

A perfect gem, by Fesca, arranged, as a quintette for organ and brass instruments, was performed by the cornet party, accompanied by Mr. Morgan, at which point we left, and, therefore, cannot speak of the cantata. Mr. Currie accompanied carefully.

The church was filled.

The music of this church is under the sole direction of Dr. Guilmette, and his large and efficient choir (numbering some eighty members,) gives an expression and interest to this part of the service truly delightful. Every taste can be suited, solo, quartet, chorus and congregational, for all the various styles are introduced from time to time, as the sentiment of the hymns seems to indicate. A grand old choral, with full choir and congregation uniting, we have never been more interested in, than on Sunday afternoon last, when we were privileged to join those present in this portion of the services, in their beautiful temple dedicated to worship of "the King of Kings and Lord of Lords."[28]

---

[27] Dr. Robin Leaver informed me that this is an early performance of a Bach organ piece in the United States.

[28] *Musical World,* Jan. 28, 1860.

CONCERT.—The concert given Thursday, the 17th, at the Claremont Avenue Dutch Reformed Church, Brooklyn, for the opening of the new organ built by Messrs. Hall and Labagh, attracted a fine house, notwithstanding the numerous musical entertainments on the same evening elsewhere in Brooklyn. Between the parts, Dr. Davidson delivered a lecture on music; it was very instructive and interesting.

Mrs. Clara M. Brinkerhoff, Mrs. Miller, and Mr. Wiebe, sustained vocal solos: Mr. S. Dyer and Mr. T. Fielding, the blind organist, presided at the organ. Several choruses were well sung by the choir. The God of Israel, by Rossini, was very efficiently rendered. The quartettes were not sung in tune. Mr. Fielding played a choral and fugue by Bach, and a theme, with variations, by Hesse, which was given extremely well, and displayed to great advantage the fine tones of the organ with the various combinations of stops.

Mrs. Brinkerhoff sang "I know that my Redeemer liveth," "Consider the lilies," by Topliff, which was encored; also the "Song of May," by Wallace, received in most enthusiastic manner. The song is charming: we give the words which were on the programme, as they are very pretty:

> Born in the soul of a smile,
>   And bathed in sparkling dew,
> Winging my flight through an amber light,
>   I come from the sky to you;
> I come with a glow of sun,
>   I come with a breath of flowers,
> And scatter my gold tints everyone
>   On the young wings of the hours.
> Beauty is shed by me
>   Over the sweet spring day;
> Then lend me your chorus merrily,
>   Singing the lay of May.
>
> Oh! I laugh at the winter gone!
>   Mine is a melting eye,
> Smiling at frost till its heart is lost,
>   And its ice goes weeping by.
> The tears it leaves in the earth
>   Freshen the teeming ground;

But they do quicken my beauty's birth,
  While the may-buds break around.
I am the dawn of love,
  Blossoming in to-day;
Then lend me your chorus merrily,
  Singing the lay of May.

Mr. S. Dyer accompanied on the organ and piano in a careful and artistic manner.[29]

---

[29] Ibid., May 26, 1860.

APPENDIX 4

Organs and Organists in the Dutch Reformed Church

The Contract for Henry Michael Kock for the Position of Organist at the South Dutch Reformed Church:

Dutch Church of New York

Appointment of Henry Michael Kock as Organist, December 15, 1727

Inasmuch as it has pleased his Excellency, William Burnet, Governor, etc., to present an organ to the Dutch Reformed Church here in New York, for use in their meetings for divine service, and the same has already been placed in a suitable position in our old church, (in Garden Street):

Therefore, Be it known to all whom it may concern, that the Rev. ministers, Elders, and Deacons of the said Church together with the Church-Masters, on the recommendation of his Excellency, have appointed Mr. Hendrick Michael Kock as Organist.

They hereby also declare that the said Mr. Kock, as Organist, is to render service upon the said Organ, according to these conditions and limitations, namely:

The Rev. Consistory appoints the said Mr. Kock as Organist for two years, and no longer, namely, from December 15, 1727, to December 15, 1729, and upon the following voluntary subscription for his salary. But this appointment is with the definite understanding that you are not to receive compensation, except for the time that you personally play on the Organ, and in the following manner: You must play the organ in the Zangtrant* of our Dutch Reformed Church on Sundays, before and after preaching, both in the morning and afternoon; also on Wednesdays, and at such other times as there shall be preaching; as well as on Mondays when there is catechizing. When the Benediction has been pronounced, you will play a suitable piece as the congregation is leaving the church; and you will do the same at other times, after prayers or catechizing. Before the sermon you will play one entire portion—or pause—of a Psalm; but after sermon only one or two stanzas as the minister may direct. On mornings when the Lord's Supper is administered, the Organ shall not be played.

That all this may be performed in the best manner, and according to the wishes of the congregation, you agree, that as often as you are to play you will be on hand and at the organ before the last ringing of the bell; that whenever you are absent, except for sickness, nine shillings shall be deducted from your salary; and that you will not take any friends up to the organ with you except some one who is to do the blowing (trappen).

You are to receive twelve pounds, New York currency, for the "blower", but for this you are to teach John Pieter Zenger, the blower; or in case of his death or removal, whomsoever the Consistory puts in his place; until he also becomes proficient in playing the organ; and the said Zenger, or a substitute, shall also always be ready at the fixed times when you are to play. During the week, apart from church-meetings, the organ shall not be played, except when you yourself are teaching Zenger; and the Psalm which is to be played must be made known to the Rev. Consistory a full hour previously. In extraordinary cases, you shall according to custom, have free access to the Rev. Consistory to make any representations to them. You shall also keep the organ clean and in its place, and further, observe all the directions touching your duties which the Rev. Consistory shall impose.

Upon all these conditions, and upon each of these limitations as herein expressed, and not otherwise, we enter into this engagement with you as Organist; and we, thereupon, promise you, that the Elders, Deacons and Church-Masters, or some one of their number, will for the ensuing years pay you for your faithful services, the sum of one hundred pounds each year, New York currency; and that the righteous half of this sum shall be paid you each half year, beginning with December 15, 1727.

And they also promise to pay you for teaching Pieter Zenger to play the organ – of whose progress therein the Consistory will expect evidence, at least each half year, if not oftener – and for the blowing of the same, the sum of twelve pounds yearly, to be paid at the end of each year; or the sum of twelve pounds at any time during the first year when the said Zenger shall have attained the art of playing.

Hereto the Elders, Deacons and Church-Masters bind themselves, qualitate qua, and also their successors after them; and for the confirmation of this our promise, and your agreement to comply with the foregoing requirements at the times fixed upon, the instrument of appointment is made to you with out seal affixed. This done in our ecclesiastical meeting at New York, December 28, 1727.

I promise to conform hereto,

Henry Michael Kock.[1]

This editorial note by Hugh Hastings appears beneath the text of the contract:

* Zangtrant means, literally, Song-style; or according to the style of music and singing employed in the Dutch Churches. There are many of the old Psalm books, with this kind of music, yet existing in our old Dutch families.

---

[1]   Hastings, *Ecclesiastical Records of the State of New York*, Vol. 4, 2397-99.

A Subsequent Consistory Minute (December 27, 1750)

The consistory met at the request of three members of the Congregation. Brant Schuyler, Matthew Ernest and Pieter Kateltas. They presented a Memorial, signed by various other members, containing a request, with reasons attached, that the organ should be played during worship, and that, for this purpose, a suitable person should be employed. This being read and considered, it was unanimously agreed to, that is, so long as the subscription continued, or the requisite funds could be obtained from the special lovers of the organ, and without burdening the treasury of the church, and also, so long as the organist bore himself properly.

The applicants were also permitted, at their request, to choose such persons as they saw fit, to go around the congregation and solicit money by subscription. When enough or more than enough was obtained, such moneys should be deposited with the Church Masters to pay the organist, and in case of need, to repair the organ.

Whereupon the organist appeared. He was informed that he would be required to play upon every occasion of public worship except when the Lord's Supper was celebrated.

In order to avoid abuses, he must the day before the service, repair to the ministers, to obtain the Psalm. His yearly salary should be 30 pounds New York currency. All this he accepted. J. Ritzema.[2]

This consistory minute indicates that sometime after the end of Kock's appointment in 1729 and the year 1750 the use of the organ during worship had been suspended. One can speculate that the cost of maintaining the instrument and paying an organist may have been the cause, since consistory minutes from this period frequently cite financial shortfalls.

[2]   Ibid., 3146.

A Letter from E & G. G. Hook Organ Builders to First Church Albany in 1845[3]

The following is a personal communication from E & G. G. Hook to the members of the organ committee for the First Albany Reformed Church (North Dutch).

> Boston May 7. 1845.
>
> Gentlemen.
>
> We have rec'd your favour of the 2d inst. containing the annexed list of stops for an organ, with enquiries relation to our price, earliest time of finishing &c.
>
> We would build an organ containing said stops enclosed in case painted in imitation of Oak put up in your church ready for use & warranted in every respect a first rate instrument for $ 2275,00 payable upon delivery and approval of the organ. or we would substitute an elegant Mahogany case which we have on hand rich wood, very similar to the one in St. Peters Ch. in your city for $ 50,00 more, though to make such a case would cost at least $ 150,00 more.
>
> We could deliver the organ (if ordered before we make other contracts) within three months & if the mahogany case we have on hand is adopted we could deliver it within two months.
>
> Very Respectfully Yours
> E. & G.G. Hook.
>
> To S. H. Pumpelly
> Thomas Mc Elroy
> M. M. Van Alstyne.
>
> P.S. By dispensing with the Sesquialtra in the Gr: Or and the Cornet in the swell we would discount $ 150, — one hundred + fifty dollars
> E. & G.G. H.

[3] Courtesy of the archives of First Church, Albany, Dr. James D. Folts, curator.

Although somewhat difficult to read them here, the letter provides the specifications for the organ and a price of $2,275, after what appears to be a negotiation saving the church $150 by not including a sesqualtera and cornet stop.

Selected Criticism and Support Regarding Organs and Organists

1. A rebuttal, signed D. D., on an article in the *Christian Intelligencer* by
   S. N.,

> March 25, 1847:
> S. N., condemns the *prelude.* "The playing of the tune over
> before singing, is, we suppose, simply for the information of the
> congregation, which, surely, is about as well as was the custom
> formerly, in Scotland, (we think) of elevating a board, bearing
> upon it, in large letters, the tunes to be sung; and as well as to
> have the first, second, and perhaps third line of the first verse
> sung by a few, before it can be known by the congregation what
> has been selected...."

> "Besides this, an *interlude* is sometimes played between the
> verses."(Although D. D. goes on to say that sometimes this goes
> on too long.)

> But S. N.'s anathemas falls upon yet other atrocities. "The sounds
> of the organ during the taking up collections! At this we opened
> our eyes wide. Most persons like the clink of filthy lucre, it is true,
> when there is a prospect of their gain; but, in the innocency of our
> heart, we had imagined that the organ's notes were as harmonious,
> as little disturbing to a right frame of spirit, as the tinkle of silver
> coin, or the dull fall of copper, muffled by green baize....

> "When the congregation is leaving the church, striving to retain
> and carry with us the gentle and wholesome influences of the
> place, again the gingling banquo assails our ears, and exorcises
> from our minds and hearts all we have assayed to garner. It is true,
> it may be questioned by some, whether is the more conducive to
> our meet departure, the tones of harmony, or the inharmony of,
> it mayhap, a thousand foot-falls reverberations."[4]

2. "Opera Music in Church"

> We give the following from an address of Dr. Shackleford before
> the Ecclesiological Society of this city. If their labors were always
> as sensibly directed they might count on more sympathy from the
> Protestants than they now have;—

4   *Christian Intelligencer* 27, no. 46, WN 878 (May 27, 1847), 151-52.

An organist is engaged, who plays popular orchestral music, and the greater the novelty of his effects, the more genius he is supposed to possess. If he be a heretic, or infidel, or a libertine, or a sot, it is not necessarily a disqualification for his leading the praise of the house of God. Four singers are then engaged with sole reference to their musical attainments, and if they have a reputation in the fashionable world, so much the better; it adds to their salaries and to the *éclat* of the congregation. Selections and adaptations from Beethoven, Mendelssohn, Schubert, or Donizetti, are served up Sunday by Sunday to the delight of the audience, many of whom come expressly to hear the music. It is very comfortable for the voluptuous worldling, who frequents the opera during the week, to hear his own favorite music, from his favorite singers, on Sunday also; and the voice of the preacher, with his denunciations of worldliness will seldom be loud enough to dispel the echoes of the more welcome strains from the gallery, at the opposite end of the church. All this while the old music is suffered to lie forgotten. Yet if it were revived and used as it ought to be, it would be a great instrument in the growth of the church, and in increasing the heartiness of her worship, and the piety and zeal of her members.[5]

3.   Portions of article from the *Christian Inquirer*:

In many churches, the proportion of voluntary on the organ to singing by the choir is unpardonably excessive. In some instances we have thought that the hymn was considered as affording opportunity for the organist to show his skill, and not the occasion to sing praise unto the Lord, and give thanks unto the name of the Most High...

We would have briefer interludes between the verses on the organ; often none, as the sense demands; and would increase the number of verses usually sung...

There is another point on which we wish to touch, now we have put pen to paper. It is the voluntary on the organ at the close of the service. This as well as the concluding hymn, is a matter of great importance. If any impression has been made by the sermon, the concluding singing and the voluntary on the organ should aid in deepening it.[6]

5   Ibid. 21, no. 6, WN 1046 (Aug. 15, 1850), 24.
6   Ibid. 23, no. 13, WN 1157 (Sept. 30, 1852), 52.

4. Portions of an article from the *Musical World*, "Church Music in New-York," by Prof. Julius Erikson:

> Between the verses, you very often hear the organist, in a too light and secular movement, play fragments of opera pieces, and every kind of music, in fact, except solemn organ music; thereby displaying his vanity, and forgetting that the contents of each verse are in close connection, and that, therefore, the interludes—according to every idea of rhetoric—ought to be in full harmony with the sentiments of the words. You may easily imagine how the closing voluntary in most case—is performed. The organist sometimes draws out every stop in his organ, and, quite forgetting the place where he is playing, and only thinking of displaying the dexterity of his fingers, performs overtures, grand marches, etc.; and it has sometimes seemed to me as though he aimed to drown the impression made by a solemn sermon, or as though he wished to express his joy that the sermon was ended....

> The organists in this country are generally employed with little, or perhaps no reference at all to their moral character and religious sentiments, which manner of proceeding, both directly and indirectly, must be the cause of much trouble and wrong influence, as well as plunging the churches themselves into needles danger and risk....

> As to the manner in which music, in my opinion, ought to be regulated during the divine service, I would recommend the following: In the opening voluntary, while the minister is ascending to the pulpit, the organist should try as far as possible, by some soft and melodious chords, to prepare the congregation for the solemn and holy purpose for which they have met. And then, when the minister is seated, let a good anthem, or chant be performed by the choir; but in choosing this, the organist ought to take great care, both in regard to its character and the effect it will produce upon the congregation.

> In giving out the tunes, the organist, ought to use such a combination of stops,   and (if the construction of the instrument allow of it) so arrange them, that the melody may predominate.

> During the taking of the collection, some devotional subjects from the works of Handel, Bach, Rink, Mozart, or Beethoven,

should be played alternately on the swell and choir organ; and sometimes with some of the solo stops, this would be acceptable.

Finally, as to the concluding voluntary, I think there is so large a field for section in the masterly fugues of Sebastian Bach, Handel, &c, that an intelligent organist would have no difficulty in selecting such pieces as are suitable.[7]

5.   The Organ in Public Worship

But a yet more serious cause of offence to many persons is found in the length and character of the solos to which, now-a-days, we are compelled to listen....One Sunday evening, no long since, we heard a very solemn sermon followed by a "fandango," as one of the audience called it, more like a march than any thing else, and would hardly been out of place in an Ethiopian concert room.[8]

---

[7]   Ibid. 23, no. 15, WN 1159 (Oct. 14, 1852), 60.
[8]   Ibid. 24, no. 41, WN 1237 (Apr. 13, 1854), 162.

Some Patterns of Church Architecture in the Reformed Church in America, 1628-1849, with an Emphasis on the Location of Instruments and Musicians in Public Worship

Introduction

As the study of church architecture offers valuable insight into the changing culture, theology, and practice of public worship, examining the accommodations for instruments and musicians reveals much about the value and practice of worship music in each setting.

This appendix is in two parts. The first part shows three prevailing types of Dutch Reformed church buildings in colonial America. Included is a description of how and from where congregational singing was led prior to the advent of choirs. The second part is a pictorial journal of four buildings erected by the South Dutch Reformed Church in Manhattan in a 170-year period, demonstrating an archetypal (but not exhaustive) progression of some of the forms of church architecture adopted by many congregations in the Reformed Church in America throughout the era. Where known, the location of musicians and instruments will be indicated in each setting.

It is important to note that many congregations have constructed and maintained only one building, with many eighteenth- and early nineteenth-century examples still in existence. Typically, these churches have undergone renovations to align with changing worship attitudes, including accommodations for organs and choirs, which are consistent with the patterns of new construction described above.

Dutch Reformed Architecture in Colonial America

Records of the first religious meetings of the Dutch West India Company indicate that settlers heard scripture readings and recited the creed in the upper room of a horse mill near the Fort on the Battery, now lower Manhattan. Shortly after 1633, a plain wooden building was erected on the shore of the East River in the vicinity of Pearl and Bridge Streets. In 1642, a church was constructed within Ft. Amsterdam of stone, seventy feet long, fifty-two feet wide, and sixteen feet high, at a cost of 2,500 guilders.[1] The pre-Reformed style church, with an A-frame roof and a square, dome-topped bell-tower portico, is depicted in the drawing below.

Figure 6. The Old Church in the Battery Fort, 1642.
[Photo of a drawing from Historical Sketch of the South Church (Reformed) of New York City, *Frederick C. White and Roderick Terry, D.D.]*

An early Dutch Reformed church is pictured below. The distinctive square church with high-pitched roof and weathervane-

---

[1]   Approximately equal to $1,081. Architectural dimensions and building description found in the *Ecclesiastical Records of the State of New York*.

Figure 7. The Six Mile Run Reformed Church, Franklin Park,
New Jersey, probably built before 1745.
(Reformed Church Roots, Arie R. Brouwer)

topped steeples was adopted from country churches found in the
Netherlands and in continental Europe.[2] As a rule, in the colonial era,
the church interiors contained benches or chairs arranged in a manner
that separated the sexes, either with the women and children seated in
the center and the men seated along the walls, or facing each other on
two sides with an open space or center aisle between them. Seating was
provided for elders, minister's family, scripture reader (*voorlezer*), and
song leader (*voorzanger*)[3] near the pulpit (hourglass type common) and
reading desk. Many of these churches had a centrally placed, temporary

[2]   Hexagonal (six-sided) and octagonal (eight-sided) shapes were also common.
[3]   The same individual often performed the role of the *voorlezer* and *voorzanger*. The
voorzanger set the pitch either with his voice or a pitch pipe. Aside from psalm
singing, the only other "music" heard in this era was the ringing of the bell or the
beating of a drum to summon the congregation to worship.

Figure 8. The First
Reformed Church,
Fishkill, New York, 1751.
*(By Grace Alone, Donald J.
Bruggink and Kim N. Baker)*

or permanent Communion table with benches for men and women on opposing sides. At a prescribed point during the Communion liturgy,[4] the assembly moved from its regular worship seating to the benches at the table.[5]

The city or town church pictured above conforms to the widespread practice of adopting New England meetinghouse balconied church designs in the eighteenth century. The rectangular churches with an A-frame roof and center square portico bell tower have either two rows of dome-shaped clear glass windows or one row of two-story windows on two sides. The interior often contains a center aisle with pews on each side and the pulpit opposite the entrance.[6] Presider, elder,

---

[4]   Held monthly, more or less, depending on how each congregation chose to observe the feasts of the liturgical year.

[5]   A good example of a centrally placed Communion table can still be seen at the Old Mud Meeting House, a rural Kentucky Reformed church built in 1800.

[6]   Some floor plans place the pulpit on a long wall and have perimeter aisles with seating in the center. Examples of churches still exist with a Communion table attached to the sides of the pews, which folds up into the center aisle. In other churches a table was set up in the center aisle on Communion Sundays.

PLAN OF PEWS AND NAMES OF PEW HOLDERS IN FIRST
CHURCH, 1785.

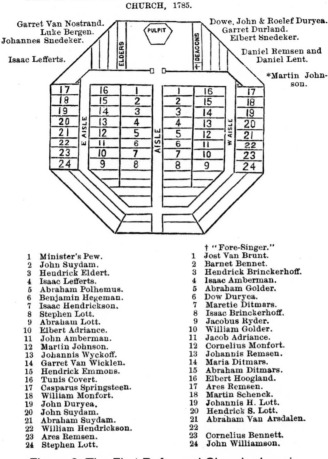

Garret Van Nostrand.
Luke Bergen.
Johannes Snedeker.

Isaac Lefferts.

Dowe, John & Roelef Duryea.
Garret Durland.
Elbert Snedeker.

Daniel Remsen and
Daniel Lent.

*Martin Johnson.

1	Minister's Pew.
2	John Suydam.
3	Hendrick Eldert.
4	Isaac Lefferts.
5	Abraham Polhemus.
6	Benjamin Hegeman.
7	Isaac Hendrickson.
8	Stephen Lott.
9	Abraham Lott.
10	Elbert Adriance.
11	John Amberman.
12	Martin Johnson.
13	Johannis Wyckoff.
14	Garret Van Wicklen.
15	Hendrick Emmons.
16	Tunis Covert.
17	Casparus Springsteen.
18	William Monfort.
19	John Duryea.
20	John Suydam.
21	Abraham Suydam.
22	William Hendrickson.
23	Ares Remsen.
24	Stephen Lott.

† "Fore-Singer."

1	Jost Van Brunt.
2	Barnet Bennet.
3	Hendrick Brinckerhoff.
4	Isaac Amberman.
5	Abraham Golder.
6	Dow Duryea.
7	Maretie Ditmars.
8	Isaac Brinckerhoff.
9	Jacobus Ryder.
10	William Golder.
11	Jacob Adriance.
12	Cornelius Monfort.
13	Johannis Remsen.
14	Maria Ditmars.
15	Abraham Ditmars.
16	Elbert Hoogland.
17	Ares Remsen.
18	Martin Schenck.
19	Johannis H. Lott.
20	Hendrick S. Lott.
21	Abraham Van Arsdalen.
22	
23	Cornelius Bennett.
24	John Williamson.

Figure 9. The First Reformed Church, Jamaica, New York, 1785, pew plan, showing location of "foresinger" on deacon's bench.
(History of the First Reformed Dutch Church of Jamaica, L.I.,
Henry Onderdonk, Jr.)

and *voorlezer/voorzanger* seating near the pulpit was like the previously described country church. Pew holders occupied the first floor, while all or part of the balcony bench seating was free for use by the poor, servants, and slaves.[7]

A poem written by Professor David Murray for the 150th anniversary celebration at the First Reformed Church in New Brunswick

7   The primary financial support of a church and its leaders came from the sale of pews. In effect, it was an annual rental that was charged, the price of the pew rental determined by the size of the seating and the distance from the pulpit.

in 1867 contains these charming descriptive lines, recalling worship and its setting in the church in the mid to late eighteenth century:

> The walls were plain, the roof was square,
> The carpets—ah! Well, they were not there;
> And the pews—of course, they were better bare,
> For cushions were deemed a carnal affair.
> In the center aisle the bell-rope hung,
> Where the sexton stood, when he puffed and rung;
> And the people said he was a cross to bear
> If any one jostled against him there.
> And the boys in the pews had a wholesome fear
> Of Johannes's anger,[8] when he was near.
> At the pulpit-front the vorsinger stood—
> His nose was large and his voice was good
> And he pitched his tune as he pitched his hay,
> To the right and left in a frantic way.
> And the Old Dutch psalms made the welkin ring,
> For Dutchmen are strong when they come to sing.[9]

The Four Buildings of the South Dutch Reformed Church, 1690-1849

The following photographs and drawings of the four buildings of the South Dutch Reformed Church in Manhattan form a pictorial journal of the sanctuaries erected between 1690 and 1849. In 1690 a new church was erected on the upper side of Garden Street, later Exchange Place, near present-day Wall Street. This imposing meetinghouse design featured round, full-length arch windows and three front entrances, including one through a central portico bell tower.[10] Here, as in the buildings described in the first part of this appendix, the *voorzanger* and/or instrumentalist(s), would have been seated by the pulpit under the watchful eyes of the deacons.

---

[8]   Johannes Leydt was the minister of First New Brunswick from 1748-86.

[9]   *Historical Discourse Delivered at the Celebration of the One Hundred and Fiftieth Anniversary of the First Reformed Church, New Brunswick, N.J., October 1, 1867*, 163.

[10]   By 1767 the growing South Dutch Church had twice branched into two other congregations, forming the North Dutch and Middle Dutch Church in the vicinity. In 1764 the Scottish preacher Archibald Laidlie became pastor of South Dutch and, in 1765, was the first to preach in English in a Dutch Reformed Church in America. In 1789, Gerardus A. Kuyper of Paramus, NJ, became pastor and preached in Dutch until 1803, the last time the language was used as the language of worship in this church.

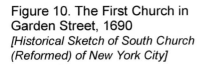

Figure 10. The First Church in
Garden Street, 1690
*[Historical Sketch of South Church
(Reformed) of New York City]*

In 1807 the first Garden Street Church was demolished. Erected was a classically appointed building, sixty feet long by fifty feet wide, with double windows and a rear apse. A bell tower was placed at the point of the roof. By the early 1830s a pipe organ and choir were located in the balcony opposite the pulpit. In a historical sermon given in 1877, the Reverend Dr. Hutton recalls his years as associate pastor at the church and his witnessed account of the fire that destroyed the building in 1835:

> Dr. Matthews (the senior pastor) and myself then took our stand on the steps of a house opposite side of the street, unable to draw ourselves away from the loved building. We stood silent, with our eyes on the pulpit. At last he exclaimed "there goes the pulpit!" our organist entered the building when almost all others had deserted it, and the organ ceased not to utter its wail until the fire commenced dropping from the ceiling; and the sexton, until the fire cut off the rope, ceased not to ring, with a wild ring, the bell which sounded as if struggling in its last agony; but the agony was in our hearts.[11]

---

[11]   *Historical Sketch of South Church (Reformed) of New York City,* 26.

Figure 11. The Second
Church in Garden Street,
1807
*[Historical Sketch of South
Church (Reformed) of New
York City]*

The congregation moved to Murray Street and dedicated its third church building, "with interesting services, lasting all day,"[12] on

Figure 12. The Church in Murray Street, 1837
[Historical Sketch of South Church (Reformed) of New York City]

[12]   Ibid., 29.

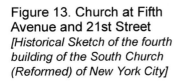

Figure 13. Church at Fifth Avenue and 21st Street
[Historical Sketch of the fourth building of the South Church (Reformed) of New York City]

December 24, 1837. The Greek Revival [*sic*, EgyptianRevival] church measured fifty by seventy-three and one-half feet, and cost a princely $32,500. A member, Dr. Ogden Doremus, proposed the purchase of a new organ, funded in part by proceeds from a concert and through subscriptions. The congregation worshiped there until March 1848. As a former pastor recalled, "A congregation consisting largely of new members was soon gathered, and by constant accessions it maintained its flourishing condition for ten years. At length however, like other down-town Churches, it began to show the effect of the tide of removal. It was surrounded by a transient population. After prayerful consideration the congregation resolved to select another situation where they could continue an efficient Church for years."[13]

While I have no description of the interior appearance of the Murray Street church, interiors in the period were often constructed or renovated to resemble theaters and featured plush carpeting, upholstered seating, and sequestered choirs as described in "Choir Location" in chapter 4.

---

[13] Ibid., 31-32. Reminiscences of South Church by John Magoffin Maculey, S.T.D. (pastor 1838-1862).

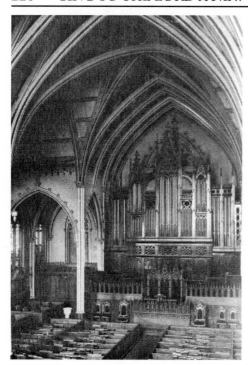

Figure 14. Interior of church at 5th Avenue and 21st Street.
[Historical Sketch of South Church (Reformed) of New York City]

The congregation's fourth church building opened for worship in June 1849 on the corner of Fifth Avenue and Twenty-First Street. The effort completed a remarkable forty-two-year transition from a New England style meetinghouse, to an Egyptian Revival building, to neo-Gothic pointed architecture, the final move inspired by the Oxford and Cambridge Movements in England and following on the heels of Richard Upjohn's (1802-78) Trinity Episcopal Church in New York City, completed in 1847. James Renwick's (1818-95) equally monumental St. Patrick's Cathedral (begun in 1853), also in New York City, helped make Gothic all the rage among upscale city congregations of many denominations. These forms found general acceptance by the last quarter of the nineteenth century and were executed in lavish detail, including stained glass, in cities, suburbs, and even in small towns on the East Coast and in the Midwest.

From the interior photograph above one can see organ facade pipes across the chancel area. In the period studied, Dutch Reformed choirs were not seated in the chancel but located near the organ console in a side or rear balcony. However, in the last quarter of the nineteenth century, many churches moved instruments and musicians out of balconies and placed them on a front platform behind the pulpit.

APPENDIX 6

Compact Disc Liner Notes

The Ensemble

The eleven-voice choir assembled for this recording consists of members of the Colts Neck Reformed Church Senior Choir and the Chamber Choir of Monmouth University. While no member of the ensemble presently earns his or her living as a singer, each has undertaken formal musical training and has sung under the tutelage of one or more church or school choir directors. A few are public school music teachers or college music majors. The rest embody the well-prepared amateur church musician. Therefore, one can speculate that the aggregate skill of this choir represents the upper echelon of the institutional (amateur) choirs that served our denomination since choirs were introduced in the late eighteenth century.

The choir is comprised of members with comparatively light, transparent voices who strive to blend well by suppressing any vocal characteristic that may cause an individual voice to be heard above the others. In this way the choir negates the imbalances that can occur when combining amateur singers with professionals who are accustomed to singing solos or performing roles in operas or musical theater. Still, much of the music from this period features passages of musical interchange between a soloist or a subset of the ensemble and the full choir, an ancient practice known as antiphonal style. In this type of music it does work well to have a professionally trained small group or quartet juxtaposed against the larger choir for musical contrast. Nevertheless, a professional quartet was not hired for this recording, deferring to the more common and economical practice of selecting compatible voices within the choir for pairings or quartets, who also sing during the full choir sections of each piece.

The members of this choir are (sopranos) Jan Applegate, Lyn Lewis, Rosanna Tinari, and Dottie Weidman; (altos) Heather Postel, Dani Richards, and Jeanne Sokol; (tenors) John Applegate and Jeff Brown; and (basses) Dan Heinzelmann and Matthew Kloufetos. An instrumental ensemble is employed in some of the pieces consisting of three professional musicians: Wayne Arndt, cello; Lyn Lewis, clarinet; and Maggie Tripold, organ and piano. A fine amateur flutist, Joy Lenz, rounds out this typical period small "church band."

The Music

I examined more than a hundred eighteenth- and nineteenth-century American tunebooks to select the fourteen pieces for this recording. My mission was to locate compositions that offer a rough representation of the types of pieces sung by choirs during the period studied. In doing so, I gathered examples for various liturgical uses and tried to assemble a diversity of pieces with contrasting musical forms and styles, both European and American. Additionally, I searched for compositions that offered a variety of accompaniment possibilities, those that may have been sung *a cappella*, those for which I adapted instrumental parts, and those that included keyboard accompaniments. I looked for pieces that are musically accomplished, that is, works that offer interest and variety, and that somehow complement the collection. I aimed to include a few musical "gems" of each genre, allied with some texts that offer keen theological statements wrapped in vivid textual imagery, along with those that perhaps are distinguished only by an ability to render a picture of quaintness or charm.

Three patterns for accompanying psalms, hymns, and anthems are found in early American Dutch Reformed worship. An early pattern required the *voorzanger* to use a tuning fork to set the starting pitch, then to use his voice to lead congregational psalm singing. For our rendition of "Psalm 46," John Applegate demonstrated two techniques of presenting a psalm with one unaccompanied voice by singing the first verse alone and then by "lining out" the second verse, using our choir as a congregation. By the late eighteenth century, the *voorzanger* had been replaced by, or retooled himself as, a chorister (choir leader), who led a choir that accompanied congregational singing. For the psalm's remaining four verses our choir demonstrated some possible textural combinations that may serve to lead congregational singing without the benefit of instrumental accompaniment.

The second pattern makes use of instrumental accompaniment. Many *voorzangers* or choristers used a cello to accompany the Dutch psalms and must have continued to do so in some churches when English hymns and anthems were first introduced. We have demonstrated this practice in William Billings's "Brookfield." By the first quarter of the nineteenth century, a number of small church bands consisting of cellos, violins, flutes, clarinets, and other instruments are reported before and after some churches had acquired organs. Accordingly, we have provided examples of pieces accompanied by a small church band and with organ and church band combined.

The third pattern uses a keyboard instrument such as the pipe organ, a reed organ—often a harmonium or melodeon—or a piano, exclusively. The latter two were commonly installed in homes, classrooms, and meeting rooms where, in all, a fulsome ecclesiastical life was replete with singing. We have selected the piano to accompany two of the pieces included in the *Music for an Ecclesiastical Life* category of this recording.

Acknowledgments

Thanks go to the Colts Neck Reformed Church for providing the splendid acoustical space of its 1856 sanctuary for our recording. I am indebted to Lyn Lewis for transcribing many of the musical examples using *Finale* software, for making the tunebook music look modern and legible for our choir members, and for transcribing instrumental parts for our church band. I am equally indebted to my colleague, George Wurzbach, for recording this CD and for the countless hours he invested in editing the recording.

Compact Disc Liner Notes

A Psalm, a Hymn, and a Spiritual Song

1. "Psalm 46" (6:04)
Music: Amos Bull (1744-1825)
Text: Isaac Watts (1674-1748)

2. "Missionary Hymn" (2:24)
Music: Lowell Mason (1792-1872)
Text: Reginald Heber (1783-1826)

3. "Brookfield" (5:06)
Music: William Billings (1746-1800)
Text: Phillip Doddridge (1702-51)

By the mid-nineteenth century a burgeoning supply of psalm and hymn texts discharged the monopoly formerly held by the Isaac Watts and John (1703-91) and Charles (1707-88) Wesley collections. The ever-expanding Reformed Church in America hymnal, *Psalms & Hymns*, struggled to keep pace with the flood of hymn texts with each new edition, resorting to publishing supplements, titled *Additional Hymns* (1831) and *Sabbath School and Social Hymns* (1843). By 1860, *Psalms & Hymns* had reached a whopping eight hundred pages![1]

Tunebooks responded with a growing supply of tunes to match the texts. Some tunebooks separated the metrical tune collection by "choir tunes" and "congregational tunes." Understood to be more difficult, "choir tunes" are either sung by the choir alone or require the choir to lead congregational singing. "Congregational tunes," then, are assumed to be easy enough to be sung by the congregation without choir leadership, and with or without instrumental accompaniment.

"Psalm 46," a "congregational tune" by American composer Amos Bull with a versification of "Psalm 146" from Isaac Watt's *Psalms of David* (1719), appears in Richard Crawford's *The Core Repertory of Early American Psalmody*. A revised, and substantially weakened, version in three-quarter time is found in *The New Brunswick Collection of Sacred Music*, seventh edition (1835) (discussed in chapter 5). Teetering between F major and F Lydian (an ancient mode differing from major mode by having a raised fourth degree), this piece offers us a sample of American tunesmith composing free from the confines of learned European art music.

---

[1]   See Brumm, *Singing the Lord's Song*, for a full account of RCA hymnals; Brumm, *Liturgy*.

Lowell Mason's "Missionary Hymn" was first published in 1823 in the long-running *Boston Handel and Haydn Society's Collection of Church Music* series. The picturesque text was written by the popular hymn writer Reginald Heber prior to his tenure as an Anglican Bishop of Calcutta. The hymn gained wide recognition by its inclusion in several regional collections, such as *Musica Sacra,* tenth edition (1835), and *The New Brunswick Collection of Sacred Music,* seventh edition (1835), and by being a mission hymn mainstay in nineteenth- and twentieth-century hymnals. However, notwithstanding its popularity, the text does not appear in the massive Reformed Church in America's hymnal, *Psalms & Hymns* (1860). [2]

While the piece is often found in F major, we found it more comfortable to sing in E-flat major. I added an eight-bar introduction to the keyboard interlude Mason prepared for this volume, a procedure sometimes suggested by tunebook compilers that unites the verses of a hymn into a "symphony." Classical music pretensions aside, the procedure more closely mirrors the form of secular ballads of the day, adding, I would think, to the popularity of hymns taking up the same form. For the second verse I employed a vocal quartet. For the fourth verse, I selected one of two alternate harmonizations included in this volume and endorsed by the composer's caption, "Improved by a harmony which brings in greater variety of chords, and which is more ecclesiastical in its character." Our small church band, consisting of flute, clarinet, and cello with organ, is employed in various combinations for this hymn.

American composer William Billings's "Brookfield," with its eerie "dry bones" Ezekiel 37:1-4 text (included in *Psalms & Hymns,* 1860), appeared in several late eighteenth-century and early nineteenth-century collections I examined. It was included by Richard Crawford in *The Core Repertory of Early American Psalmody.* Crawford notes an imaginative use of triple time, with its diverse collection of rhythmic values including half notes, quarter notes, and dotted rhythms. He also observes the irregularity of its four-line plain tune structure, whereby the fourth phrase is a near repetition in all voices of the second phrase, thus "creating the form ABCB."[3] "Brookfield" may have escaped the wholesale condemnation of American music by those allied with the New England-centered European "cultured" music movement. It was given faint praise by Thomas Hastings (1784-1872), who recognized

---

2   See chapter 5 for more information on Lowell Mason's "Missionary Hymn."
3   Richard Crawford, *The Core Repertory of Early Psalmody*, Recent Researches in American Music, vols. 11 and 12 (Madison: A-R Editions, 1984), xxviii.

Billings as a composer of "some genius, but very little learning" and admitted that "his Brookfield has been deservedly popular."[4] Indeed, "Brookfield" continued to appear into the 1850s in many of the tunebooks I examined.

I arranged this probable "choir tune" in ascending order from one- to five-voice parts, the five-voice version doubling the tune in the first soprano and tenor parts, as was often the practice in eighteenth-century America. I also added a cello part, combining the common practice of using the cello as accompaniment on the bass line with some speculation as to how the whole might be united by the cello providing a thematic introduction and postlude to the verses.

Responses

4. "Devotion" (1:10)
   Music: Attributed to Wolfgang A. Mozart (1756-91)
   Text: Unknown

5. "Sicily" (1:04)
   Music: Eighteenth-century Sicilian Melody
   Text: Attributed to John Fawcett (1740-1817), *A Supplement to the Shawbury Hymnbook*, 1773, alt.

As the nineteenth century drew on, the gradual institutionalizing of church choirs prompted tunebook compilers to include more responses in American tunebooks. Along with introits, the *Gloria Patri*, the Nicene and Apostles' Creeds, The Lord's Prayer, doxologies, and benedictions (used both in Roman Catholic and Protestant worship), Latin and English mass and office chants began to appear in what surely must have been one of the most ecumenical publications of the time, the tunebook.

After a lengthy sojourn to Germany, where he had reportedly met Felix Mendelssohn (1809-47), William B. Bradbury (1816-68) returned to New York with a cache of music for his and Thomas Hastings's (1792-1872) *Mendelssohn Collection* (1849). Having long been proponents of German music, Bradbury and Hastings were influential in broadening America's church music taste from a near entrenchment in English church music to encompass not only German music, but Italian, Swiss, and other national schools.

---

[4]   Ibid., xxviii (*Musical Magazine* I; quoted in McKay, 7; Crawford, 203.).

"Devotion," labeled an introit in this collection but also suitable as a prayer invitation or response, demonstrates the bridge between Austro-German folksong and eighteenth-century classical musical form epitomized by Joseph Haydn (1732-1809), Wolfgang Mozart, and Ludwig Beethoven (1770-1826). Consequently, this short composition could serve equally well as a (brief) third movement of a string quartet, a vocal quartet in an opera, or, as it is here with as sacred text, an introit. The piece is equipped with a charming melody, playful rhythms in a lilting 3/8 meter, a tightly woven structural and harmonic plan, and a delightful interplay between the close relations of parallel thirds and wide sonorities that lend alternately a sense of intimacy followed by one of spaciousness.

Also from the *Mendelssohn Collection*, "Sicily," with its peculiar meter of alternating eight- and seven-syllable phrases, appears with only one of the verses that usually accompany the hymn tune now called "Sicilian Mariners." It is not labeled a benediction response in this collection, yet it serves this purpose. We added the second verse and have employed a church band and organ to offer the impression of a rousing and joyful sending forth.

General Anthems

6. "Go Forth to the Mount" (1:42)
Music: Sir John Stevenson (1761-1833)
Text: Thomas Moore (1779-1852)

7. "Come Ye Disconsolate" (1:58)
Music: German. Harmonized by Sir John Stevenson
Text: Thomas Moore

8. "Daughter of Zion" (3:36)
Music: Lowell Mason
Text: Anonymous, *Fitzgerald's Collection*

By the mid-nineteenth century, tunebooks had come to include many more choral anthems than during the early part of the century. The anthem repertoire had blossomed to offer a breadth of musical styles and forms by homegrown and international composers. Pieces of all eras and worship traditions were included, such as English verse and full anthems, Renaissance motets, classical and Romantic quartets and trios, and German chorales. European art music stood beside folk music, the previously banished music of American tunesmiths, and a host of less-than-distinguished ditties, seemingly dashed off to fill tunebook pages in what had become a highly competitive marketplace.

From the *Boston Handel and Haydn Collection of Sacred Music,* III (1827), the same collection owned by First Church, Albany, in the 1820s, "Go Forth to the Mount" is an example of English or, in this case, Irish cathedral music. Owing to its continued popularity, Isaac Woodbury prepared an arrangement of it in his tune book, *The Dulcimer* (1850).

From the same collection is an anthem arrangement of the popular hymn text, "Come Ye Disconsolate," using a German folk song instead of the better known tune by Samuel Webbe (1740-1816).[5] This *H & H* collection offered an independent organ accompaniment for each anthem used in our recording. Two interpretive questions arise when performing early choral music with a modern pipe organ. The first question is whether or not it is appropriate to use an organ with an enclosed division of pipes having louvered shades on the outside of the enclosure that are opened and shut by a pedal on the console to effect volume and timbre changes. By the mid-nineteenth century, fully enclosed pipe organs or those with enclosed portions were normative, such as the E. & G. G. Hook organ constructed at First Church, Albany, in 1845 (see appendix 4 for stop list and appendix 5 for photographs), along with those manufactured for many Dutch Reformed churches by Hall and Erben, Odell, Robjohn, Ferris, Crabb, and others. Thus, when performing music composed after 1800, we find it appropriate to use a "swelling organ," as it was once called. Our "American Classic" pipe organ at the Colts Neck Reformed Church is almost fully enclosed in a reproduction period case befitting our mid-nineteenth-century sanctuary.

The second question is what organ registration is appropriate, considering the differences between modern pipe organ sound and that of nineteenth-century American organs. While not designed to mimic the sound of a nineteenth-century organ, our instrument provides a consistent, high-quality tone in all stops and registers, free of idiosyncrasy, which lends itself well to most periods and styles of hymn and anthem accompaniments and organ literature. Therefore, although our organ does not replicate the sound of nineteenth-century pipe organs, it neither "gets in the way" nor detracts from the choral performance, but lends a strong and pleasing support to the sound.[6]

---

[5]   See chapter 5 for more information on Samuel Webbe's "Come Ye Disconsolate."

[6]   The two-manual, eighteen-rank pipe organ was built by Patrick J. Murphy & Associates, Inc., Stowe, Pennsylvania, in 2003.

Published concurrently in *The Boston Handel and Haydn Collection of Church Music*, fifteenth ed. (1835); *The New Brunswick Collection of Sacred Music*, seventh ed. (1835); and *Musica Sacra*, tenth ed. (1836); "Daughter of Zion" provides a lovely example of the kind of American psalmody prepared by composers like Lowell Mason and Thomas Hastings. Mason marked *soli* and *tutti* markings to indicate frequent interchanges between a vocal quartet and the full choir to vary vocal texture. In the *H & H* collection above he recommended using the first eight bars of the anthem as instrumental introduction and the last four bars as an interlude between verses in the same manner described for "Missionary Hymn." By using our church band and organ in various combinations, we sought to underscore and add further interest to the interchanging vocal textures in Mason's anthem.[7]

Occasional Anthems

9. "Dying Christian" (3:11)
Music: Edward Harwood (1707-87), *A Set of Hymn and Psalm Tunes*, 1770
Text: Alexander Pope (1688-1744), 1712

10. "Hark! The Vesper Hymn is Stealing" (2:23)
Music: Russian Air, Anonymous, c. 1818.
Text: Thomas Moore, from John Stevenson's *A Selection of Popular National Airs*, 1818

11. "Easter Anthem" (1:24)
Music: William Billings, 1787.
Text: paraphrase Luke 24:34. Edward Young, 1798.

For funerals and graveside services, "Dying Christian" depicts a dying believer's thoughts as he leaves our earthly plane and passes into heaven. A *set piece* (a composition featuring new music with each new section of text, unlike most hymns, where multiple verses are sung to the same music), the piece changes key (from F minor to F major) and passes through four time signatures. This version of "Dying Christian" is not the more commonly encountered F-major version introduced by Andrew Law (1749-1821) and described by Richard Crawford in *The Core Repertory of Early American Psalmody*, but the earlier Edward

---

[7]   See chapter 5 for more information on Lowell Mason's "Daughter of Zion."

Harwood version found in the *New Brunswick Collection of Sacred Music*, seventh edition (1835), and in *Village Harmony*, twelfth edition (1815). Our church band accompanied the choir for this performance, in a demonstrated practical solution to accompanying a graveside rendition of the piece.[8]

Another popular hymn arranged as an anthem, "Hark! The Vesper Hymn is Stealing," is ideally suited for evening worship. From *The Boston Handel & Haydn Society Old Colony Collection of Anthems*, third edition (1823), the anthem takes up two verses, with soprano on melody above a superimposed slower moving alto, tenor, and bass repeating the words "jubilate" and "amen." The organ accompaniment, with its bell-like eighth-note figures, packages the anthem in an eight-measure introduction, a four-measure interlude, and a four-measure postlude.[9]

Notwithstanding its wide distribution and seeming popularity in the late eighteenth century, "Easter Anthem" was among those pieces eschewed by early nineteenth-century tunebook compilers that were subsequently rediscovered as American gems of ingenuity by the mid-nineteenth century. From an early reprinting in *The Devotional Harmonist* (1853), "Easter Anthem" is arranged in discrete sections, of which some are repeated. Whether due to Billings's homegrown nonschooling in the formal techniques of European Art Music, or simply by his genius, there are no smooth transitions between anthem sections. Thus the listener is afforded not a measured consideration of the unfolding story of Christ's resurrection and humanity's endowment of salvation, but a spontaneous and ecstatic expression of Christian triumph over death. Each section is characterized by the tools of tone painting, including dotted rhythms and rising scales and triads that lend well to a sense of bold and unbridled joy.

Music for an Ecclesiastical Life

12. "Temperance Hymn" (1:04)
Music: George F. Root (1820-95)
Text: George F. Root

13. "Children of the Sabbath School" "Duet and Chorus between Choir and Teachers and Scholars" (2:42)
Music: Isaac Woodbury (1819-58)
Text: Isaac Woodbury

---

[8]   See chapter 5 for more information on Edward Harwood's "Dying Christian."
[9]   See chapter 5 for more information on the hymn- anthem more often titled, "Vesper Hymn."

14. "Let Every Heart" (For Independence, Thanksgiving, or other national festivals) (3:16)
Music: Isaac Woodbury
Text: Isaac Woodbury

For the Christian faithful, a rich ecclesiastical life included weekly prayer gatherings; meetings to expand the Social Gospel movement, such as those for the Temperance and Bible societies; Sabbath (Sunday) school exercises; and celebrations of national holidays, such as Independence Day and Thanksgiving. All were occasions for singing, and most provided an opportunity to display a well-prepared church choir. "Temperance Hymn," from George Root's *Sabbath Bell* (1856), is a rallying cry to free those enslaved by "the poisoned bowl," that "for happier homes and brighter days...the wife regains a husband freed! The orphan clasps a father found!" Performed by *a cappella* quartet, the music evokes the soon-to-arrive jaunty choruses in the light operas of W. S. Gilbert (1836-1911) and Sir Arthur Sullivan (1842-1900).

"Children of the Sabbath School," from Isaac Woodbury's *The Dulcimer* (1850), was designed for annual or weekly opening exercises of the church Sabbath school and offers a delightful musical repartee between students and their teachers. A divided chorus and piano accompaniment is employed here.

Another occasional piece from Woodbury's *The Dulcimer*, "Let Every Heart" is the kind of festival song that choirs and rapt audience might enjoy at a church picnic on a national holiday. On such occasions one might enlist the church band to accompany the choir. Here we have selected the piano, since the accompaniment part is idiomatically suited for the instrument.

Bibliographic Essay

For this work of historical/archival research, information was gathered from denomination and individual church archives and publications for selected churches in New York, New Jersey, and Michigan. The materials for this investigation are located at the Gardner A. Sage Library of the New Brunswick Theological Seminary, the Alexander Library of Rutgers University, the American Organ Archives of the Organ Historical Society at the Talbot Library at Westminster Choir College of Rider University, the Joint Archives of Holland at Hope College in Holland, Michigan, and in the holdings of individual churches.[1]

---

[1] Particularly valuable to this study were the many published church histories found at the Gardner A. Sage Library and at the American Organ Archives of the Organ Historical Society. The *Christian Intelligencer*, a denominational weekly newspaper, was also an invaluable reference. Additionally, resources were gathered from several well-organized archives maintained in individual churches such as First Church, Albany, New York; First Reformed Church, Schenectady, New York; Old Brick Reformed Church, Marlboro, New Jersey; and Third Reformed Church, Holland, Michigan.

As a work also of interpretation, this study drew upon American cultural historical methods. I was guided by the method in John P. Luidens's dissertation, *The Americanization of the Dutch Reformed Church*. I was also assisted by a number of works that examined the assimilating tendencies of the Dutch in America, including Randall Balmer, *A Perfect Babel of Confusion: Dutch Religion and English Culture in the Middle Colonies*[2]; Elton J. Bruins, *The Americanization of a Congregation*[3]; Gerald F. De Jong, *The Dutch Reformed Church in the American Colonies*[4]; and Firth Haring Fabend, *Zion on the Hudson:Dutch New York and New Jersey in the Age of Revivals*.[5]

Music histories and musicological methods were valuable to this study, including H. Wiley Hitchcock, *Music in the United States: A Historical Introduction*,[6] the first work to unveil two discrete music traditions in America, the "vernacular" and the "cultivated." Richard Crawford, in *The American Musical Landscape*,[7] extended this notion to other "separate binary streams," such as "popular/classical," "light/serious," "informal/ formal," "functional/artistic," and I would add "rural/urban." Each stemmed from a tension between the "provincial forces," those that are less self-conscious of their utilitarian or "fun" music making, and the "cosmopolitan forces," those that focused on a cultivated craft "to be appreciated for its "edification—its moral, spiritual, or aesthetic values."[8] Through these lenses I examined the evidence of church choirs against the representative histories.

I was guided by three essential frames of reference found in Robin A. Leaver's *Goostly Psalmes and Spiritual Songes: English and Dutch Metrical Psalms From Coverdale to Utenhove, 1535-1566*[9] and "Lection, Sermon, and Congregational Song: A Preaching Lectionary of the Dutch Reformed Church (1782) and Its Implications" in *Pulpit, Table and Song, Essays in Celebration of Howard G. Hageman*.[10] First, from the earliest days of the Reformation in the Netherlands, the Psalms were not the only repertoire of the church; rather, constant pressure to include hymns led to the first publication of a Dutch hymnal in 1806. Second, there

2   (New York: Oxford Univ. Press, 1989).
3   Historical Series of the Reformed Church in America, no. 26, 2nd ed. (Grand Rapids: Eerdmans, 1995).
4   Historical Series of the Reformed Church in America, no. 5 (Grand Rapids: Eerdmans, 1978).
5   (New Brunswick: Rutgers Univ. Press, 2000).
6   Third ed. (Englewood Cliffs, NJ: Prentice-Hall, 1988).
7   (Berkeley: Univ. of California Press, 1993).
8   Hitchcock, *Music*, 54.
9   (Oxford: Clarendon, 1991).
10   Heather Elkins and Edward C. Zaragoza, eds. (Lanham: Scarecrow, 1996).

was a liturgical tradition transplanted in North America, with lections and preaching based on the Christian calendar, which gradually eroded when English became the language of worship. Third, the church in the Netherlands, even after America's independence, continued to influence the Reformed Church in America.

Two efforts to deal with the Dutch church music tradition in America are Bertus F. Polman, "Church Music and Liturgy in the Christian Reformed Church of North America,"[11] and Rudolf Zuiderveld, "Some Musical Traditions in Dutch Reformed Churches in America."[12] Paul Westermeyer, "Lineaments of the Reformed and Lutheran Traditions: Liturgy and Hymnody in 19th Century Pennsylvania"[13] and *What Shall We Sing in a Foreign Land? Theology and Cultic Song in the Reformed and Lutheran Churches of Pennsylvania, 1830-1900*[14] were useful guides to assess the reciprocal musical influences among religious traditions in America. James L. H. Brumm has compiled a useful history of the denomination's psalter/hymnals in *Singing the Lord's Song: A History of the English Language Hymnals of the Reformed Church in America* and *Liturgy among the Thorns, Essays on Worship in the Reformed Church in America.*[15] Here he suggested some of the demographics and catalysts for change that I carried forward to this thesis. Howard G. Hageman's 1962 *Pulpit and Table: Some Chapters in the History of Worship in the Reformed Churches*[16] inspired many of the scholarly efforts mentioned here and elsewhere, including Daniel Meeter, *The "North American Liturgy": A Critical Edition of the Reformed Dutch Church in North America, 1793,*[17] which uncovered a valuable unofficial dialogue about the colonial Collegiate Church's dilemma in creating an English psalter, but to the "old" Dutch tunes. This evidence helped set the stage for the various and complex states of affairs leading to the unwinding of the psalm-singing tradition in the Dutch Reformed Church and the onslaught of choirs and organs. None of these works, however, ventured but cursorily into the area of church choirs.

My inquiry into church choirs in the Dutch Reformed tradition was prompted by the work and suggestion of Anne Bagnall Yardley. Her articles, "Choirs in the Methodist Episcopal Church, 1800-1860"[18] and

---

[11]   Ph.D. diss., Univ. of Minnesota, 1981.

[12]   *Hymn* 36:3 (July 1985), 23-25.

[13]   *Church Music,* 80 (1980), 2-22.

[14]   Ph.D. diss., Univ. of Chicago, 1978.

[15]   (New Brunswick: Historical Society of the Reformed Church in America, 1990); (Grand Rapids: Eerdmans, 2007).

[16]   (Richmond: John Knox, and London: SCM Press, 1962).

[17]   Ph.D. diss., Drew Univ., 1989.

[18]   *American Music* (Spring, 1999), 39-63.

"What Besides Hymns? The Tune Books of Early Methodism,"[19] broke new ground by examining the makeup of individual church choirs, where and on what occasions they sang, their leaders, their repertoire, how they were accompanied, and especially how they influenced nineteenth-century Methodism. Aside from Yardley's aforementioned work, I know of no other effort to retrieve and analyze the statistical data of individual church choirs in nineteenth-century America. This scant picture has left the door open to generalizations about American church choirs and their repertoires.

[19]   *Methodist History* 37:3 (Apr., 1999).

Bibliography

Archives and Reference Sources:

Acts and Proceedings of the General Synod of the Reformed Church in America, The. Vols. 2-21. New York: Board of Publication of the Reformed Church, 1813-1907.

Acts and Proceedings of the General Synod of the Reformed Protestant Dutch Church in North America, The. Vol. I: *Embracing the Period from 1771 to 1812, Preceded by the Minutes of the Coetus (1738-1754), and the Proceedings of the Conferentie (1755-1767), and Followed by the Minutes of the Original Particular Synod (1794-1799).* New York: Board of Publication of the Reformed Protestant Dutch Church, 1859.

Archives of First Church, Albany, NY, The. Dr. James Foults, historian.

Calvin, John. *Ioannis Calvini Opera quae supersunt omnia.* Ed. Wilhelm Baum, Edward Cunitz, and Edward Reuss. 59 vols. Brunsviqae: A. Swetsche and Son, 1843-48.

_____. *Ioannis Calvini Opera Selecta.* Ed. Peter Barth, Wilhelm Niesel, and Dora Scheuner. 5 vols. Munich: C. Kaiser, 1926-62.

243

_____. *Commentary on the Book of Psalms.* Grand Rapids: Eerdmans, 1949.

_____. *Institutes of the Christian Religion.* Ed. John T. NcNeill, John Baille, and Henry P. Van Dusen. Trans. Ford Lewis Battles. Vols. XX and XXI of *The Library of Christian Classics.* Philadelphia: Westminster, 1960.

_____. *Calvin: Theological Treatises.* Trans. with introductions and notes by J.K.S. Reid. Louisville: Westminster John Knox, 1978.

Constitution of the Reformed Church in the United States of America, The. New York: William Durrell, 1793.

Corwin, Edward Tanjore. *A Manual of the Reformed Church in America.* 1st, 2d, 3d, 4th and 5th eds. New York: Board of Publication, Reformed Church in America, 1859, 1869, 1879, 1902.

_____. *A Digest of Constitutional and Synodical Legislation of the Reformed Church in America.* New York: Board of Publication, Reformed Church in America, 1906.

Ecumenical Creeds and Reformed Confessions. Grand Rapids: CRC Publications, 1987.

Hastings, Hugh. *Ecclesiastical Records of the State of New York.* 7 vols. Albany: James B. Lyon, 1901-1916.

Heidelberg Catechism: 400th Anniversary Edition, The. Philadelphia and Boston: United Church Press, 1963.

Organ Historical Society Archives, Westminster Choir College of Rider University, Princeton, NJ.

Diaries or Journals

Morse, George Francis. *Unpublished Worship Diary, 1901-1911.* (Organist and director of the choir of the Flatbush Reformed Church, Brooklyn, NY). Owned by the Flatbush Reformed Church, Brooklyn, NY.

Wansey, Henry. *Journal of an Excursion to the United States of America in the Summer of 1794,* published as *Henry Wansey and his American Journal,* ed. D. J. Jeremy. Philadelphia: American Philosophical Society, 1970.

Magazines, Newspapers, Organ Manufacturers Publications, and Websites

Christian Intelligencer: Weekly Newspaper of the Reformed Dutch Church, The. (New York), August 7, 1830 –September 15, 1934.

Collegiate Reformed Protestant Dutch Church of the City of New York, Organized April, 1628, The. http://www.collegiatechurch.org/history.html. Internet accessed March 14, 2006.

Colonial News, The. Freehold, NJ: April 7, 1968.

Dwight's Journal of Music. (Boston, MA), 1852-1881.

Henry Erben & Co., Organ Manufactury, 235, 237 & 239 East 23rd St. Between 2d and 3rd Aves., New York. New York: George F. Nesbitt, 1874.

Magazine of the Reformed Dutch Church, The. (New Brunswick, NJ), 1827-1830.

Message Bird, The. New York. 50:222R (Apr. 1, 1850) and 50:294 (May 1, 1850).

New York Times, The. "All Ideas are Political" (New York: Oct. 8, 2005).

Odell's Concert Notices. New York, 1831.

Redway Notices, Announcements, etc., on Music from the "Commercial Advertiser," 1838.

Reformed Church in America. http://www.rca.org/NETCOMMUNITY/ Page.aspx?&pid=230&srcid=183. Internet accessed October 2004 – May 2006

Van Pelt, William T., compiler. *The Hook Opus List, 1829-1916 in Facsimile with a Compiled List of Organs 1916-1935 and Facsimiles of Promotional Publications* (Richmond: The Organ Historical Society, 1991).

Willis, Richard Storrs, ed. *The Musical World & Times.* (New York), 1846-1860.

Liturgy and Music Resources

Allen, Francis D. *The New-York Selection of Sacred Music, Containing a great number of plain Tunes, carefully arranged, and particularly designed for Church Worship, and generally suited to the several metres in the Psalms and Hymns used in the Dutch Church to which an Appendix, containing both plain and repeating tunes, intended for the various metres in Watts, Dwight, Dobell, Rippon and others. The whole of the Work has been carefully compiled from the best American and European Authors by F.D. Allen* (New York: F.D. Allen, 1818).

Boston Handel and Haydn Society Collection of Church Music; Being a Selection of the Most Approved Psalm and Hymn Tunes; Together with Many Beautiful Extracts from the Works of Haydn, Mozart, Beethoven, and Other Eminent Modern Composers. Harmonized for Three and Four Voices, With a Figured Bass for the Organ or Piano Forte. 2d ed., with additions and improvements. Boston: Richardson and Lord, 1823.

Boston Handel and Haydn Society Collection of Sacred Music; Consisting of Songs, Duetts [sic], Trios, Chorusses [sic], Anthems, & c. Selected from the Works of the Most Celebrated Authors. Arranged for the Organ or Piano Forte, By the Handel and Haydn Society, The. Vol. III. Boston: James Loring, 1827.

Calvin, John. *Aulcuns pseaulmes et cantiques mys en chant a Strasburg 1539.* (Reimpression phototypographique precede d'un avant-propos par D. Deletra, Geneva), 1919.

Collection of the Psalm and Hymn Tunes, Used by the Reformed Protestant Dutch Church of the City of New York, agreeable to their Psalm Book, published in English: In four Parts, viz. Tenor, Bass, Treble, and Counter, A. New York: Hodge and Shober, 1774.

Dathenus, Peterus. *De CL Psalmen des Propheten Davids (1566).* Kruiningen, NE: v.d. Peijl, 1950.

De Ridder, Richard R., with the assistance of Peter H. Jonker and Leonard Verduin. *The Church Orders of the Sixteenth Century Reformed Churches of the Netherlands Together with their Social, Political, and Ecclesiastical Context.* Grand Rapids: Calvin Theological Seminary, 1987.

Douen, Orientin. *Clement Marot et la Psautier Huguenot.* 2 vols. Paris: 1878-79, rep. Nieuwkoop, 1967.

Fulton Street Hymn Book, The. New York: Board of Publication of the Reformed Protestant Dutch Church in North America, 1862.

Hastings, Thomas, and Wm. B. Bradbury. *The Psalmodist: A Choice Collection of Psalm and Hymn Tunes, Chiefly New; Adapted to the Very Numerous Metres Now in Use, Chants, Anthems, Motets, and Various other Pieces; For the Use of Choirs Congregations, Singing Schools and Musical Associations.* New York: Mark H. Newman, 1844.

_____. *The New York Choralist: A New and Copious Collection of Psalm and Hymn Tunes, Adapted to All the Various Metres in General Use. With a Large Variety of Anthems and Set Pieces.* New York: Mark H. Newman, 1847.

_____. *The Mendelssohn Collection, or Hastings and Bradbury's Third Book Of Psalmody: Containing Original Music and Selections from the Best European and American Composers; Consisting of Tunes, Anthems, motets, Introits, Sentences, and Chants, with an Appendix of the Most Approved Standard church Tunes, for Congregational Singing.* New York: Mark E. Newman; Cincinnati: Wm. H. Moore, et al, 1849.

_____. *Psalmista, or Choir Melodies, an Extensive Collection of New and Available Church Music; The Choicest Selections From the Former*

Publications of the Authors, For Choir and Congregational Use. New York: Mark H. Newman, 1851.

Hastings, Thomas, and Solomon Warriner. *Musica Sacra, or the Utica and Springfield Collection United. Consisting of Psalm and Hymn Tunes, Anthems, and Chants Arranged for Two, Three, or Four Voices, with a Figured Bass for the Organ or Piano Forte.* 10th rev. ed. with an appendix. Utica, NY: William Williams, 1835.

Hopkinson, Francis, ed. *The Psalms of David, with Hymns and Spiritual Songs, Also the Catechism, Confession of Faith, Liturgy, &c. Translated from the Dutch: For Use of the Reformed Protestant Dutch Church of the City of New-York.* New York: James Parker, 1767.

Hymns of the Church, The. New York: A.S. Barnes, 1869.

Knox, John, et al., eds. *Sabbath School and Social Hymns of the Reformed Protestant Dutch Church in the United States of America.* New York: Board of Managers of the General Synod Sabbath School Union, 1843.

Livingston, John Henry, ed. *The Psalms and Hymns of the Reformed Protestant Dutch Church in North America.* New York: Board of Publication of the Reformed Protestant Dutch Church in North America, 1789.

_____. *The Psalms and Hymns of the Reformed Protestant Dutch Church in North America.* New York: Board of Publication of the Reformed Protestant Dutch Church, 1813.

_____. *Psalms and Hymns.* New York: Board of Publication of the Reformed Protestant Dutch Church in North America, 1848.

Mason, Lowell. *The Hallelujah: A Book for the Service of Song in the House of the Lord; Containing Tunes, Chants and Anthems, Both for the Choir and the Congregation.* New York: Mason Brothers, 1854.

Mason, Lowell, and George James Webb. *The National Psalmist; A Collection of the Most Popular and Useful Psalm and Hymn Tunes; Together with a Great Variety of New Tunes, Anthems, Sentences, and Chants; The Whole Forming a Most Complete Manual of Church Music for Choirs, Congregations, Singing-Schools, and Musical Associations.* Boston: Tappan, Whittemore, and Mason; New York: Geo. F. Cooledge and Brother, et al., 1848.

Meeter, Daniel J. *The "North American Liturgy": A Critical Edition of the Reformed Dutch Church in North America, 1793.* Ph.D. diss., Drew Univ., 1989.

Pidoux, Pierre. *Le Psaltier Hugenot du XVIe Siecle.* 2 vols. Basel: Edition Baerenreiter, 1962.

Tate, Nicholas, and Nahum Brady. *A New Version of the Psalms of David, by N. Tate & N. Brady. Together with some Hymns...as used in the English established Church in Amsterdam. And set to Musick by J.Z. Triemer.* Amsterdam: Henry Gartman, 1757.

Thompson, Bard: "The Palatinate Liturgy, Heidelberg, 1563" [trans. with notes by Bard Thompson]. *Theology and Life* 6/1 (Spring 1963), 49-67.

Van Deventer, Cornelius. *The New-Brunswick Collection of Sacred Music; A Selection of Tunes From the Most Approved Authors in Europe and America. Designed Principally for the Use of Churches.* 7th ed., enlarged and improved. New Brunswick: Terhune & Letson, 1835.

Woodbury, I.B. *The Dulcimer: or The New York Collection of Sacred Music. Constituting a Large and Choice Variety of New Tunes, Chants, Anthems, Motets, &c., From the Best Foreign and American Composers, with all the Old Tunes in Common Use.* New York: F.J. Huntington, Mason Brothers, 1850.

Church Histories and Anniversary Publications

Alexander, Robert S. *Albany's First Church: And Its Role in the Growth of the City, 1642-1942.* Albany: First Church in Albany, 1988.

Beekman, Rev. P. S., compiler. *History of the Reformed Church of Flatbush, NY 1807-1907.* Kingston, NY: R. W. Anderson, 1907.

Birch, John J. *The Pioneering Church of the Mohawk Valley.* Schenectady: The Consistory of the First Reformed Church, 1955.

_____. Stated Clerk of Classis. *As the Fields Ripened: Being a History of the Schenectady Classis of the Reformed Church in America.* Publ. by the Schenectady Classis, 1960.

Blanchard, Frank D., minister. *History of the Reformed Dutch Church of Rhinebeck Flats, New York.* Albany: J.B. Lyons, 1931.

Brotherton, Mary F. ed. *The History of the Old Brick Reformed Church: In Celebration of the Three Hundredth Anniversary of the Congregation 1699-1999.* Marlboro, NJ: The Old Brick Reformed Church, 1998.

Brower, William Leverich, and Henry P. Miller, coll. and ed. *1628-1928 Collegiate Reformed Protestant Dutch Church of the City of New York: Her Organization and Development. A record of the proclamation of the truth over three centuries, now written in the annals of eternity and "Safe in the hallowed quiets of the past." Published by the Consistory of the Collegiate Reformed Dutch Church to commemorate the Tercentenary of her organization on Manhattan Island.* New York, 1928.

Celebration on the Fiftieth Anniversary of the Founding of the Second Reformed (Dutch) Church of New Brunswick, New Jersey, 19, 20. February, 1893. Publ. by the Consistory. Trenton: J.L. Murphy, 1893.

Celebration of the Quarter Millennial Anniversary of the Reformed Protestant Dutch Church of the City of New York, November 21st, 1878, In the Church, Fifth Avenue and Twenty-Ninth Street, 1628-1878, The.

Centennial of the Theological Seminary of the Reformed Church in America. New York: Board of Publication, Reformed Church in America, 1885.

Cole, David, D. D. *Historical Address Delivered at the Twenty-Fifth Anniversary of the Reformed Church of Yonkers, NY on the Twenty-Third of April, 1868.* Yonkers, NY: The Consistory of the Reformed Church of Yonkers, 1868.

Corwin, Edward Tanjore. *Historical Discourse on Occasion of the Centennial Anniversary of the Reformed Dutch Church of Millstone.* New York: J. J. Reed, 1866.

_____. *Manuel and Record of the Church of Paramus, 1859.* Rev. and enlarged. Published by the Consistory. New York: Hosford Stationers and Printers, 1859.

Cox, Henry M. *History of the Reformed Church of Herkimer, NY from the Settlement of Herkimer County in 1723.* Herkimer: L.C. Childs, 1886.

Dailey, W.N.P. *The History of the Montgomery Classis R.C.A.* Amsterdam, NY: Recorder Press, date unknown (c. 1915).

Demarest, W. H. S. *Anniversary of the First Reformed Church, Walden, N. Y. October 1st and 2nd, 1893. The Fifty-fifth of the Church, the fifth of the Existing Pastorate.* Walden, NY: The Consistory of the First Reformed Church of Walden, 1893.

Discourse Delivered in the North Reformed Dutch Church (Collegiate) in the City of New York, on the Last Sabbath in August, 1856 by Thomas De Witt, D.D, one of the ministers of the Collegiate reformed Dutch Church, A. Publ. by the Consistory of the Collegiate Reformed Dutch Church. New York: Board of Publication of the Reformed Protestant Dutch Church, 1857.

Erickson, Martha, and Leonard Neil. *200 Years of Brick Church History.* Waldwick, NJ: Waldwick Printing, 1974.

First Reformed Church Memory Book. New Brunswick: Unpub. ms., 1943.

Gifford, Millard M. *The Phoenix of the North: For Ministers and Supply Pastors Who Served the Fort Miller Reformed Church, Fort Edward, NY 1817 to 1972.* New York: Kwik Kopy, 1971.

Gleason, William H., D.D. *1836-1886, Semi-Centennial Celebration of the First Reformed Protestant Church, Hudson, NY.* Hudson: M. Parker Williams, Register and Gazette, 1886.

Haefner, Scott, et al. *A Serving People: A History of the Niskayuna Reformed Church.* Niskayuna, New York: The Consistory, 2000.

Historical Discourses and Addresses, 175th Anniversary of the Reformed Church, Readington, NJ. Somerville, NJ: The Unionist-Gazette Association, 1894.

Historical Discourse Delivered at the Celebration of the One Hundred and Fiftieth Anniversary of the First Reformed Church, The. New Brunswick, NJ, Oct. 1, 1867.

Historical Sketch of the South Church (Reformed) of New York City. New York: Gilliss Brothers & Turnure, The Art Age Press, 1887.

History of the Classis of Paramus of the Reformed Church in America, (1800-1900): Containing the Proceedings of the Centennial Meeting of the Classis, The Historical Discourse, and the Addresses, Statistical History and the Histories of the Individual Churches, A. New York: Board of Publication, R.C.A., 1902.

Irish, Edward B. *Historical Highlights of the Harlingen Reformed Church, 1727-1951.* Harlingen, NJ: The Consistory, 1951.

Keator, Eugene H. *Anniversary Memorial, 1736-1936 First Reformed Church, Pompton Plains, New Jersey.* Paterson, NJ: Lont and Overkamp, 1936.

_____. *Historical Discourse, Two Hundredth Anniversary of the Six-Mile Run Reformed Church.* Franklin Park, NJ: The Consistory, 1910.

Keefer, Donald A. Scotia Village Historian. *A History of the Reformed Church of Scotia, New York, 1818-1968.* Scotia, NY, The First Reformed Church of Scotia, 1968.

Knox, Taber, et al. *1804-1904, The Record of a Century of Church Life of the Reformed Church, Warwick, NY.* New York: Warwick Valley Dispatch, 1904.

Labaw, George Warne (pastor of the church). *Preakness and the Preakness Reformed Church, Passaic County, New Jersey. A History. 1695-1902. with Genealogical Notes, the Records of the Church and Tombstone Inscriptions.* New York: Board of Publication of the Reformed Church in America, 1902.

Leiby, Adrian C. *The United Churches of Hackensack and Schraalenburgh New Jersey, 1686-1822.* Drawing by Richard G. Belcher. River Edge, NJ: Bergen County Historical Society, 1976.

Marsh, Robert T. *History of the Reformed Church, Bedminster, New Jersey.* Bedminster: The Consistory, 1958.

Martine, A.I. *Bi-Centennial Celebration 1699-1899 Reformed Church of the Navasink and its Two Branches The First Reformed Church of Freehold Now Known as the Brick Church of Marlboro, N.J. and the Reformed Church of Holmdel Formerly Known as the White Meeting House, Tuesday, October 24, 1899.* New York: P.F. Collier, 1899.

McCain, Walter L. *The First Hundred Years: A History of the Reformed Church of Closter, 1862-1962.* Closter NY: The Consistory, 1962.

McNomee, Harry Gale. *The Church of the Ponds, 1710-1935.* Pompton Lakes, NJ: The Bulletin, 1935.

Memorial of the Second Reformed Church, Albany N.Y. Corner-Stone Ceremonial of *the New Church, Closing Exercised in the Old Church Dedication of the New Church.* Albany: Weed, Parsons & Company, 1881.

Miller V. Walter and John Jurkowski. *St John's Low Dutch Reformed Church, 200th Anniversary 1788-1988.* Upper Red Hook, NY: St. John's Dutch Reformed Church, 1988.

Muyskens, J. David. *"The Town Clock Church" History of the First Reformed Church New Brunswick, NJ.* New Brunswick: The Consistory, 1991.

"Old First" Church Tercentenary 1654-1954, The. The Corporation of the Reformed Dutch Church of the Town of Brooklyn. New York: The Consistory, 1954.

Onderdonk, Henry, Jr. *History of the First Reformed Dutch Church of Jamaica, L.I. with an Appendix by Rev. Wm. H. DeHart, the Pastor.* Jamaica, LI: The Consistory, 1884.

One Hundred and Fiftieth Anniversary of the Founding of New Brunswick Theological Seminary, The. New Brunswick: New Brunswick Theological Seminary, 1934.

One-Hundredth Anniversary of the Second Reformed Church, New Brunswick, N.J., 1843-1943, The. Publ. by the Consistory. New Brunswick, NJ: Thatcher-Anderson, 1943.

One Hundredth Anniversary of the First Reformed Church of Walden, New York, April 23-30th, 1939. Walden, NY: The Consistory, 1939.

One Hundred and Seventy-Fifth Anniversary of The Second Reformed Church of Wyckoff. Wyckoff, NJ: The Consistory, 2002.

Our Two Hundred and Fifty Years. A Historical Sketch of the First Reformed Church, Albany, N.Y. Published by the Officers of the Church, 1899.

Partlan, Martha B., and Dorothy A. DuMond. *The Reformed Protestant Dutch Church of Kingston, New York. Three Hundred and Twenty-Fifth Anniversary.* Martha B. Partlan and Dorothy A. DuMond, 1984.

Patterson, Maurice L., et al., eds. *A History of the Interlaken Reformed Church: 1830-1980.* Interlaken, NY: I-T Publishing, 1980.

Pearson, Jonathan. *The History of the First Reformed Church of Schenectady, 1680-1980.* Vol. 1. Schenectady: The Consistory, 1980.

Pontius, James W. *The Five Buildings of The First Reformed Church of Schenectady. Prepared for the Occasion of the Rededication of the Church Rebuilt During 1948 and 1949 and Now Completed with Spire Twenty-Two Years after the Fire of February 1, 1948.* Schenectady: The Consistory, 1970.

Pontius, Kathryn Sharp, et al. *The History of the First Reformed Church of Schenectady, 1680-1980.* Vol. 2. Schenectady: The Consistory, 1980.

Proceedings at the Centennial Anniversary of the Dedication of the North Dutch Church, May 25th, 1869 and also, at the Laying of the Cornerstone of the New Church on Fifth Avenue and Forty-Eighth Street, on the Same Day. New York: The Consistory, 1869.

Record of Two Centuries 1804-2004: A Compilation of Two Books, Warwick Reformed Church, The. Warwick, NY: The Bicentennial History Committee, 2004.

Riley, Isaac, and Peter Stryker. *Jubilee: The Fiftieth Anniversary of the Organization of the Thirty-Fourth Street Reformed Church of New York City. December 14-21, 1873.* New York: The Consistory, 1874.

Romeyn, Theodore B. *Historical Discourse Delivered on the Occasion of the Re-opening and Dedication of the First Reformed Dutch Church at Hackensack, N.J., May 2, 1869.* New York: Board of Publication, R.C.A., 1870.

Romig, Edgar Franklin, ed. *The Tercentenary Year: A Record of the Celebration of the Three Hundredth Anniversary of the Founding of the First Church in New Netherland, Now New York, and the Beginning of Organized Religious Life under the Reformed (Dutch)Church in America.* New York: The General Synod of the Reformed Church in America, 1929.

Sherwood, Louis. *A History of the Lafayette Reformed Church of Jersey City. Prepared for the Fiftieth Anniversary Services, May, 1913.* Jersey City: The Consistory, 1913.

Smith, Daniel U. *A Short History of the Hillsborough Reformed Church, Millstone, NJ.* Millstone: The Consistory, 1966.

Spring, John C. *Let's Start from the Beginning – The Early Church of Schraalenburgh.* Dumont, NJ: The Consistory, 1964.

Steele, Richard H., D.D. *Historical Discourse Delivered at the Celebration of the One Hundred and Fiftieth Anniversary of the First Reformed Dutch Church, New Brunswick, N.J., October 1, 1867.* New Brunswick: The Consistory, 1867.

Strauss, Preston F.A.M. *History of the Harlingen Reformed Church, Harlingen, N.J. 1727-1927.* Harlingen, NJ: Christie Press, 1927.

Stryker, Elise B. *Centennial Historical Account, Middlebush Reformed Church,* 1934.

Taylor, Benjamin C., D.D. *Annals of the Classis of Bergen, of the Reformed Dutch Church, and of the Churches Under its Care: Including the Civil History of The Ancient Township of Bergen, in New Jersey.* New York: Board of Publications of the Reformed Protestant Dutch Church, 1857.

Thomas, Norman Edwin. *A History of St. John's Reformed Church Formerly the Reformed Calvinist Church of the Upper Part of Palatine in the County of Montgomery.* (Rev. ed. by the Bicentennial Historical Book Committee, St. Johnsville, New York: The Consistory and the Congregation of St. John's Reformed Church, 1947.) St. Johnsville: Enterprise and News, 1970.

Tilton, Edgar, Jr., D.D. *The Reformed Low Dutch Church of Harlem, Organized in 1660, Historical Sketch.* Harlem, NY: The Consistory, 1910.

Tower, Maria Bockee Carpenter. *The Records of the Reformed Dutch Church of New Hackensack, Dutchess County, New York.* Collections of the Dutchess County Historical Society. Vol.V. Poughkeepsie, NY: 1932.

Two Hundredth Anniversary of the First Reformed Protestant Dutch Church of Schenectady, NY June 20th and 21st 1880. New York: Steam Printing House, 1880.

Two Hundred Fiftieth Anniversary of the Six-Mile Run Reformed Church. Franklin Park, NJ: The Consistory, 1960.

Two Hundred and Fifty Years of Service, 1694-1944. Tappan, NY: Tappan Reformed Church, 1944.

Van Dyke, A. H. *One Hundred Fifty Years of Service for Christ and His Church, 1795- 1945.* Glen, NY: Glen Reformed Church, 1945.

Van Pelt, Daniel. *Picture of Early Church Life in New York City*. New York: Board of Publication, 1877.

Van Woert, H. S. *History of the First Reformed Church of Bethlehem, NY 1763-1913*. Albany, NY: J.B. Lyon, 1913.

Vincent, Lorena Cole. *Readington Reformed Church, Readington, NJ, 1719-1969*. Somerset, NJ: Publ. by the Consistory and Somerset Press, 1969.

Walker, Mrs. Harry and La Mont A. Warner, eds. *A History of the Reformed Church of Bronxville: in Commemoration of its Centenary November 5, 1950*. Bronxville, NY: The Consistory of the Church of Bronxville, NY, 1951.

Ward, Emory. *Faith of our Fathers Living Still: The Story of Marble Collegiate Church*. New York: Marble Collegiate Church, 1978. (Publ. on the 350th Anniversary of the Collegiate Church in NYC.)

Wells, Cornelius L., D. D. *Reformed Dutch Church of Flatbush. Celebrated February 9th, 1904, in the Reformed Dutch Church, of Flatbush, N.Y. 1654-1904*. Flatbush, 1904.

Wells, Theodore, W. *The Pastor and the Church or Rev. John H. Duryea, D. D. and the Second Reformed Church of Yonkers, 1868*. Yonkers, NY: The Consistory of the Reformed Church of Yonkers, 1868.

_____. *Brick Church Memorial, 1699-1877, The Days of Old and their Commemoration. Wednesday, September 5, 1877*. Marlborough, NJ:Publ. by the Consistory, 1877.

White, Frederick C., and Roderick Terry. D.D. *Historical Sketch of the South Church (Reformed) of New York City*. New York: Gilliss Brothers & Turnure, The Art Age Press, 1887.

Whitehead, Joseph H., et al., eds. *1800-1900, A History of the Classis of Paramus in the Reformed Church in America: Containing the Proceedings of the Centennial Meeting of the Classis, the Historical Discourse, and the Addresses, Statistical History and the Histories of the Individual Churches*. New York: The Board of Publication, R.C.A., 1902.

Whittemore, Henry, ed. *History of the First Reformed Protestant Dutch Church of Breuckelen, Now Known as The First Reformed Church of Brooklyn, 1654-1896*. New York: Comp. by the Consistory, 1896.

Wilcox, John C. *"The Old Church on the Green" the History and Traditions of the First Reformed Church, Hackensack, N.J. Founded 1686*. Publ. by the Congregation in the Church's 278th year on the occasion of the New Jersey Tercentenary Celebration, 1964.

Woodruff, Stanley, R., et al. *The First Reformed Church, Bayonne, NJ, On the Occasion of the One Hundredth Anniversary, 1828-1928.* Bayonne: 1928.

Zabriskie, F.N. *History of the Reformed P.D. Church of Claverack, A Centennial Address.* Hudson, NY: Stephen B. Miller, 1867.

Story of the Old North Reformed Church, Dumont, NJ, 1794-1975, The. Dumont: The Consistory, 1976.

Secondary Sources:

Addleshaw, G.W.O., and Frederick Etchells. *The Architectural Setting of Anglican Worship: an Inquiry into the Arrangements for Public Worship in the Church of England from the Reformation until the Present Day.* London: Faber & Faber, 1948.

Augustine, Saint. *Confessions.* Trans. with an Introduction by R.S. Pine-Coffin. London: Penguin Books, 1961.

_____. "On Music (De musica)." Trans. Robert Catesby Taliaferro. *The Fathers of the Church.* New York: Cima Publishing, 1947.

Balmer, Randall. "The Historiographical Neglect of Religion in the Middle Colonies," *Pulpit, Table, and Song: Essays in Celebration of Howard G. Hageman.* Heather Murray Elkins and Edward C. Zaragoza, eds. Drew Studies in Liturgy, No. 1. Lanham, MD, and London: Scarecrow Press, 1996.

_____. *A Perfect Babel of Confusion: Dutch Religion and English Culture in the Middle Colonies.* New York: Oxford Univ. Press, 1989.

_____. The Social Roots of Dutch Pietism in the Middle Colonies," *Church History,* LIII, 1984.

Beardslee, John W. III. "The Reformed Church and the American Revolution." *Piety and Patriotism.* The Historical Series of the Reformed Church in America, no 4. Grand Rapids: Eerdmans, 1976.

_____. "Makers of the Modern Reformed Church: John Henry Livingston and the Rise of the American Mission Movement," *Historical Highlights* (Issue No. 30, Vol. 8, No. 2, Oct. 1989).

_____. ed. *Vision from the Hill: Selections from Works of Faculty and Alumni,* published on the bicentennial of New Brunswick Theological Seminary. The Historical Series of the Reformed Church in America, no. 12. Grand Rapids: Eerdmans, 1984.

Beeke, Joel R., ed. *Forerunner of the Great Awakening: Sermons by Theodorus Jacobus Frelinghuysen (1691-1747)*. The Historical Series of the Reformed Church in America, no. 36. Grand Rapids: Eerdmans, 2000.

Bratt, James D. "American Culture and Society: A Century of Dutch-American Assessments." Reformed Church Press, 1977.

_____. *Dutch Calvinism in Modern America: A History of a Conservative Subculture*. Grand Rapids: Eerdmans, 1984.

Bratt, John H., ed. *The Heritage of John Calvin*. Heritage Hall Lectures, 1960-1970. Grand Rapids: Eerdmans, 1973.

Brown, Willard Dayton. *History of the Reformed Church in America*. New York: Board of Publication of the Reformed Church in America, 1928.

Brouwer, Arie R. *Reformed Church Roots: Thirty-five Formative Events*. New York: 1977.

Bruggink, Donald J. "The Reformation of Liturgical Space." *Reformed Liturgy and Music*. Vol. 16 (Spring 1982).

Bruggink, Donald J., and Carl H. Droppers. *Christ and Architecture: Building Presbyterian/Reformed Churches*. Grand Rapids: Eerdmans, 1965.

Bruggink, Donald J., and Kim N. Baker. *By Grace Alone: Stories of the Reformed Church in America*. The Historical Series of the Reformed Church in America, no. 44. Grand Rapids: Eerdmans, 2004.

Bruins, Elton, J. *The Americanization of a Congregation*. The Historical Series of theReformed Church in America, no. 26. 2nd ed. Grand Rapids: Eerdmans, 1995.

Bruins, Elton, J., Jeanne M. Jacobson, and Larry Wagenaar. *Albertus C. Van Raalte: Dutch Leader and American Patriot*. Holland, MI: Hope College, 1996.

Bruins, Elton J., and Robert P. Swierenga. *Family Quarrels: The Dutch Reformed Church of the 19th Century*. The Historical Series of the Reformed Church in America, no. 32. Grand Rapids: Eerdmans, 1999.

Brumm, James H., ed. *Liturgy Among the Thorns: Essays on Worship in the Reformed Church in America*. Historical Series of the Reformed Church in America, no. 57. Grand Rapids: Eerdmans, 2007.

Centennial Discourses. A Series of Sermons Delivered in the Year 1876. By the Order of the General Synod of the Reformed (Dutch) Church in America. 2nd ed. New York: Board of Publication of the Reformed Church in America, 1877.

Coakley, John. "The Theological Roots of the RCA's Ecumenical Disposition," in *Concord Makes Strength: Essays in Reformed Ecumenism.* John Coakley, ed. The Historical Series of the Reformed Church in America, no. 41. Grand Rapids: Eerdmans, 2002.

Conklin, Paul K. *The Uneasy Center: Reformed Christianity in Antebellum America.* Chapel Hill: Univ. of North Carolina Press, 1995.

Corwin, Edward Tanjore. *History of the Reformed Church, Dutch.* New York: The Christian Literature Co., 1895.

Davies, Horton. *Worship and Theology in England.* 5 vols. Princeton: Princeton Univ. Press, 1961-1975.

Davis, Natalie Z. "From 'Popular Religion' to Religious Cultures" *Reformation Europe: A Guide to Research.* Steven Ozment, ed. St. Louis: Center for Reformation Research, 1982.

De Jong, Gerald F. *The Dutch in America 1609-1974.* The Immigrant Heritage of America Series. Ed. Cecyle S. Neidle. Boston: Twayne Publishers. G. K. Hall and Co., 1975.

_____. *The Dutch Reformed Church in the American Colonies.* Historical Series of the Reformed Church in America, no. 5. Grand Rapids: Eerdmans, 1978.

DeJong, Peter Y., ed. *Crisis in the Reformed Churches: Essays in Commemoration of the Great Synod of Dort, 1618-1619.* Grand Rapids: Reformed Fellowship, 1968.

Demarest, David D. *History and Characteristics of the Reformed Protestant Dutch Church.* 2nd ed. New York: Board of Publication of the Reformed Protestant Dutch Church in America, 1856.

_____. "Liturgical Spirit and Features of the Reformed Church in America," in *Centennial Discourses of the Reformed Church in America.* New York: Board of Publication, 1877.

_____. *The Reformed Church in America: Its Origins and Characteristics.* 4th ed. rev. and enlarged. New York: Board of Publication of the Reformed Church in America, 1889.

Demarest, David D., Paul D. Van Cleef, and Edward T. Corwin, eds. *Centennial of the Theological Seminary of the Reformed Church in America, 1784-1884.* New York: Board of Publication of the Reformed Church in America, 1885.

Demarest, William H. S., et al. *Tercentenary Studies, 1928, Reformed Church in America: A Record of Beginnings Compiled by the Tercentenary*

Committee on Research and Publication. New York: The General Synod of the Reformed Church in America, 1928.

Eekhof, A. *Jonas Michaeleus: Founder of the Church in New Netherland.* Leyden: A. W. Sijthoff, 1926.

Fabend, Firth Haring. *A Dutch Family in the Middle Colonies, 1660-1800.* New Brunswick: Rutgers Univ. Press, 1991.

_____. *Zion on the Hudson: Dutch New York and New Jersey in the Age of Revivals.* New Brunswick: Rutgers Univ. Press, 2000.

Finke, Roger, and Roger Stark. *The Churching of America 1776-1790: Winners and Losers in Our Religious Economy.* New Brunswick: Rutgers Univ. Press, 1992.

Geertz, Clifford. "Religion as a Cultural System" *The Interpretation of Cultures.* New York: Basic Books, 1973.

Gehring, Charles Theodor. *The Dutch Language in Colonial New York: An Investigation of a Language in Decline and its Relationship to Social Change.* Ph.D. diss., Indiana Univ., 1973.

Hackett, David G. *The Rude Hand of Innovation: Religion and Social Order in Albany, New York, 1652-1836.* New York: Oxford Univ. Press, 1991.

Hageman, Howard G. *Lily Among the Thorns.* New York: Board of Education Reformed Church in America and the Half Moon Press, 1953.

_____. *Pulpit and Table: Some Chapters in the History of Worship in the Reformed Churches.* Richmond: John Knox, 1962 (Also London: SCM Press, 1962).

_____. "The Liturgical Origins of the Reformed Churches." *The Heritage of John Calvin.* John H. Bratt, ed. Heritage Hall Lectures, 1960-1970. Grand Rapids: Eerdmans, 1973.

_____. "William Bertholf: Pioneer Domine of New Jersey," *Reformed Review,* XXIX, 1976.

_____. *Two Centuries Plus: The Story of New Brunswick Seminary.* The Historical Series of the Reformed Church in America, no. 13. Grand Rapids: Eerdmans, 1984.

Harinck, George, and Hans Krabbendam, eds. *Sharing the Reformed Tradition: The Dutch – North American Exchange, 1846-1996.* Amsterdam: VU Uitgeverij, 1996.

Harmelink, Herman III. *Ecumenism and the Reformed Church.* The Historical Series of the Reformed Church in America, no. 1. Grand Rapids: Eerdmans, 1968.

_____. et al. *The Reformed Church in New Jersey.* Woodcliff-on Hudson: Synod of New Jersey, 1969.

Harms, Richard H. "Forging a Religious Identity: The Christian Reformed Church in the Nineteenth-Century Dutch Immigrant Community." *Dutch-American Experience.* Amsterdam: VU Uitgeverij, 2000.

Harrison, Edward N., and Shirley B. Harrison. *Dutch Reformed Influence on Education in New Jersey for Over Three-and-a-half Centuries.* 2 vols. Harrogate, TN: Lincoln Memorial Univ. Press, 1992.

Hatch, Nathan O. *The Democratization of American Christianity.* New Haven: Yale Univ. Press, 1989.

Hesselink, I. John. *On Being Reformed: Distinctive Characteristics and Common Misunderstandings.* 2nd ed. New York: Reformed Church Press, 1988.

Hoff, Marvin. "The Fulton Street Prayer Meeting," *Reformed Review* (Sept., 1963).

House, Renee S., and John W. Coakley. *Patterns and Portraits: Women in the History of the Reformed Church in America.* The Historical Series of the Reformed Church in America, no. 31. Grand Rapids: Eerdmans, 1999.

Huizinga, John. *Erasmus and the Age of Reformation.* Princeton: Princeton Univ. Press, 1984.

Hyma, Albert. *The Christian Renaissance: A History of the "Devotio Moderna."* 2nd ed. Hamden CT: 1965.

Janssen Allan, J. *Gathered at Albany: A History of a Classis.* The Historical Series of the Reformed Church in America, no. 25. Grand Rapids: Eerdmans, 1995.

Jones, Cheslyn, Geoffrey Wainwright, Edward Yarnold SJ, and Paul Bradshaw. *The Study of Liturgy.* Rev. ed. London and New York: SPCK; Oxford Univ. Press, 1992.

Kerr, Hugh T. "Building the Reformed Image." *Reformed Liturgy and Music* 26 (Fall, 1992).

Kilde, Jeanne Halgren. *When Church Became Theatre: The Transformation of Evangelical Architecture and Worship in Nineteenth-Century America.* London: Oxford Univ. Press, 2002.

Krabbendam, Hans, and Larry J. Wagenaar, eds. *The Dutch-American Experience: Essays in Honor of Robert P. Swierenga.* Amsterdam: VU Univ. Press, 2000.

Leiby, Adrian C. *The Early Dutch and Swedish Settlers of New Jersey.* The New Jersey Historical Series. Princeton: D. Van Nostrand, 1964.

Lodge, Marin Ellsworth. *The Great Awakening in the Middle Colonies.* Ph.D. diss., Univ. of California, Berkeley, 1964.

Luidens, Donald A., and Roger J. Nemeth. "Dutch Immigration and Membership Growth in the Reformed Church in America." *Dutch-American Experience.* Amsterdam: VU Uitgeverij, 2000.

Luidens, John P. *The Americanization of the Dutch Reformed Church*, Ph. D. diss., Univ. of Oklahoma, 1969.

McKim, Donald K., ed. *Major Themes in the Reformed Tradition.* Grand Rapids: Eerdmans, 1992.

McNeil, John T. *The History and Character of Calvinism.* New York and London: Oxford Univ. Press, 1954.

Meeter, Daniel J. *Meeting Each Other in Doctrine, Liturgy & Government.* The Historical Series of the Reformed Church in America, no. 24. Grand Rapids: Eerdmans, 1993.

Nemeth, Roger J., and Donald A Luidens. "The Persistence of Ethnic Descent: Dutch Clergy in the Reformed Church in America." *Journal for the Scientific Study of Religion* 34 (June 1995).

Nichols, James H. *Corporate Worship in the Reformed Tradition.* Philadelphia: Westminster, 1968.

_____. *Romanticism in American Theology: Nevin and Schaff at Mercersberg.* Chicago: Univ. of Chicago Press, 1961.

Niebuhr, H., Richard. *Christ and Culture.* New York: Harper & Row, 1951.

Noll, Mark A., Nathan O. Hatch, and George M. Marsden. *The Search for Christian America.* Expanded ed. Colorado Springs: Helmers & Howard, 1989.

Pointer, Richard W. *Protestant Pluralism and the New York Experience: A Study of Eighteenth-Century Religious Diversity.* Bloomington: Indiana Univ. Press, 1988.

Rowe, Kenneth E. "The Palatinate Liturgy and the Pennsylvania Germans." *Pulpit, Table and Song: Essays in Celebration of Howard G. Hageman.* Heather Murray Elkins and Edward C. Zaragoza eds. Drew Studies in Liturgy, No. 1. Lanham, MD and London: Scarecrow Press, 1996.

Schaff, Phillip, et al., gen. ed. *The American Church History Series*. Vol. 7: *A History of the Reformed Church, Dutch, the Reformed Church, German, and the Moravian Church in the United States*. 2nd ed., by E. T. Corwin, J.H. Dubbs, and J.T. Hamilton. New York: Scribner's, 1902.

Schama, Simon. *The Embarrassment of Riches: An Interpretation of Dutch Culture in the Golden Age*. New York: Knopf, 1987.

Schenck, George. *Music—an Address Delivered in the first Reformed Dutch Church of Sommerville, NJ at a Concert of Music from the "Young Ladies" of the "Sommerset Institute."* Sommerville, NJ: 1849.

Shorto, Russell. *The Island at the Center of the World. The Epic Story of Dutch Manhattan and the Forgotten Colony that Shaped America*. New York: Vintage Books, 2005.

Smith, Gary Scott. *The Seeds of Secularization: Calvinism, Culture, and Pluralism in America, 1870 – 1915*. Grand Rapids: Christian Univ. Press, 1985.

Tanis, James. *Dutch Calvinistic Pietism in the Middle Colonies: A Study in the Life and Theology of Theodorus Jacobus Frelinghuysen*. The Hague: Martinus Nijhoff, 1967.

_____. "Frelinghuysen, the Dutch Clergy, and the Great Awakening in the MiddleColonies." *Reformed Review* 28 (1985).

ten Zythoff, Gerrit J. *Sources of Secession: The Netherlands Hervormde Kerk on the Eve of the Dutch Immigration to the Midwest*. Historical Series of the Reformed Church in America, no. 17. Grand Rapids: Eerdmans, 1987.

Tercentenary Studies, Reformed Church in America. New York: Board of Publication, Reformed Church in America, 1928.

Tercentenary Year: The Musical Supplement of the Tercentenary Pageant of the Reformed Church in America, 1628-1928, The. New York: Tercentenary Committee, 1928.

Thompson, Bard. *Liturgies of the Western Church*. 1st Fortress Press ed. Philadelphia: Fortress, 1980.

_____. *Humanists and Reformers: A History of the Renaissance and Reformation*. Grand Rapids: Eerdmans, 1996.

Van Cleef, Paul D. "The Catholic Spirit of the Reformed Dutch Church Toward all other Christians," in *Centennial Discourses of the Reformed Church in America*. New York: Board of Publication, 1877.

Vander Leeuw, Gerardus. *Liturgiek*. 2nd edition. Nijkerk, 1946.

Van Hoeven, James W., ed. *Piety and Patriotism: Bicentennial Studies of the Reformed Church in America, 1776-1976*. The Historical Series of the Reformed Church in America, no. 4. Grand Rapids: Eerdmans, 1976.

_____. ed. *Word and World: Reformed Theology in America*. The Historical Series of the Reformed Church in America, no. 16. Grand Rapids: Eerdmans, 1986.

Vischer, Lukas. *Christian Worship in Reformed Churches Past and Present*. Grand Rapids: Eerdmans, 2003.

Wall, Alexander J. "The Controversy in the Dutch Church in New York Concerning Preaching in English, 1754-1768." *New York Historical Society Quarterly Bulletin* 12 (Apr. 1928).

White, James F. *Protestant Worship: Traditions in Transition*. Louisville: Westminster/John Knox, 1989.

_____. *A Brief History of Christian Worship*. Nashville: Abingdon, 1993.

Yates, Nigel. *The Oxford Movement and Anglican Ritualism*. London: The Historical Association, 1984.

Secondary Sources on Music:

Allwardt, (Anton) Paul. *Sacred Music in New York City, 1800-1850*. S.M.D. diss., Union Theological Seminary, 1950.

Bisgrove, Mildred E. *Sacred Choral Music in the Calvinistic Tradition of the Protestant Reformation in Switzerland and France from 1541-1600*. Ph.D. diss., New York Univ., 1968.

Blume, Friedrich, et al. *Protestant Church Music*: New York: W.W. Norton, 1974.

Bristol, Lee Hastings, Jr. "Thomas Hastings, 1784-1872," *The Hymn* 10 (Oct. 1959).

Britton, Allen Perdue, Irving Lowens, and completed by Richard Crawford. *American Sacred Music Imprints, 1698-1810: A Bibliography*. Worcester, MA: American Antiquarian Society, 1990.

Bruinsma, Henry A. *The Souterliedekens and its Relation to Psalmody in the Netherlands*. Ph.D. diss., Univ. of Michigan, 1948.

_____. "The Organ Controversy in the Netherlands Reformation to 1640." *Journal of the American Musicological Society* 7 (Fall, 1954).

Brumm, James L. H. "Singing the Lord's Song: A History of the English Language Hymnals of the Reformed Church in America."

New Brunswick: The Historical Society of the Reformed Church in America, 1990.

Cameron, Peter T. "A History of the Organs of the Collegiate Church of New York City, 1727-1861." *The Tracker* (Journal of the Organ Historical Society). 25th Anniversary Issue. Vol. 25, No. 1 (Fall 1980).

Chase, Gilbert. *America's Music: From the Pilgrims to the Present.* Rev. 3rd ed. Urbana: Univ. of Illinois Press, 1987.

Corwin, Charles E. "First Organ in New York in 1727; Story of Early Days," *The Diapason.* 23/1 (Dec 1931).

Crawford, Richard. *The Core Repertory of Early Psalmody*, Recent Researches in American Music, vols. 11 and 12, Madison: A-R Editions, 1984.

_____. "Psalmody," in *The New Grove Dictionary of American Music.* Hitchcock, H. Wiley, and Stanley Sadie, eds. New York: Grove's Dictionaries of Music, 1986.

_____. "Psalms, metrical" in *The New Grove Dictionary of American Music.* Hitchcock, H. Wiley, and Stanley Sadie, eds. New York: Grove's Dictionaries of Music, 1986.

_____. "Set-piece" in *The New Grove Dictionary of American Music.* Hitchcock, H. Wiley, and Stanley Sadie, eds. New York: Grove's Dictionaries of Music, 1986.

_____. *The American Musical Landscape.* Berkeley: Univ. of California Press, 1993.

_____. *Introduction to American Music.* New York: Norton, 2001.

Crawford, Richard R., Allen Lott, and Carol J. Oja, eds. *A Celebration of American Music: Words and Music in Honor of H. Wiley Hitchcock.* Ann Arbor: Univ. of Michigan Press, 1990.

Crawford, Richard, and David Warren Steel. "Singing Schools," in *The New Grove Dictionary of Music and Musicians.* 20 vols. Stanley Sadie, ed. London: 1980.

Crookshank, Esther Rothenbusch. "'We're Marching to Zion': Isaac Watts in Early America," *Wonderful Words of Life: Hymns in American Protestant History and Theology.* Richard Mouw and Mark Noll, eds. Grand Rapids: Eerdmans, 2004.

Daniel, Ralph T. *The Anthem in New England before 1800.* Evanston: Northwestern Univ. Press, 1966.

Doughty, Gavin L. *The History and Development of Music in the United Presbyterian Church in the United States of America*. Ph.D. diss., Univ. of Iowa, 1966.

Ellinwood, Leonard. *The History of American Church Music*. New York: Morehouse-Gorham, 1953.

Engle, Randall Dean. *A Devil's Siren or an Angel's Throat? The Organ Controversy in the Netherlands from Calvin to Huygens*. Ph.D. diss., Univ. of Wales, 2006.

Eskew, Harry, and Hugh T. McElrath. *Sing with Understanding: an Introduction to Christian Hymnology*. Nashville: Broadman, 1980.

Etherington, Charles L. *Protestant Worship Music: Its History and Practice*. New York: Holt, Rinehart, and Winston, 1962.

Fellowes, Edmund H. *English Cathedral Music*. Rev. 2nd ed. London: Methuen, 1945.

Foote, H.W. *Three Centuries of American Hymnody*. Hamden: Harvard Univ. Press, 1940. Rep. 1961, 1968.

Frantz, John B. *Revivalism in the German Reformed Church in America to 1850, With Emphasis on the Eastern Synod*. Ph.D. diss., Univ. of Pennsylvania, 1961.

Garside, Charles, Jr. "The Origins of Calvin's Theology of Music: 1536-1543," *Transactions of the American Philosophical Society* 69:4. Philadelphia: The American Philosophical Society, Aug. 1979.

_____. "Calvin's Preface to the Psalter: A Re-Appraisal," *The Musical Quarterly*, XXXVII: 4 (Oct. 1951).

Glover, Raymond, ed. *The Hymnal 1982 Companion*. 4 vols. New York: Church Hymnal Corporation, 1990 and 1994.

Gould, Nathaniel D. *Church Music in America, Comprising Its History and Peculiarities At Different Periods, with Cursory Remarks on Its Legitimate Use and Its Abuse; With Notices of the Schools, Composers, Teachers, and Societies*. Boston: A.N. Johnson, 1853. Rep., New York, 1972.

Grout, Donald Jay, and Claude V. Palisca. *A History of Western Music*. 5th ed. New York: Norton, 1996.

Hamm, Charles, *Music in the New World*. New York: Norton, 1983.

Hammond, Joseph W. *Sing to the Lord! A History of Music at the Old Brick Reformed Church in Marlboro, New Jersey*. Unpubl. paper, 1994.

Harms, John K. "Music of the Radical Reformation," *Church Music* (1977/2) and (1978/1).

Hastings, Thomas. *Dissertation on Musical Taste or General Principals of Taste Applied to the Art of Music.* New York: Da Capo, 1974, republ. of the 1st ed., 1822.

_____. *The History of Forty Choirs.* New York: Mason Bros, 1854.

Heller, George N., and Carol A. Pemberton. "The Boston Handel and Haydn Society Collection of Church Music (1822): Its Context, Content, and Significance," *The Hymn* 47:4 (Oct. 1996): 27.

Hitchcock, H. Wiley. *Music in the United States: A Historical Introduction.* 3rd ed. Englewood Cliffs, NJ: Prentice-Hall, 1988.

Honders, A.C. "Das Abendmahl nach der Ordnung des Petrus Dathenus 1566." In *Coena Domini I: Die Abendmahlsliturgie der Reformationskirchen im 16./17. Jahrhundert.* Ed. Irmgard Pahl. Freiburg, Switzerland: Universitatsverlag, 1983.

Huygens, Constantijn. *Use and Non-Use of the Organ in the Churches of the United Netherlands.* Trans. Erica Smit-Van Rotte. New York, 1964.

Julian, John. "Dutch Hymnody," in *Dictionary of Hymnology.* Grand Rapids: Kregel, 1985.

Kaufman, Charles H. *Music in New Jersey, 1655-1860: A Study of Musical Activity and Musicians in New Jersey from its First Settlement to the Civil War.* Rutherford: Fairleigh Dickenson Univ. Press, 1981.

Kist, N. C. "Het Kerkelijke Orgel-Gebruik bijzonder in Nederland," *Archief voor Kerkelijke Geschiedenis inzonderheid van Nederland X* (1840).

Leaver, Robin A. "Dutch Secular and Religious Songs in Eighteenth-Century New York," in *Amsterdam-New York Transatlantic Relations and Urban Identities   Since 1653.* Ed. George Harinck and Hans Krabbendam. Amsterdam: VU Uitgeverij, 2005.

_____. "Lection, Sermon, and Congregational Song: A Preaching Lectionary of the Dutch Reformed Church (1782) and Its Implications," *Pulpit, Table, and Song: Essays in Celebration of Howard G. Hageman.* Heather Murray Elkins and Edward C. Zaragoza, eds. Drew Studies in Liturgy, No. 1. Lanham, MD and London: Scarecrow Press, 1996.

_____. *Goostly Psalmes and Spiritual Songes: English and Dutch Metrical Psalms From Coverdale to Utenhove, 1535-1566.* Oxford: Clarendon, 1991.

Leaver, Robin A., and Joyce Ann Zimmerman, eds. *Liturgy and Music: Lifetime Learning*. Collegeville, MN: Liturgical Press, 1998.

Lenselink, Samuel J. *De Nederlandse Psalmberijmingen van Souterliedekens tot Datheen*. Doctoral diss., Assen, 1959.

_____. "De Netherlandse Hymnologie in internationaal Perspectief," *Netherlands Archief voor Kerkgeschiedenis* (Nieuwe Serie) 56 (1975).

Leslie, Robert Homer, Jr. *Music and the Arts in Calvin's Geneva: A Study of the Relation between Calvinistic Theology and Music and the Arts, with Special Reference to the "Cent cinquante pseaumes" (1538) of Pascal de L' Estocart*. Ph.D. diss., McGill Univ., 1969.

Lowens, Irving. "The Easy Instructor: (1798-1831): A History and Bibliography of the First Shape-Note Tune Book." *Journal of Research in Music Education* 1 (1953).

_____. *Music and Musicians in Early America*. New York: Norton, 1964.

Luth, Jan R. "Where do Genevan Psalms Come From?" *Reformed Liturgy and Music* 5 (1993).

Marini, Stephen A. "Rehearsal for Revival: Sacred Singing and the Great Awakening in America." *Sacred Sound: Music in Religious Thought and Practice*. Joyce Irwin, ed. Chico, CA: Scholars Press, 1983.

_____. *Sacred Song in America: Religion, Music, and Public Culture*. Urbana: Univ. of Illinois Press, 2003.

Mason, Lowell. *Letters from Abroad*. New York: Mason Brothers, 1854. This ed. with an introduction by Elwyn A. Wienandt. New York: Da Capo, 1967.

Maxwell, Jack Martin. *Worship and Reformed Theology. The Liturgical Lessons of Mercersberg*. Pittsburgh: Pickwick, 1976.

Meeter, Daniel J. *"Bless the Lord, O My Soul": The New-York Liturgy of the Dutch Reformed Church, 1767*. Lanham, MD: Scarecrow Press, 1998.

_____. "Genevan Jigsaw: The Tunes of the New York Psalmbook of 1767." *Ars et musica in liturgia*. Metuchen, NJ: Scarecrow Press, 1994.

Music, David W. *Hymnology: A Collection of Source Readings*. Studies in Liturgical Musicology, No. 4. Lanham MD and London: Scarecrow Press, 1996.

Ogasapian, John. *Organ Building in New York City, 1700-1900*. Braintree, MA: Organ Literature Foundation, 1977.

_____. *Music of the Colonial and Revolutionary Era.* Westport: Greenwood, 2004.

Osche, Orpha. *The History of the Organ in the United States.* Bloomington: Indiana Univ. Press, 1975.

Pidoux, Pierre. "Polyphonic Settings of the Genevan Psalter: Are They Church Music?" in *Cantors at the Crossroads.* Johannes Riedel, ed. St. Louis: Concordia, 1967.

Pinel, Stephen L. "Henry Erben: New York Organbuilder." *de Mixtur, tijdschrift over het orgel.* Nummer 60, (Juni 1988).

Plank, Steven. *"The Way to Heavens Doore:" An Introduction to Liturgical Process and Musical Style.* Studies in Liturgical Musicology, No. 2. Lanham: Scarecrow Press, 1994.

Polman, Bertus F. *Church Music and Liturgy in the Christian Reformed Church of North America.* Ph.D. diss., Univ. of Minnesota, 1981.

_____. "Dutch Reformed Church, music of the," *New Grove Dictionary of American Music.* Hitchcock, H. Wiley, and Stanley Sadie, eds. New York: Grove's Dictionaries of Music, 1986.

Rainbow, Bernarr. *The Choral Revival in the Anglican Church 1839-1872.* New York: Oxford Univ. Press, 1970.

Redway, Virginia L. "James Parker and the 'Dutch Church.'" *The Musical Quarterly,* 24 (Oct., 1938).

Reese, Gustave. *Music in the Renaissance.* Rev. ed. New York: Norton, 1959.

Rosewall, Richard Byron. "Singing Schools of Pennsylvania." Ph.D. diss., Univ. of Minnesota, 1969.

Sadie, Stanley, ed. *The New Grove Dictionary of Music and Musicians.* 20 vols. London: Macmillan, 1980.

Schoep, Arthur P. *The Harmonic Treatment of the Dutch Psalter of the 18th and 19th Centuries.* M.M. thesis, Eastman School of Music, 1945.

Smith, Carleton S. "The 1774 Psalm Book of the Reformed Protestant Dutch Church in New York," *The Musical Quarterly,* 34 (Jan., 1948).

Stackhouse, Rochelle A. *Language of the Psalms in Worship: American Revisions of Watts' Psalter* (Lanham: Scarecrow Press, 1997).

Stevenson, Robert. *Protestant Church Music in America: A Short Survey of Men and Movements from 1564 to Present.* New York: Norton, 1966.

Temperley, Nicholas. "The Old Way of Singing: Its Origins and Development." *Journal of the American Musicological Society* 34 (Fall 1981).

_____. *The Music of the English Parish Church*. 2 Vols. Cambridge: Cambridge Univ. Press, 1979.

Van Andel, Cornelius P. *Tussen de Regels, De Samenhang van Kerkgeschiedenis en Kerklied*. The Hague: 1968.

Van Amstel, Piet. "The Roots of Genevan Psalm Tunes." *Reformed Music Magazine* 3 (1992).

Weber, W.A., "The Hymnody of the Dutch Reformed Church in America, 1628-1953," *The Hymn* 26: 2 (Apr. 1975).

Westermeyer, Paul. "What Shall We Sing in a Foreign Land? Theology and Cultic Song in the Reformed and Lutheran Churches of Pennsylvania, 1830-1900." Ph.D. diss., Univ. of Chicago, 1978.

_____. "Lineaments of the Reformed and Lutheran Traditions: Liturgy and Hymnody in 19th Century Pennsylvania." *Church Music* 80 (1980).

_____. *Te Deum: The Church and Music*. Minneapolis: Fortress, 1998.

Wienandt, Elwyn A., and Robert H. Young. *The Anthem in England and America*. New York: Free Press, 1970.

Willis, Richard Storrs. *Church Chorals and Choir Studies*. New York: Clark, Austin & Smith, 1850.

Witvliet, John D. *Worship Seeking Understanding: Windows into Christian Practice*. Grand Rapids: Baker Academic, 2003.

Yardley, Anne Bagnall. "Choirs in the Methodist Episcopal Church, 1800-1860." *American Music*, Spring, 1999.

_____. "What Besides Hymns? The Tune Books of Early Methodism," *Methodist History*, Vol. 37:3 (Apr. 1999).

Young, C.W. "Effects of the Reformation on Church Music in 16th Century Strasbourg," *Church Music* (69:2).

Zuiderveld, Rudolf, "Some Musical Traditions in Dutch Reformed Churches in America," *The Hymn* 36:3 (July 1985).

Index